P9-CQW-951

THE BEAVERTON STORY

THE BEAVERTON STORY

"Harvest of Dreams"

Written and Published
by the
History Committee
of the
Beaverton Thorah Eldon Historical Society

1984

First Published May 1984
Ontario Publishing Company Limited
Established 1893

ISBN: 0-919354-04-1

Financial assistance given by the New Horizons Programme of the Department of Health and Welfare of the Federal Government of Canada is gratefully acknowledged.

Printed and bound in Canada by

T.H. Best Printing Company Limited
33 Kern Road
Don Mills, Ontario
M3B 1S9

Dedicated to the memory of the stalwart pioneers who planted the seeds of Beaverton and Thorah and the faithful custodians who nurtured the growing community through the years so that we, today, reap the harvest of their dreams.

ERRATA

page 53 line 5: "village" should read "township"

page 199 line 18: "1979" should read "1978"

TABLE OF CONTENTS

TABLE OF CONTENTS

FOREWORD

As the present and former residents of Beaverton and the surrounding countryside celebrate the centennial of this village's incorporation, it is natural that thoughts turn to the past. The Beaverton Thorah Eldon Historical Society was formed to investigate and preserve the history and artifacts relating to this area's early years. In an attempt to share with the community the results of our historical research, we have written *The Beaverton Story*.

This book covers Thorah's pioneer period and Beaverton's formative years. One chapter takes a close look at the Village in 1884 as Farmer Baldy takes an extensive jaunt through its streets. Successive chapters take the reader into the Twentieth Century. However, the emphasis in this history is on the Nineteenth Century. We have left the more recent eras to be covered in depth at some later date.

Settlers began arriving in Thorah Township in the 1820's, and settlement continued for the next two to three decades. As the Township "grew up," Beaverton, with a growing population, became the centre of business, church, social, and recreational life. By 1884 this village was ready to become a separate political entity.

Some thirty years ago Mary Houston Ritchie wrote her delightful history *A Township on the Lake*. It must be pointed out that *The Beaverton Story* does not replace the earlier book.

While many sources have been consulted and studied, early issues of the Beaverton Express, which the management of that newspaper have kindly allowed us to microfilm, have been extremely valuable in learning about the past. We are most grateful to those who have preserved newspapers as well as documents and other resources for our examination.

Many of the pictures used in this book come from our Society Archives, but originally from people in our community. Others were loaned to us by the Women's Institute, the Public Library and certain individuals whose names appear with the pictures. We wish to express our gratitude to all who have helped us make pictures a very special part of this book.

We wish, also, to thank many of the senior members of our community who have given us vivid glimpses into the past.

For the alphabetical arrangement of the index our gratitude goes to Mr. Ron Link for the indexing computer program, for the use of his "Indexing Program List Creator," and the Computer Awareness students at Brock High School for typing entries.

Mr. Jack Little, too, has devoted much time doing photographic work for us. We thank him for his contribution.

In this book we have striven for accuracy based on the information available to us. We trust that our readers will forgive any errors which may exist.

Our hope is that this history will familiarize the readers with the dreams of our pioneers and bring into focus the ways in which these aims and desires were realized.

The History Committee of the
Beaverton Thorah Eldon Historical Society.

Committee Members:

Helen A. Alsop	Audrey I. Jones
Janet H. Alsop	Mary E. McGill
Kenneth R. Alsop	Kathleen Morrison
E. Margaret Baillie	Russell Morrison
Dorothy M. Burcher	P. Ian Murray
Robert P. Burcher	Donalda E. Nicholls
Morrison Colville	Harry H. Rogers
M. Elizabeth Furniss	Jane L. Veale
Harry J. Furniss	Garry W. Veale

Chapter 1

THE FISHING GROUNDS OF THE HURONS

From early times Lake Simcoe was a major link in two main waterway routes for the Indians. One started from Toronto Carrying Place to Lake Simcoe, Couchiching and the Severn River to Lake Huron. La Salle travelled this route three or four times on his way to Mackinac Island between the years 1680-83. The second, from Georgian Bay via Lake Simcoe and the Talbot River along the Trent system to Lake Ontario, was used by Champlain after wintering in Huronia in 1615. Thorah Island, therefore, was well known to the Hurons as was the mouth of the Beaver River.

Three Indian sites have been located on Thorah Island and cover a period of over 2,000 years. In the Beaverton area two sites which have never been excavated are known. A large site, between the present railway and Marina, had a population of about 200. Another on today's Fair Grounds near the harbour covered a period of possibly 3,000 years.

Early settlers mention an Indian graveyard "under the shadow of the Old Stone Church" and a "little city of the dead" along the banks of a creek near the house of the former Gunn farm north of Beaverton. In those days Indians made regular pilgrimages to perform ceremonies for the dead. A rumour still persists that a young Indian "princess" or chief's daughter is buried there "under the shade of a great balsam tree".

The Hurons were a trading and agricultural nation. They grew great crops of Indian corn, beans, pumpkins, and tobacco, with the women tending and gathering the crops. In their trade monopoly between the Petuns and Neutrals to the south and the Ottawa, Chippewas and Winnebagos to the north, they traded their produce, flints, copper ornaments, nets, and bags, for furs, buffalo robes and birchbark canoes from tribes to the northwest, and for materials to make nets from the Petuns to the south.

An early pioneer from the area near Barrie gave the following interesting account of Huron customs in his diary.

> "I have seen", he said "as many as 100 teepees in the woods on the south side of Kempenfeldt Bay. It was an interesting sight to see the making of an Indian home in the winter. The head of the

family carrying a bow and arrow, tomahawk and knife, strides ahead. The mother, carrying one or two papooses on her back as well as the household belongings followed. When the site selected for the camp was reached, the Indian chopped down a few saplings with crotched tops. The squaw meantime, with a cedar shovel, formed a circular hole in the snow. The crotched sticks were set around this and covered with bark or evergreens, boughs were spread on the ground and covered with fur. A fire was started in the middle of the tent and in half an hour the house was ready for occupation. While the work of preparation was going on, the papooses, strapped to flat boards, were hung up on trees by hooks at the head of the boards. If one cried, the mother would stop work for a moment and soothe the child with a gentle rocking accompanied by a lullaby.

All the Indians of that day from Lake Simcoe and Georgian Bay country came to Toronto once a year to receive money and goods which the government gave them in return for the surrender of their lands. They have been seen coming down Yonge Street in twos and threes, magnificent specimens of manhood, their head-dresses decorated with eagle feathers and carrying war spears in their hands. Too often they went back in an entirely different condition (sic). The white man knew this fondness for whiskey of the Indians, and whites waylaid these "children of the forest" and supplied them freely with firewater in exchange for the goods the Indians had received from the government. Frequently by the time the reds reached home, they had neither goods, blankets nor money and had to beg food for maintenance. Notwithstanding the manner in which they had been robbed, and the fact that they were armed, I never heard of a white man being killed by them. Eventually, however, the scandal became so great that the government adopted the plan of carrying the annuities for the Indians to their reserves and paying them there."

By 1630 Huronia stretched only from Lake Simcoe to Georgian Bay with a population of 30,000 living in villages of 1200 to 1800 people containing from 50 to 100 longhouses. The French, however, brought with them the dreaded smallpox and the Indians, with no immunity, succumbed in large numbers. By 1635 their numbers had shrunk to 12,000 and in their fear they blamed the Jesuits with witchcraft.

Although the Hurons had once possessed the territory comprising Rama, Mara and Thorah townships, after their defeat by the Iroquois in 1649, the lands were gradually taken over by the Mississaugas and

Chippewas with the Snake (Georgina) and Rama tribes of the Chippewas acquiring title to the eastern Lake Simcoe area.

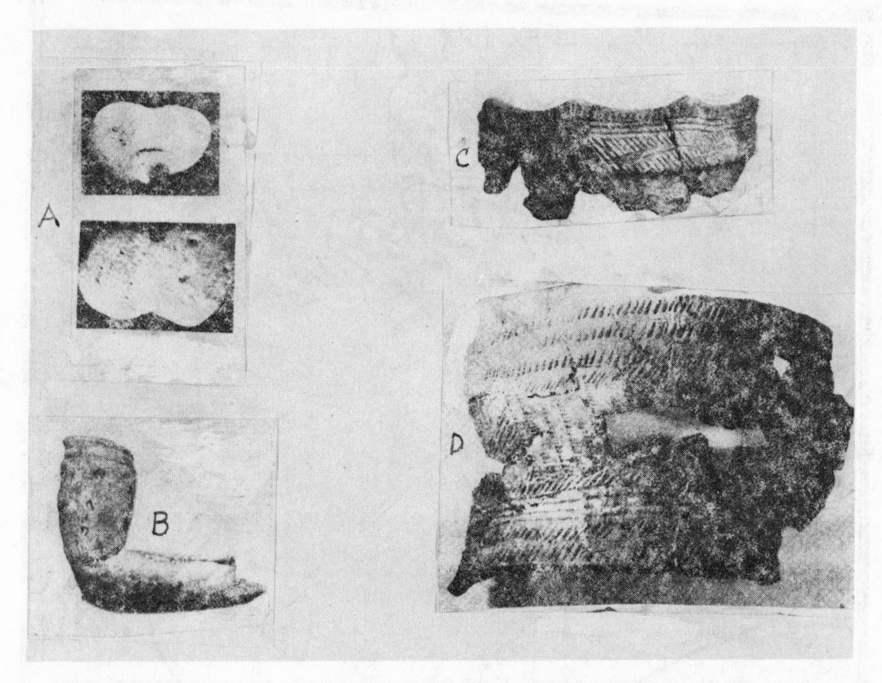

HURON INDIAN SHARDS FROM P. SWEETMAN DIGS AT THORAH ISLAND AND ELDON TOWNSHIP

Decorations appeared on the rims of jugs. Sticks, cords, cloth, and leather thongs and sometimes hollow bones to form circles, were pressed into the wet clay to form variegated or indented designs.

A. *Fish-Net sinkers from Bristow site, Thorah Island. It was primarily a temporary fishing site.*
B. *Stone pipe.*
C. *Ceramic rim type from the Bristow site, Thorah Island.*
D. *Reconstructed portion of a large vessel, showing complex cording. Pre-Huronic Indian.*

BIBLIOGRAPHY

Johnson, Leo A., *History of the County of Ontario 1615-1875.*
Sweetman, Paul. Letter re excavations.
Leitch, Adelaide. *The Visible Past.* County of Simcoe Ontario, 1967.

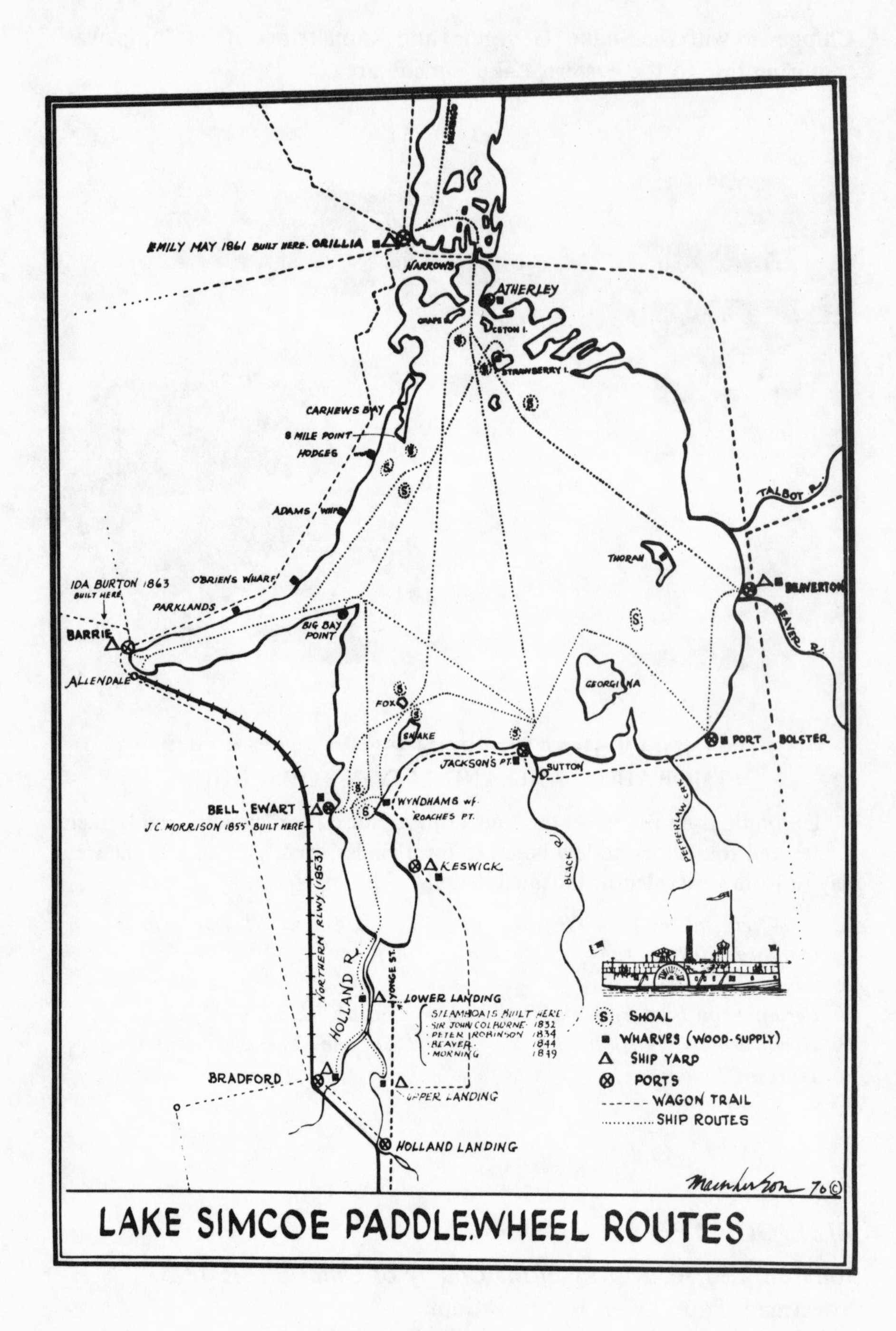
EMILY MAY 1861 BUILT HERE. ORILLIA
NARROWS
ATHERLEY
STRAWBERRY I.
CARNEWS BAY
8 MILE POINT
HODGES
ADAMS WHF
TALBOT R.
THORAH
O'BRIENS WHARF
IDA BURTON 1863 BUILT HERE
PARKLANDS
BEAVERTON
BEAVER R.
BIG BAY POINT
BARRIE
ALLENDALE
GEORGINA
FOX
SNAKE
PORT BOLSTER
JACKSON'S PT.
SUTTON
BELL EWART
J.C. MORRISON 1855 BUILT HERE
WYNDHAMS wf.
ROACHES PT.
KESWICK
BLACK R.
PEFFERLAW CRK.
NORTHERN RLWY. (1853)
HOLLAND R.
YONGE ST.
LOWER LANDING
STEAMBOATS BUILT HERE
SIR JOHN COLBORNE 1832
PETER ROBINSON 1834
BEAVER 1844
MORNING 1849
SHOAL
WHARVES (WOOD-SUPPLY)
SHIP YARD
PORTS
WAGON TRAIL
SHIP ROUTES
BRADFORD
UPPER LANDING
HOLLAND LANDING
LAKE SIMCOE PADDLEWHEEL ROUTES

Chapter 2
EARLY NAVIGATION

Early settlers striving to reach their new homes in lands surrounding Lake Simcoe, had to hire small boats to transport them across the waters. The first schooner ever mentioned on the Lake was noted in 1819 in a diary as having been seen at Holland Landing.

In 1834 Beaverton was "only a bush, store and a few shanties in a clearance on the Beaver River"[1] and yet by that date a ketch, the Sultana, and the schooner, Sara Jane Harris, had been built there.

James MacPherson owned a stone quarry in Rama Township on the east side of Lake Couchiching and built the schooner "Couchiching" to transport stone to Barrie and Belle Ewart. The "Couchiching" sailed only on Lake Simcoe. James' father, Captain MacPherson, settled in Rama in 1835. The "Couchiching's" wreck lies in Lake Simcoe about two miles from Jacksons Point.

The schooners, "St. George" and "Queen" were built in Orillia in 1851 and 1852. The remains of the "St. George" lie near Thorah Island according to the *Barrie Examiner* and the "Queen" at Bear Point near Barrie. Two other schooners are also known to have sailed the lake: the "Edward John" of Belle Ewart (1859) and the last, the "Lucille Bacon" of Holland Landing. No doubt there were others.

While the sailing boats were still riding the waves, the first paddle wheel steamboats made their appearance. The "Sir John Colborne" named after the Lieutenant Governor, was launched in 1832 at the lower landing of the Holland River, the northern terminal of Yonge Street which was only a trail at that time. On its inaugural trip it was met with great rejoicing and festivities by the settlers. It took one week to circle the lake, making numerous stops at wharves to load timbers for fuel. Its regular schedule was from the Holland River on Mondays and Thursdays to Shingle Bay (Orillia) steaming up the east side of Lake Simcoe. She returned to the Holland River on Tuesdays and Fridays down the west coast of the lake. Captain Borland ran the ship and Mr. Thornbury was engineer. The construction costs of building the "Colborne" were raised by subscriptions of two pounds, ten shillings per share, but after her launching Charles Thompson of Summerhill bought these subscriptions.

[1] Tatley, Richard. *Steamboating on the Trent-Severn*. Belleville, 1978.

He was an entrepreneur of many interests, controlling hotels in York (Toronto) and all stage travel north of York as well as possessing the Royal Mail contract. Later he became a founder of the Northern Railway which joined York with Allandale. He was also either owner or co-owner of the first five paddle wheelers on Lake Simcoe.

The "Colborne's" speed was only four miles per hour and she had such a deep draught, similar to schooners, that she could not pass through the Narrows into Lake Couchiching and had to stand offshore to load.

The second ship, the "Peter Robinson" (1834), was built on the same lines but was lighter and faster with a newer style engine. Her schedule was identical to that of the "Colborne". She was run by Captain MacIntosh and engineer David Robinson, and was abandoned at the Narrows near Atherly after sailing Lake Simcoe for ten years.

Both ships were later converted to schooners. The paddle wheelers, "Beaver", "Morning", "J.C. Morrison", "Emily May", and "Ida Burton" all prospered by transporting freight and passengers. Excursion parties and picnics were also encouraged to such places as Strawberry Island.

Later screw-propelled steamers followed the paddle wheelers. The "Geneva", "Islay", "Carella", "Orillia", "Lillie" and "Enterprise" all stopped at Beaverton while the "Priscilla", "Enterprise", "Longford", "Siesta", "Queen of the Isles" and "Lady of the Lakes" also operated on Lake Simcoe. As late as 1887 we read in the *Beaverton Express* that "Jas. Bates of Toronto informs us he has purchased a new little steamer the 'Mascot' in Toronto, which he intends running at Beaverton next summer if any harbor accommodation is offered."

At least 250 steamships are known to have sailed on portions of the Trent-Severn system from 1832 to 1951 but the appearance of the railways spelled doom to transportation on the waterways for commercial purposes.

Until the later years of the 19th century, residents of Thorah Island had to depend on privately-owned sail boats to reach Beaverton for supplies and mail. In the winter, of course, the heavy ice on the lake made the entire area of Lake Simcoe a broad roadway and sleighs could travel as far as Barrie and Orillia.

In the late 1800's, John Maclean, a salt-water sailor, owned a three-masted sail boat and carried passengers, as well as hauling limestone from Thorah Island to Beaverton.

In 1903, Thos. Warren Sr. of Thorah Island built a gasoline-powered boat the "Belle of Thorah" and began a passenger service to the mainland. In 1912, as his father's boat was aging, Thos. Warren Jr. built a second gasoline-powered boat named "Thorah Belle" and transported both

PADDLEWHEEL PAINTING
by Duncan McPherson "SIR JOHN COLBORNE."

passengers and mail. Later in 1926, Thos. Jr. purchased the "Darontal" from Arthur Emes and added it to his service. He augmented his fleet in 1934, by having the "Wawanessa" built by Farquhar McRae at Thorah Island. It also carried passengers as well as mail. Later in 1960, a ferry service was run by Bob Smith who carried out service to the island with his boat "Miss Beaverton" and later on with a larger boat.

The present day ferry service is run by Roy Camplin with his boat "Rusty Spike."

Mrs. Donalda Nicholls and members of the Davidson family.
MacPherson, Duncan. Printed notes of research on early paddle wheelers and steamers. Also map showing original lake route.
Hunter, A.F. *A History of Simcoe County*. Barrie, 1909.
Leitch, Adelaide. *The Visible Past*. The pictorial history of Simcoe County. Compiled and written for the County of Simcoe, Ontario, Canada. 1967.
Ritchie, Mary Houston. *A Township on the Lake*, Beaverton and Thorah 1820-1952.

S.S. GENEVA

A View of Beaverton Harbour circa 1910. The three tall buildings to the right were sail-boat houses.

Chapter 3

THE LURE OF THE LAND

Holding the deed for property registered in one's own name is certain to give any person a feeling of satisfaction; yet in a country where land ownership is very much taken for granted, we do not easily grasp the significance that owning property played in the lives of men and women whose families in Britain had been mere tenants for generations. What was formerly dismissed as completely out of reach in their native land could become a reality in Canada.

Their individual reasons for coming to this land were probably as many and as varied as the districts and stations of life which Thorah's pioneers represented. However, it is common knowledge that Britain, and most specifically Scotland, homeland of most Thorah settlers, was undergoing difficult economic times, that the use of land was changing, machines were replacing workers, veterans of the Napoleonic Wars were being released into the work force, and immigration from Ireland was putting strains on an already overpopulated land. High unemployment and a sluggish economy, then, were the two greatest factors which drove Scots to the colonies. Various emigration schemes aided by government funds eased, for many, the difficulties of departing from the Old Land. The prospect of owning property on the other side of the Atlantic undoubtedly took much of the sting out of leaving their homeland, family, and friends for a place in the wilderness of Upper Canada.

For some of these people the "promised land" would be Thorah on the east shores of Lake Simcoe, a township whose name from the Hebrew means "the Pentateuch, the revealed word of God."[1]

The task of surveying the Township was given to John Edward White, although some of this work was done later by David Gibson. In return, White received grants of land in 1821[2] amounting to five per cent of the land surveyed[3] and totalling about 1,700 acres. Like all such grants, his acreages were scattered about the township, but as settlement increased, the sale of these lands brought remuneration. The White family built a home and cleared land along the lake just north of Beaverton. James

[1] Gardiner, H.F., *Nothing But Names*, Toronto, Geo. N. Morang and Co., 1899.
[2] Index to Abstract Land Deeds for Thorah Township.
[3] Minutes of Home District Council, 29.12.1819.

White, the first male white child born in Thorah and his wife, Jeanette Waddell, the first female white child born in Mara, the township bordering Thorah to the north, later farmed on lot 13, Concession 7.

Other grants of land were made to military men who had served during the Napoleonic Wars. The majority of these grantees were Scottish, but the earliest one to settle in Thorah, Ensign William Turner of the Sicilian Regiment, was an Irishman.[4] Turner was located on lot 23 of the 1st Concession in 1821.[5] There on the shore of Lake Simcoe was built a home, a log structure, which still stands today. Lumber for this house was brought, it is said, from Holland Landing by rowboat, there being, of course, no saw mill closer. A letter written by Mr. Turner two years later requested that land he held in lots 11 and 12 in Concession 8 be exchanged for lot 21, Concession 1 because the "petitioner has four miles of road to make, no intervening settler to assist him, a bridge to construct over a river 60 yards wide."[6] Little did Mr. Turner realize that he was relinquishing one of the finer farm properties in the Township.

Turner's daughter, Elizabeth, later to become Mrs. Robert McTaggart, was the first white female child born in Thorah.

Numerous grants were made to soldiers as part of efforts designed to ease Britain's economic problems in a time of recession worsened by the discharge of thousands of soldiers into civilian life. It appears that some of these half-pay officers and pensioners never took up their land. Some who did were not able to adapt to the rigors of pioneer life with the result that their land was abandoned or sold and vocations more to their liking were pursued.

One military grantee who put other talents to use was Donald Cameron, that colonizer responsible for bringing so many Scots to this township. Previously a transporter of immigrants to Canada,[7] Cameron turned his attention in 1823 to land speculation and the placing of settlers on land. Many of these locatees were from the Eastern District, in the Townships of Lancaster, Lochiel, and Charlottenburgh (all part of Glengarry County in later years), but others came directly from Scotland. It seems that many to whom location tickets were issued never put foot on Thorah soil. Finally the colonial government became suspicious of Cameron's settlement, commissioned Arad Smalley to investigate and report his findings in 1830, and subsequently charged Cameron with

[4] Tombstone Inscription of Ensign Turner.
[5] Public Archives of Ontario, Land Records Index.
[6] Letter written by Ensign Turner, 19.7.1823.
[7] Hill, Douglas, *Great Emigrations: The Scots to Canada*. London, Gentry Books, 1972, page 110.

perjury; later he was indicted for high treason. Was Cameron really a villain bent on misrepresentation of facts for personal gain, or was he merely the victim of circumstance? We might also ask if the settlement requirements imposed on him by the colonial government were really practicable. At any rate, Donald Cameron's efforts were responsible for bringing many fine Scottish families to this Township, including the McRaes, the McPhersons, the McEwens, the Campbells, the Camerons, the Stewarts, and many others. Examination of the innumerable letters written by settlers located in Thorah by Cameron shows no complaints or criticism of his treatment of them.

Those who received location tickets were required to clear and fence five acres for every hundred acres granted, to build a dwelling house 16 feet by 20 feet, and to clear one-half of the road in front of each lot. These duties were to be performed within two years from the date of the ticket.[8] Even those soldiers who received grants were compelled to carry out these requirements.

With almost unbroken forest and no such man-made markers or boundaries as fences for guides, the likelihood of errors in locating property, in defining limits, and staying within those bounds was great. John Campbell of the 2nd Concession was mistakenly shown the wrong property on which he built a house and cleared eight acres of land. When the surveyor ran the line, "behold, all the improvement is on the south half."[9] In such cases the land on which the improvements were made was usually granted except where claims by other locatees had already been made. In many instances the improved land was superior and so the mistake turned out to the settler's advantage.

Among those settlers taking up land in the 1820's were the Campbells, Camerons, and McRaes in the south part of the Township, Lieut. Cameron in the 8th Concession, and the McDonalds of the 9th Concession.

Each settler could look forward to years of toil in clearing the forest. Not only was the chopping of trees hard labour, it was dangerous as well, and many the man was injured through the misuse of tools, or lost his life when crushed by a falling tree. Dougal Gillespie was one such pioneer who, while chopping trees was killed when a branch fell on his head. His widow Mary and five of his seven children still at home, carried on after his death on land granted to them in the 2nd Concession. Some of their descendants still reside in Thorah and Beaverton.

[8] Settling Duties required by an Order-in-Council, 20.10.1818.
[9] Letter written by Mr. Campbell, 15.3.1833.

A shelter, however crude, was the immediate concern of each pioneer family and the first shanty was built of logs with the spaces caulked with moss. Logs, often of basswood were split, hollowed out, and placed side by side with inverted ones placed over the edges to make a roof. By 1830 about 35 houses had been built in the Township, but five of these were classed as huts.[10]

An important product of the forest was the ash left after the branches or trunks of hardwood trees were burned. Many settlers leached the wood ash by piling alternate layers of ash and straw in a barrel and adding water. The run-off was caught after it seeped through, and evaporated over a fire. The residue, or potash, was used for making soaps. It is said that some settlers made a bigger profit from potash than from grain. In 1842 Thorah had three potasheries.[11]

Clearing the land continued as the years passed and more settlers located in Thorah. Only a few more than 400 acres were cleared by 1830,[12] but by 1842 five times this area (2,174 acres) was classed as "improved land."[13]

Donald Gunn of Gunn's Limited, father of General John Gunn, recalled his years as a young man in Thorah when he would put in 10 hours a day cradling grain on the farm of his neighbour, Col. Cameron, and then cut grain at home in the early morning and late evening.[14] Donald, a son of John Gunn who settled in the south half of lot 11 Concession 7 in 1830[15] was able to cut four or five acres of grain in a day.[16]

Sitting on a lonely hillside on the estate of the Duke of Sutherland, Scotland, John Gunn, Donald's father, watched his home, the house in which he was born, devoured in flames.[17] We can imagine the bitterness, the anger, the utter helplessness which must have been felt by this victim of the Clearances; yet he, like so many of these evicted crofters, did not allow this misfortune to defeat him. He was ready to create for himself and his family a new life in the Canadian wilderness.

During the pioneer years in Thorah John Gunn was a leader in the religious community, ministering to the spiritual needs of the people before a church was established or a regular minister was engaged, and

[10] Smalley's Inspection Report of 1830.
[11] 1842 Census of Thorah Township.
[12] Smalley's Inspection Report of 1830.
[13] 1842 Census of Thorah.
[14] Smith, op. cit., page 149.
[15] Coleman, Thelma, *The Canada Company*, Stratford, County of Perth and Cumming Publishers, 1978, page 225.
[16] Smith, op. cit., page 149.
[17] "Early Days in Thorah", *Weekly Sun*, Toronto. 1.9.1909.

instrumental in getting a grant of land on which the Church of Scotland could erect a place of worship. He possessed skill in healing the sick and his help was much in demand in a community without a physician.[18] By trade, John Gunn was a stone mason and it is said that he worked at the building of Government House in Toronto.[19]

Gunn's name is often associated with temperance. In the early days whisky was available in abundance at all bees. In some cases, swamp water, alive with polliwogs and other small creatures, was the only alternative. While the men usually worked harder after some indulgence, the increase in accidents and rowdiness was often a problem. On one occasion at John Gunn's farm, two logging gangs, well fortified with whisky, were vying to be the first to finish their section. When one man cheated by shoving a log from his section to the rival gang, the fight was on. John Gunn, it was said, jumped between the fighters and calling on his remarkable strength, was able to subdue their anger. Atop a heap of logs Gunn gave the group a quiet lecture, vowing then that never again would he allow liquor at a logging bee on his property.[20]

Settling directly north of the Gunns were two other Sutherlandshire natives, John Bruce and his wife, Roberta Fraser. Married in 1829, this couple came to Canada that year, living in Bytown, or Ottawa, for about a year before arriving in Thorah. Their son, George Fraser Bruce, played an important role in this community, serving as the Reeve of Thorah, County Warden, and later as the first Reeve of Beaverton.

The first permanent residents of what is now Beaverton were the Calders who arrived about 1828.[21] They were among a group of Scots from Islay who had emigrated to North Carolina in 1818.[22] Finding the climate not to their liking, feeling uncomfortable with the system of slavery, and finally refusing to swear allegiance to the United States, these families looked northward. One young man, Archibald McMillan,[23] went ahead in 1827 to investigate the land. In Canada he met Donald Cameron who persuaded him to come to Thorah.

Thus began the long trek to Upper Canada. The Calders, along with a black baby girl, the first of her race north of Toronto, settled along the Beaver River near the lake while the other families went farther east near the Thorah-Eldon townline. Archibald McMillan, already men-

[18] Smith, op. cit. page 153.
[19] As told by Peter McMillan, 1947.
[20] Smith, op. cit., page 154.
[21] Reminiscences of A.C. Campbell in the *Canadian Post*, 1915.
[22] A.C. Campbell.
[23] Kathleen McMillan.

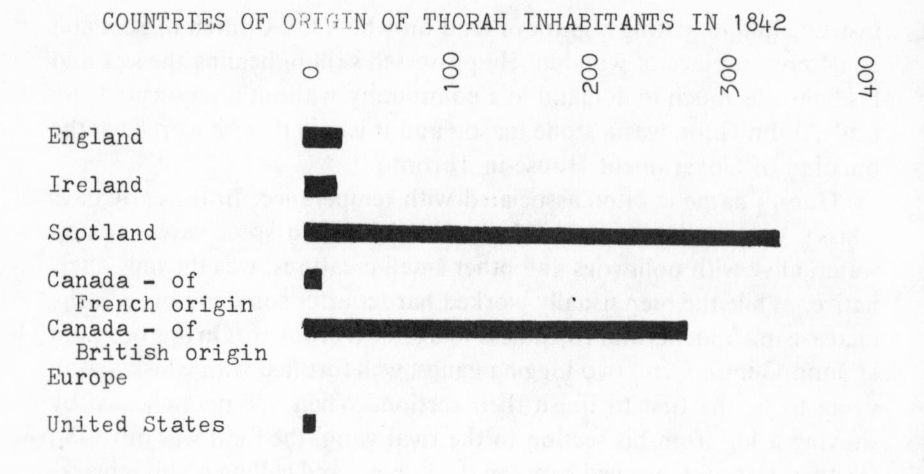

tioned, and his wife, Mary Currie, settled on lot 2 Concession 4 where their great-grandson, John, and later his son Rick farmed until recently. Hugh McMillan, brother of Archibald, and his wife, Elizabeth McCuaig, farmed at lot 2, Concession 5. This farm was sold in 1981 by their great-grandchildren, Gordon and Kathleen McMillan.

Others of the North Carolina settlers in this area were the Campbells, McFadyens, and Rays. The Thorah-Eldon townline became known as Islay Street. These Carolina settlers had horses, oxen, wagons, ploughs, and some tools with which to begin life in the Thorah bush.[24] Surely they had an advantage over many Thorah pioneers.

The Calders built the first grist mill on or near the site of the mill at Simcoe Street and Mara Road which burned to the ground in 1978. Surely this mill was a god-send to the early settlers. Alex McDougall, quoted in the book *Pioneers of Old Ontario* by W.L. Smith, said, "One man with nine children was forced to carry all the grain he used that winter to Newmarket on his back and to carry the flour back the same way. He was kept going and coming all winter because no sooner had he carried in one load of flour than he had to start back for another."[25]

Some families ground their wheat at home between two stones made to revolve with a crank turned by hand. The wheat was poured by hand through a hole in the upper stone.[26]

[24] A.C. Campbell.
[25] Smith, op. cit., page 146.
[26] Ibid. page 141.

The story is told of one Eldon pioneer who carried on his back a bag of wheat to have it ground at Beaverton 10 miles away. Overtaken by a neighbour on horseback on the return trip, the weary man asked for a ride. When the neighbour replied that he could not give both him and his bag of flour a ride, the quick-thinking pedestrian replied, "You give me a ride and I'll carry the flour on my own shoulder."[27]

Beaverton's second family, the Gordons, natives of Sutherlandshire, Scotland, made their way about 1831 from Holland Landing in a rowboat to the Beaver River after a four-month voyage from their motherland.[28] James Gordon was Beaverton's first blacksmith and "his smithy with the mill that adjoined it was the rendezvous of all the first settlers of Thorah, Mara, Eldon, Mariposa, and Brock."[29]

Near the grist mill where Donald Calder's son, Duncan, ground grain and distilled whisky, another son, Alexander, a turner and cabinet maker, operated a sawmill. The small settlement which grew up on what is now downtown Beaverton was known as Mill Town, or Milton, or even Calder's Mills.[30]

In 1833 the Calders sold property to Kenneth Cameron[31] who opened Beaverton's first store. Before this time, provisions had to be brought in across the lake.

One story told by Mr. McFadyen of Eldon suggests that Beaverton had its share of lawlessness even in the early days. His uncle, Dougall Carmichael, had his belongings sent by boat to Beaverton in 1832 while he walked from Sutton by land. When he went to pick up his goods, some men started shooting and Carmichael fled. Upon his return later, he found that his trunk had been broken into and sixty sovereigns as well as some clothing stolen. McFadyen recalled that years later a man told him of the robbery and stated that the robber had buried the gold under his hearthstone in Beaverton.[32]

Another tale of treasure buried by an Irishman by the name of Lampier was remembered by some of the old-timers. John Usher, a well-diviner of this area in years past spent much time searching for the treasure which he declared was in an oak box 15 to 18 inches square. In fact, he claimed to have touched the chest, but every time the treasure

[27] A.C. Campbell.
[28] *Beaverton Express* of 27.3.1896 (Obituary of Mrs. Gordon)
[29] loc. cit.
[30] Letter written to John McKay was addressed to Calder's Mills.
[31] Index to Abstract Land Deeds.
[32] Smith, op. cit., page 141.

seemed to be within his grasp, the 'durn thing shifted."[33]

The Proctors arrived about 1833 and set up the second store. In 1834 George Proctor bought 100 acres in lot 8 Concession 3.[34] Was this property through which the Beaver River passed purchased with the intention of starting a mill? In 1839 land in lot 13 Concession 5 was bought[35] and six years later Proctor erected a mill[36] on the Beaver River about a half mile upstream from Calder's Mill. In connection with the mill, Proctor distilled whisky, as did Duncan Calder and Archibald Stewart.[37]

As well as the Calders, others from that Inner Hebridean Scottish island called Islay were to come to Thorah. In fact, the McDougalls who settled in the 9th Concession are said to have come as a result of representations made by Donald Calder.[38] Angus and Margaret McDougall arrived in Thorah in 1831[39] along with their five children, settling on lot 9 Concession 9. During their first winter, their four sons, Duncan, Alexander, Peter, and Angus, chopped 15 acres of bush while their father, in order to provide for his family, took jobs threshing grain with a flail.[40] Wheat was cleaned by being thrown up in the air from a sheet.[41]

During the 1830's many names well-known in the Beaverton area, generations later appear on land records. John McKay, the Township's first clerk, settled in the 4th Concession where his descendants carried on for several decades. John Morrison and his family took up land in Concession 3. It was said that it was on their farm that the first sow thistle of the neighbourhood appeared. The Morrison boys dug deep for its roots and smothered it with straw.[42]

Other families arriving to take up land in Thorah in the 1830's include the Leslies, McBains, Robinsons, and Edgars in the south of the Township, the French, Galloway, Carmichael, McCallum, and McCuaig families in the east, and the Frasers, McBrides, McEwens, and Westcotts in the north.[43] In the area surrounding Beaverton were the Thompson,

33 *Beaverton Express*, 8.12.1951.
34 Index to Abstract Land Deeds.
35 loc. cit.
36 *Beaverton Express*, Christmas Issue, 1882.
37 Lovell, John, *Canada Directory*, 1851.
38 "Early Days in Thorah", *Weekly Sun*, Toronto, 1.9.1909.
39 Smith, op. cit., page 146, as quoted from Alex McDougall.
40 loc. cit.
41 loc. cit.
42 Reminiscences of A.C. Campbell.
43 Index to Abstract Land Deeds.

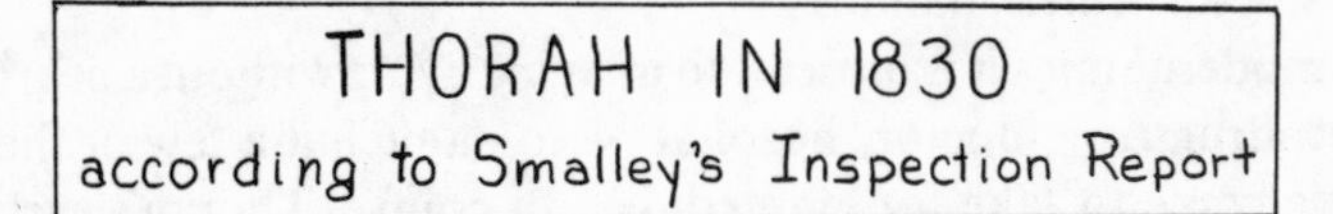

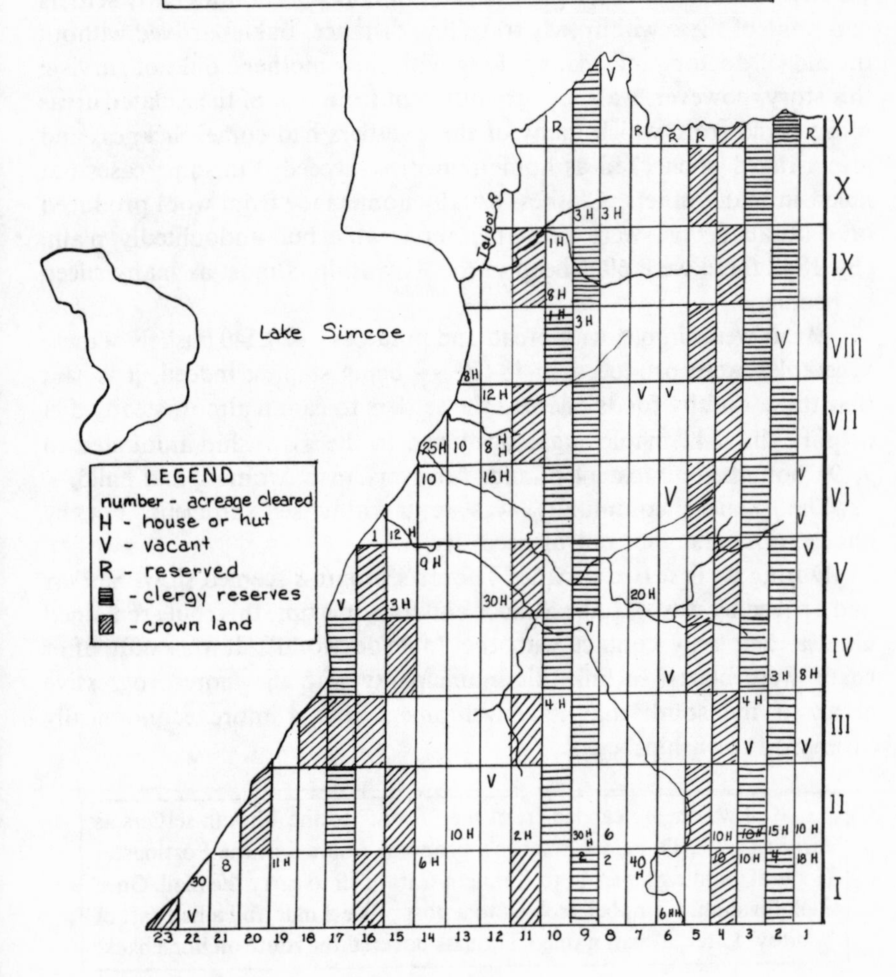

An annual event in this area in the early days was the migration of pigeons which passed through in swarms. "They hung in a thick cloud quite low down in the air," one hunter recalled in a conversation with Mr. J.K. Kohl, a German visitor to this area in 1853. In fact, this same man feared being suffocated, so thick were the birds.

Furniss, and Murray families.[44]

In modern times it is difficult to imagine living without a nearby supermarket, drugstore, doctor, hospital — to name but a few of the services we have come to take for granted; yet, of course, Thorah's early settlers had none of these within easy travelling distance. Babies arrived without the aid of doctors and many, along with their mothers, did not survive; this story, however, was not very different from that of the isolated areas of Scotland from which many of these settlers had come. Sickness and fevers raged unchecked as home-remedies succeeded in some cases but failed in many others. Clothes, usually homemade from wool produced on Thorah farms, were probably serviceable but undoubtedly plain. (By 1842 there were 602 sheep in the Township, almost as many sheep as people.)[45]

Meals were simple, with bread and potatoes — 20,540 bushels of these vegetables were produced in 1842[46] — being staples; indeed, it is said that these starchy foods enabled the settlers to eat an almost steady diet of pork. in 1842 maple sugar produced in the Township amounted to 9,191 pounds,[47] almost 14 pounds for every man, woman, and child.

The pioneer community was remarkably self-sufficient, not by choice, of course, but out of necessity.

During its first two decades Thorah's progress seemed slow. Settlers had arrived by way of Lake Simcoe and for some time this route remained almost their only contact with the "outside world". It was only after roads were blazed to link this municipality with the more progressive areas to the south that its development into a more economically diversified township began.

Mail was being carried from the "Front" to the Thorah settlers as early as 1827. Donald Cameron's proposal resulted in the Postmaster General granting a permit to Kenneth Campbell to carry the mail. Once each fortnight Campbell walked to a post office a mile and a half east of Whitby. Later, a man named Thomas covered the route on horseback.

The 1848 Census of Thorah states that there were in the Township: 146 farmers, 26 labourers, 1 merchant, 1 physician, 1 surgeon, 1 innkeeper, 1 fuller, 2 churches, 4 schools, and 1 inn.

[44] loc. cit.
[45] 1842 Census of Thorah.
[46] loc. cit.
[47] loc. cit.

Chapter 4
CROSS ROADS ON THE BEAVER

Thorah Township of 160 years ago was very different from the one we know today. If we could be transported back all those years and allowed to see it from the air, possibly only two tiny clearings would be found, both hugging the shore of Lake Simcoe.[1] The balance of Thorah was composed of dense bush, streams, creeks, swamps and beaver meadows. What would become good farm land grew tall stands of maple, oak, birch, ash, cedar, pine, spruce and tamarack. The swamps were prevalent and of such size that they defied for many years the best attempts of man and beast to conquer them. Many Thorah crops are grown where once was a home for beaver, cranes, ducks and other creatures of the water. These areas bred great hosts of mosquitoes and black flies and frequently came to be blamed as the source of the ague and other ailments. Thorah was relatively flat; thus ground water was slow to drain to creeks and rivers. It was covered with dense bush rooted in centuries of decaying vegetation and made an excellent sponge. Under these conditions the land had a great capacity to retain moisture and only released it slowly to the streams that drained it. For this reason Thorah's rivers and creeks ran at a more constant volume all year.

Clearing the land reduced the humus content of the soil and allowed rapid evaporation from the surface. Road building necessitated the digging of ditches. These two factors, when combined with other drains, slowly eliminated the swampland. The result is that today nearly all the run-off occurs in the spring, leaving the streams low for the balance of the year.

When White and Gibson conducted their surveys in the 1820's they not only marked out parcels of land but also road allowances. Early arrivals were required to clear half of the road allowance in front of their property as a condition to own the land.[2] But if the nearest neighbour was a mile away, the intervening road allowance might go unopened for years. It is easy to appreciate the transportation problems that some early pioneers faced.

The only reliable routes for the traveller and inhabitant alike were

[1] York Almanac, 1825.
[2] A condition stated in the Location Ticket.

those that had been used for generations by the aboriginal people. These were not random trails from one point to the other but common sense roads or portages that could be used safely for most of the year. They could be 100 yards or 40 miles in length and followed the natural heights of the land.

These important trails crossed the land with no regard for the neat gridwork of properties that had been established by the surveyors. Think of the settler who through long toil had grown his first crop of golden wheat by chance across the path of such a road. He might awake one morning to find a portion trampled by strangers who found his field the only possible route. Such problems led to these Indian trails becoming legally surveyed roads. All that was necessary was a petition of twelve inhabitants of Thorah to give birth to new roads or alterations in existing ones.[3] It is possible that a new road could be surveyed because a leading citizen had the right friends at York.

At the time of the arrival of the first permanent white settlers in Thorah, every aspect of administration was controlled from York, and remained so for years. This power was in the hands of the Court of the General Quarter Sessions of the Peace for the Home District.[4] The justices or magistrates, as they were called, were appointed for life by the Lieutenant-Governor on the advice of the Legislative Assembly.[5] A supposed passionate fear of republicanism after the war of 1812, but more likely a fervent desire to transplant the British class system to the Canadas, resulted in only "true blue" Tories being appointed to these posts.[6]

Until 1837 the Home District comprised all of the more recent counties of Peel, York, Ontario, Simcoe and great portions of Dufferin and Grey Counties.[7] Every detail of both municipal and judicial administration came under their scrutiny.[8] At that time the Home district was reduced to nearly half of its earlier size but still included Thorah Township.[9]

[3] Public Archives of Ontario, M.S. 251, Reel 1, Minutes of the General Quarter Sessions of the Peace for the Home District, York. Confirmation of survey by Arad Smalley, surveyor of highways for the Home District, July 9, 1830.

[4] Ibid., Introduction to Reel 1.

[5] Johnson, Leo A., *History of the County of Ontario, 1615-1875.* Page 59.

[6] Loc. cit.

[7] Jonasson, Eric, "The Districts and Counties of Southern Ontario, 1777-1979, Two Centuries of Evolution", *Families,* Vol. 20, No. 2, 1981, page 96. Map 3.

[8] PAO, M.S. 251, Introduction to Reel 1.

[9] Jonasson, op. cit. Page 96.

Judicially, this court tried all but the most serious crimes. A study of the minutes of the court reveals cases of larceny, theft, assault, arson, and public nuisance with occasional occurrences of manslaughter or murder.[10]

Municipally, they appointed assessors, clerks and licensed taverns.[11] In 1827 they issued a tavern license to a Thomas Balderson for a location that was described only as: "beyond Lake Simcoe."[12] They also licensed non-conforming clergymen. On March 1, 1842, the Rev. John McMurchy, minister of the Church of Scotland for West Gwillimbury, was "ordered to receive the usual license to solemnize marriages."[13] At that time McMurchy was also serving Thorah Township[14] and later became permanently established in Eldon Township.

The magistrates also appointed surveyors and coroners. One man who appears to have held both these posts was Arad Smalley.[15] His name may seem remote to our story but Smalley may have ultimately cast the seed for the village of Beaverton. It was Smalley who brought into existence those roads that sprang from those early Indian trails that proved to be such vital economic links for Thorah and thus for Beaverton. In 1827 he surveyed what was to become the Cameron Road.[16] His line started at the lake shore just south of the mouth of the Beaver River at the present Beaverton Harbour. From there it ran roughly to the south-east through the present village then more or less followed the high ground just west of the Beaver River. From Thorah the road extended southerly through Brock Township to a point southwest of the present site of Cannington. Here he crossed the Beaver River and continued southeasterly to the site of Manilla. A present-day drive from Manilla to Oshawa, down Simcoe St. to Lake Ontario, roughly recreates the balance of this survey line.[17]

This survey may have remained just a trail for a number of years, but increased pressure to sell the produce of the township to larger markets would not have allowed this for long. Squire Donald Cameron is reputed to have been a leader in opening at least part of this road, which became Thorah's most important avenue of commerce, especially in the formative

[10] PAO, M.S. 251, Reel 2, Vol. 6, page 90, Nov. 14, 1834.
[11] Ibid., Vol. 7, page 294.
[12] Ibid., Reel 1, Jan. 5, 1827.
[13] Ibid., Reel 2, Vol. 7, Mar. 1, 1842.
[14] PAO, G.S. 6397, Parish Registers of Reverend John McMurchy.
[15] PAO, M.S. 251, Reel 1, page 99, Vol. 5, May 4, 1830.
[16] Ibid., Nov. 29, 1827. Map R-H Home Gore and Simcoe Districts, 1846.
[17] PAO, Map Collection; Map Home and Simcoe Districts, C. Rankin, 1841.

years.[18] Wheat seemed to be the most marketable crop and was therefore most popular.[19] Small amounts of oats and barley for malting were shipped in some years.[20] All old Thorah families have oral traditions of the menfolk hauling grain by sleigh or wagon to Prince Albert along the Cameron Road. Prince Albert was near the Plank Road which diverted traffic from Oshawa Harbour to the better harbour at Whitby.[21] Here grain dealers bought grain all winter in anticipation of selling it when navigation opened up on Lake Ontario in the spring. This market served many of the so called back townships including Fenelon, Eldon, Mariposa, Brock and, of course, Thorah.[22] Shipping the grain in the winter had two great advantages. First, winter was when the farmer had the most time to spare. Second, roads were at their best when the creeks and low areas were frozen over. The farmer would rise before dawn to begin his trek. If he made good time he could expect to spend that night in Prince Albert. He could also expect to spend part of that night waiting in line to unload.[23] All the grain was handled by hand and scores of sleighs might arrive on one day, creating line-ups of over a half mile in length.[24] No doubt there was time for conversation and exchange of news as he helped other farmers in front of him unload. The next day necessary goods would be purchased early and the return trip began.

The time period and vantage point had a great effect upon what name was chosen when referring to this road. An inhabitant of the southern part of the county would probably always refer to it as Simcoe St., simply because a road frequently takes the name of its destination. At the Thorah end this road was called the "Whitby Road" by Smalley himself in 1829.[25] This name was used in Thorah until about 1862 when the name Cameron Road suddenly came into use.[26] One plausible theory for this name change might be mentioned. It was about this time that the centre road was being opened into Thorah. Though not passable through Thorah at that time, it did make direct communication with the

[18] Beers, J.H. & Co., *Historical Atlas of the County of Ontario 1877*. Cumming reprint. Page 12.

[19] Johnson, op. cit. page 200.

[20] Ibid., page 201.

[21] Farmer, Samuel, *By the Shores of Scugog*, page 49.

[22] Ibid., page 68.

[23] Ibid., page 69.

[24] Ibid., page 68.

[25] PAO, M.S. 251, Reel 1, Dec. 8, 1829.

[26] PAO, M.S. 348. Thorah Council Minutes. The term "Whitby Road" was used at the May 25, 1861 meeting of Thorah Council but at the April 26, 1862 meeting the name "Cameron Road" was used and continued from that date.

town of Whitby and thus was no doubt competing with the older road for this title. Possibly to end this confusion the old Whitby Road was renamed the Cameron Road in honour of Squire Cameron. The Whitby Road, later Cameron Road, was named after the township of Whitby and not after the town which came into existence long after the road was surveyed.

In a report to the Court of the General Quarter Sessions at York on December 8, 1829, Arad Smalley stated that: "having been requested by certain inhabitants to the number of twelve of the Township of Thorah... to lay out a road from the north west corner of Brock along the lakeshore to the Talbot River. . ."[27] he had done so. This road surveyed by Smalley skirted the shore of the lake northward from the Brock townline remaining inland just far enough to avoid certain ravines. It joined with the 5th Concession line at the lakeshore and continued to the 6th line. From here it turned easterly to enter the present site of Beaverton crossing the Beaver River near the present museum. This line ran diagonally to the 7th Concession, then straight to the 8th Concession following between lots 12 and 13. At the 8th it returned to the shore line and continued to the mouth of the Talbot river.[28]

With this survey Smalley had placed Beaverton at a cross roads when there was possibly only one family on the site, and several years before the Calder mill was built.[29] Thus Beaverton was at a focus of transportation by Smalley's hand.

In 1830 Smalley was at work again in Thorah surveying detours in the line of the 2nd Concession, as requested by a number of inhabitants.[30] A detailed study of the survey notes reveals that these changes were necessary to avoid three large swampy areas. The most easterly low area was in front of the former Alf Cockburn farm at lots 3 and 4 of the 2nd Concession. This area seems fairly dry today, but close observation shows stands of cattails at a number of locations marking natural springs. The road ditches here are quite deep for the purpose of conducting ground water over the slight rise at lot 5, which prevents natural drainage to the Beaver River. To avoid this wet area Smalley turned the new line of the road southwesterly at lot 2, crossing diagonally in front of the present

[27] PAO, M.S. 251, Reel 1, Dec. 8, 1829.
[28] Loc. cit.
[29] PAO, R.G. 1, A-VI-9, Vol. 2, Report of Arad Smalley. There is much dispute regarding actual date of construction of Calder's first mill. At the time of Smalley's inspection report he gave Calder credit for a house and nine acres of cleared land but made no mention of a mill.
[30] PAO, M.S. 251, Reel 1, Vol. 5, July 14, 1830.

Rickard farm buildings. It continued across lot 3, turning nearly west to follow the ridge across the former Cockburn farm. From here it ran west to the Beaver River, following the south line fence of the former Clarence Ritchie farm.[31] A short distance past the river it returned north to the original line, probably along the Whitby Road. At lot 11, until recently the Bob Ross farm, Smalley ran a new line southwest then westward to lot 16, the David Lancaster farm, where it returned to the old line. Once more Smalley detoured the road southward at lot 19 to follow the slightly higher ground along the centre of the 1st Concession. This new line connected with the Lakeshore road at or near Ensign Turner's buildings.[32]

The original purpose of the new line was to provide an all-season route across the south of the township, which was relatively well settled at an early date. There appears to be much more to it, however, as the most easterly detour, at least, seems to have been a favoured road to destinations outside the township for a period of perhaps 40 years. This eastern section was definitely in use by 1840.[33] In fact, it was used early enough to have become the boundary line between the former Ritchie farm and the John Lotton property.[34] These farms extend in an east to west direction instead of the normal north to south alignment. In 1844 this road was described as "leading strait (sic) from Eldon to Georgina."[35] From that date it was known variously as the Eldon Road,[36] the Post Road,[37] or the Peterborough Road.[38] It appears that not only was mail carried on this route, but it must have been a favourite way to Peterborough. On arriving at the Thorah-Eldon townline a traveller must have been compelled to turn south. Only that portion of the townline between the 1st and 2nd lines appears to have been open at an early date.[39] In 1844 Samuel Richardson, a surveyor for the government, chose this road as part of his route from Toronto to Eldon township. His diary states that he spent the night at Widow Stewart's, and had breakfast the following morning

[31] Interview with Clarence Ritchie, July 3, 1983.

[32] PAO, M.S. 251, Reel 1, July 14, 1830.

[33] Registry Office, Whitby, Instrument #3499. Nov. 1, 1840 Lots 5 and 6 Concession 1 — "road now travelled."

[34] Loc. cit.

[35] Registry Office, Whitby, Instrument #26209, Oct. 12, 1844.

[36] Registry Office, Whitby, Instrument #14190, Nov. 14, 1855, "limit of the Eldon road passing through the said lot. . ."

[37] PAO, M.S. 348, Sept. 1, 1853.

[38] Registry Office, Whitby, Instrument #50293, July 21, 1853 ". . . so much of said N½ of said lot situate on the north side of the road to Peterborough. . ."

[39] PAO, M.S. 348, Thorah Council Minutes, Feb. 18, 1850. This is the only portion of townline laid out in the Road divisions, being part of division #1.

at Irish's Tavern[40] (now Woodville). Mrs. Stewart lived with her sons in a log house[41] that stood beside the Peterborough road in lot 4 of the 1st Concession.[42] They emigrated from Islay, Scotland,[43] and settled in Thorah before 1837.[44] Just west of their home, on this road, the first Riverview School was erected.[45]

The point at which the Peterborough Road crossed the Beaver River was the site of a substantial bridge built prior to 1854.[46] Before its construction an early traveller may have had to use a ford in the river just south of the bridge site.[47] This is a possible explanation for a once deeded road allowance along the south edge of the north half of lots 7 and 8 which just happens to be aligned with this river ford.[48]

By the early 1870's the line of the 2nd Concession had been improved enough to make the eastern detour redundant. In 1873 a bylaw was passed closing the road across the lots 2, 3, and 4.[49] The remainder was in service for a few more years. On February 5, 1876, William Skinner, a nearby resident, was instructed to: "Barricade the bridge across the Beaver River on lot 7 Concession 1, and to post up notices warning persons that the said bridge is dangerous."[50] And so ended what was for a time, through its connection with the Cameron Road, Beaverton's link with points to the southeast. The other detours along the 2nd Concession are less well documented, and may have been abandoned much earlier. The detour between lots 11 and 16 may account for the location of the former Bill Bursby and the present Alan Ross buildings being so far removed from roads we know today.

In the north of the township the Portage Road is cited as the traditional Indian portage from Lake Simcoe to Balsam Lake. It seems doubtful that our aboriginal friends would have chosen a route that exactly

[40] PAO, R.G. 1, CB-1, Box 9, Diary of Samuel Richardson, 1844.
[41] Canada West Census, Thorah, 1851.
[42] Walton, George, *The City of Toronto and the Home District Commercial Directory and Register with Almanac and Calender for 1837*, Toronto.
[43] Transcriptions; Old Stone Church Cemetery, Cemetery Committee of the Beaverton Thorah Eldon Historical Society, 1979.
[44] Walton, op. cit.
[45] Registry Office, Whitby, Instrument #720, Lot 4, Concession 1, Thorah. Oct. 18, 1873.
[46] PAO, M.S. 348, Reel 1. Thorah Council Minutes, July 25, 1854. "Sum of money be granted in aid of covering the bridge across the Beaver River at Arch. McBains." In view of the fact that this road was in use long before this date it is reasonable to guess that the bridge may have been constructed by at least 1840.
[47] Of course there is no guarantee that this ford existed 140 years ago.
[48] Registry Office, Whitby, Instrument #46148, April 1, 1852.
[49] PAO, M.S. 348, Thorah Township Bylaws, #8, 1873.
[50] PAO, M.S. 348, Thorah Council Minutes.

coincides with the road allowance that was surveyed in front of the 11th Concession. It is possible that they very nearly followed it as far as lot 6, however. Gamebridge would have made a good disembarkation point since the Talbot is navigable for light craft to this point.[51] The country that the present Portage Road crosses between lots 6 and 1, at the town-line, was reported to have been a large swamp. For this information we have a man by the name of Wellesley Ritchey to thank. In his letter dated August 3, 1835, to Peter Robinson, he reported on work being done on what was to become the Portage Road.[52] He states that "the road runs through a cedar swamp in the township of Thorah from lot 6 to lot 1, the townline of Eldon, which will require causewaying a greater part of the way as it is low and no way of getting around it, and water in the swamp at present." This was certainly not very dry land if water was still present in the first week of August. Wellesley continued by stating that "unless it is causewayed neither wagons, sleighs nor horses could pass through." A Mr. Willson, the contractor, constructed nearly 15 miles of road that summer.[53] The road was only 16 feet wide, and would have seemed to be a very narrow swath through the towering forest that stood along most of this route.

This road was possibly constructed as a substitute for part of the proposed Trent Canal. A report of 1835 recognized that the most expensive section of the canal would be from Lake Simcoe to Balsam Lake, at an estimated cost of 121,212 pounds.[54] The 562 pounds spent on this narrow road would certainly have been a bargain.[55] Willson pushed the road through the swamp on instructions from some bureaucrat. The more logical route would have been to cross the Talbot and follow the higher north shore.[56] A road may have crossed the Talbot at this point very early, making use of a ford. By 1861 it crossed at or very near the present road, just below the Pickerel Dam.[57] The Portage Road, whatever its course before or after 1835, was an important route to and from the north of Eldon Township. Travellers along this road would have been compelled to go through or to Beaverton.

The 5th Concession road, and possibly the 6th to a lesser extent,

[51] Interview with Harry Furniss.
[52] PAO, R.G. 1, A-1-7, Vol. 13, Roads, information regarding various roads in the province.
[53] Loc. cit.
[54] Fleming, Rae Bruce, *The Early Life of Sir William MacKenzie 1849-1891,* a thesis, University of Saskatchewan, 1981, page 15.
[55] PAO, R.G. 1, A-1-7, Vol 13.
[56] The geography on the north shore is much better suited for a road.
[57] PAO, M.S. 348. April 13, 1861 refers to an established road on Lot 6 Concession 11.

A HALLOWE'EN TRICK

One Hallowe'en the Gunn boys, ready for a little fun, arrived, under the cover of darkness, at the farm of their uncle and neighbour, Hector Grant, the present site of Mac-Mar. Grant had a wagon loaded with grain ready to leave early in the morning for Prince Albert, the great grain depot of that time. The boys unloaded the wagon, took it apart, and resituated it astride the peak of the barn. Then each sack of grain was carried to be placed on the wagon.

Morning came and Grant rose before sunrise to get an early start. Where was his load of grain? A chance glance at his barn in the first rays of light showed his wagon all ready to go but for one minor detail. He needed some able hands and soon decided which strong young men in the neighbourhood should be called on; so off to the Gunn home he went.

Many years later, Donald recalled that the morning task did not seem nearly as easy as that of a few hours earlier.

were in regular use before 1850.[58] The fifth line would have been the most heavily travelled due to the earlier presence of bridges.[59] Heavy use of these roads cannot be accounted for by saying that all properties along the way were settled. There were numerous vacancies along both roads.[60] These were direct routes from Eldon to Beaverton.

At the February 18, 1850, meeting of Thorah Council the road divisions were set up for the township.[61] It is interesting to note that the six above mentioned roads were very nearly the only ones set out at the meeting. The only significant addition was the logical connecting link between the Portage Road and the Lakeshore Road. When drawn on a map the trend is obvious. Beaverton was clearly at a hub of local travel, a trend that was established before 1830.

It is not to be assumed that the above mentioned roads were the only routes in use. A family living some distance from one of these must have, through necessity, used some sort of road or trail through the bush. All that can be said with certainty is that these were main avenues, and that was no guarantee that they were open in all seasons.

One technique for improving roads over wet land was the use of causewaying, now commonly called corduroy road. This involved placing

[58] PAO, M.S. 348, Thorah Council Minutes, Feb. 18, 1850.
[59] Ibid., Nov. 19, 1853, June 14, 1853.
[60] PAO, M.S. 251, Assessment of Thorah Township, 1852.
[61] PAO, M.S. 348, Thorah Council Minutes.

logs in series crosswise to the intended roadway on top of larger timbers or stringers. High causewaying must have involved placing one or two more levels of stringers to further elevate the roadway in very wet land. Both these types of construction were used on the Portage Road in 1835.[62] The section of road skirting the shore of Lake Simcoe between the front of the 9th Concession of Thorah and the Talbot River is a very old section of corduroy road and is still known to some as "the causeway."[63] The causeway led to the only known bridge between Beaverton and Mara Township in the early 1850's.[64] Though it may have been a solid structure at that time, later it was reported to have been a floating bridge.[65]

What would an inhabitant of the fledgling village of Beaverton of the early 1850's have called the roads that met there? He may have called the lakeshore road, north of town, "the Mara Road", but this has not been documented before 1858.[66] Within the bounds of the village the name Simcoe Street applied as it does today.[67] East from Osborne one had the option of calling it either the Whitby Road[68] or the Eldon Road[69] depending upon the intended destination. The road running south from Simcoe Street was known by many names; Toronto Road,[70] Brock Road,[71] Lakeshore Road[72] and Georgina Road.[73] The term Osborne Street came into use a little later. The 6th Concession took the name Main Street no later than 1856.[74]

To these main avenues, and lesser streets, came the tailors, merchants, harnessmakers, shoemakers, carpenters, hotelkeepers, weavers, blacksmiths, and assorted other businessmen. Each in his own way, whether rich or poor, made a contribution to Beaverton's growth.

[62] PAO, R.G. 1, A-1-7, Vol. 13.
[63] Interview with Mrs. Harry Furniss, 1983.
[64] PAO, M.S. 348, Thorah Council Minutes, April 12, 1854. A Donald Cameron was serving notice that he wished to remove this bridge in order to bring a rather large vessel down the Talbot River. This is the only bridge he mentions and thus seems to be the only one spanning the river.
[65] Interview with Mrs. Harry Furniss.
[66] PAO, M.S. 348, Nov. 12, 1858.
[67] Registry Office, Whitby, Instrument #37028 Lot 14, Concession 5, Sept. 18, 1846.
[68] Registry Office, Whitby, Instrument #48136, Lot 14, Concession 5. Feb. 28, 1853.
[69] Loc. cit.
[70] PAO, M.S. 348, Thorah Council Minutes, May 4, 1858.
[71] Ibid., Nov. 9, 1852.
[72] Ibid., July 4, 1858.
[73] Registry Office, Whitby, Instrument #48136, Feb. 28, 1853.
[74] Registry Office, Whitby, Abstracts to Land Titles.

Chapter 5

THE CHURCHES OF BEAVERTON — THE EARLY YEARS

Our earliest settlers, once they had managed to put up a dwelling, sought religious services, even if they had to furnish them themselves.

John Gunn, an ordained elder of the Church of Scotland, held prayer services in both English and Gaelic, not only at his home in Thorah, but at other settlers' homes in Eldon and Mariposa.[1] The first Church of Scotland services were held on the banks of the Talbot River in 1831 by Rev. George Galloway.[2] Shortly after, building of churches started. By 1837 there was a Presbyterian church in Woodville, built of logs, complete with pulpit, pews and communion table, but no minister. By 1844 a larger church had been built in Woodville and Rev. John McMurchy was called as minister. He had spent some time previously as a visiting minister to congregations in Eldon, Mariposa and elsewhere.[3] Before there was a church in Beaverton, Presbyterian services were held in Calder's grist mill. Attendance was so large at a baptismal service in 1843 that the mill floor collapsed.[4]

Rev. Adam Elliott, an Anglican missionary travelling this area to assess church needs, reported: "On Sunday evening, February 1, 1835, I performed divine service at the house of Mr. Stephenson. Though the weather was exceedingly cold, about 200 people were present."[5]

The first Roman Catholic services in the area were held by Fr. Edward Gordon, who walked across the frozen Lake Simcoe from West Gwillimbury to hold services in 1830.[6]

[1] *History of the Presbyterian Church at Beaverton.*
[2] Loc. cit.
[3] The Founding of Woodville Presbyterian Congregation. Page 28.
[4] Smith, W.L., *Pioneers of Old Ontario.* Geo. N. Morang: 1923.
[5] Archives, Anglican Diocese of Toronto, notes on the Deanery of Victoria, compiled by Rev. Canon R.W. Allen, October 1945.
[6] *History of the Northern Region*, Catholic Women's League Councils 1981.

The earliest record of Methodist work in the vicinity of Beaverton was the first Quarterly Meeting of the Point Mara Wesleyan Mission, on August 11, 1860.[7]

There were reports of marriages performed in Eldon and Brock in the 1840's by a Baptist circuit rider named Hugh Reid, but there were not enough people to start a church in Beaverton.[8]

In 1835, as a result of petitions to the Legislature of Upper Canada, two one hundred acre tracts of land were set aside on the fourth Concession of Thorah as glebe lands for the use of the Roman Catholics and the Church of Scotland, the Roman Catholics getting the west half of lot 10, the Church of Scotland, the east half of lot 10.[9]

Shortly, thereafter, the Church of Scotland had a log church built on their property, close to the Beaver River.[10]

The first Anglican services were held in the Orange Lodge clubrooms, in the building later occupied by the Beaverton Express office.[11] This original building which burned down many years ago, was just west of the present newspaper office on Victoria Avenue.

The Anglican, Rev. Adam Elliott, had reported in the 1830's that the people of Brock and Thorah were mostly Scottish Presbyterians,[12] so it was no small wonder that the south end of Brock, settled by people from Ireland, was the scene of early Anglican and Roman Catholic work.

The Roman Catholic parish of Brock was formed in 1854 by Father Edward Walsh at Vroomanton, where there was a rectory and cemetery.[13] Geographically the parish extended from Reach, Uxbridge and Scott to Georgina, North Gwillimbury, Thorah and Mara. Travelling conditions were so difficult in those days that Fr. Walsh, or his successor (in 1857) Fr. John Lee, could only get around once a month to say mass. The mission of Beaverton was served by a log Church built in 1855 on the glebe lands on the fourth concession of Thorah, lot 10.[14]

The original grant of 100 acres for the Presbyterian Church was made to John Gunn, Alexander Calder and Christopher Robinson. They

[7] *Sketch of Church Life in Beaverton* 1929.
[8] Public Archives of Ontario, Peterborough County Marriage Registration.
[9] Press Release — Ontario Dept. of Public Records and Archives Sept. 1971, Historical Plaque to be Unveiled, Commemorating "The Old Stone Church" Beaverton.
[10] *History of the Presbyterian Church at Beaverton.*
[11] *Beaverton Express*, July 26, 1978, fact sheet compiled by Mrs. Nettie King Pearson for Special Edition.
[12] Archives, Anglican Diocese of Toronto, notes on the Deanery of Victoria, compiled by Rev. Canon R.W. Allen, October 1945.
[13] *History of Roman Catholicism in Georgina Township* 1963.
[14] Conversation with Father Edward Jackman, Historian, Archdiocese of Toronto.

DR. DAVID WATSON first minister of St. Andrew's Church 1853-1898. courtesy of Mrs. Helen Crockford

were to use it for a church, manse and burial ground. Under the direction of John Gunn, a skilled stone mason, construction of the Stone Church was started in 1840.[15] The grant of land was made to the Church of Scotland which, as the established church, accepted government funding and patronage. Rejection of the idea of patronage led to the *Disruption* in Scotland in 1843,[16] resulting in the founding of the Free Church. The three trustees sided with the policies of the Free Church. This stopped construction on the Stone Church which was, of course, vested in the (Established) Church of Scotland.[17] Having lost the best builders, construction slowed down to the point that the church was used in an uncompleted state for several years. With only a sand floor underfoot, services were held with planks stretched between stumps in lieu of pews.[18]

Without an organized congregation or funds, the Free Church people held services in their own homes. On September 30, 1849, they were able to form the united charge of Thorah and Eldon.[19] In 1850 the first church, a rough cast building was erected on Main St.[20] The minister of both Beaverton and Woodville churches was Rev. John McTavish.[21] By 1861 sufficient growth had taken place so that Woodville and Beaverton churches were separated, with Rev. John McLaughlin as Beaverton's first Free Church minister.[22]

By 1853 the Stone Church was practically completed. Its walls were built of field stone, drawn from the neighbouring fields and even from Thorah Island. The interior was built of pine and oak hauled from the banks of the Talbot River.[23]

In the year 1853 the congregation extended a call to Rev. David Watson.[24] Born in Scotland in 1823, he came to Canada at the age of 21. The family settled near London, Ontario where he was tutored in Latin and Greek. In order to finance a university education he took up teaching

[15] *Sketch of Church Life in Beaverton* 1929.
[16] *The United Church Observer*, May 15, 1943. The Scottish Disruption, page 18.
[17] *Sketch of Church Life in Beaverton* 1929.
[18] Press Release — Ontario Dept. of Public Records and Archives Sept. 1971 Historical Plaque to be Unveiled, Commemorating "The Old Stone Church" Beaverton.
[19] United Church Archives, *The Presbyterian* 1900 (Exact date not known), photocopy from a volume.
[20] *Sketch of Church Life in Beaverton* 1929.
[21] The Founding of Woodville Presbyterian Congregation. Page 34.
[22] Ibid. Page 46.
[23] Press Release — Ontario Dept. of Public Records and Archives 1971 Historical Plaque to be Unveiled, Commemorating "The Old Stone Church" Beaverton.
[24] *Sketch of Church Life in Beaverton 1929.*

PEWTER COMMUNION TOKEN from the old St. Andrews (Stone Church) X2. Front and back. courtesy of Mr. & Mrs. Harry Furniss

for several years, a profession in which he was highly proficient. By 1848, while still teaching, he was granted an A.B. degree from Queen's followed by an A.M. in 1850, and a theology degree in 1853.[25]

In 1867, at a meeting held in Mara, steps were taken to build a Methodist church in Beaverton.[26] Members of the building committee were James Todd, George Cain, George Drake and John Fox. The church was built on a lot of one third of an acre, the gift of Artemus Thompson, on Main St. adjoining the original Knox Presbyterian Church. The church, built of brick, was opened in 1869.[27] Still standing, the church is in use today as the Victory Tabernacle.

On March 6, 1871, the deed for land for an Anglican church was transferred from Alexander Calder to C.H. Davidson and others, in trust. Though unfinished, services were started in 1872.[28] Its first rector, Rev. Taylor, reported: "People were few in numbers, but faithful and zealous."[29]

[25] Conversation with Miss Mary Fowler, great grand-daughter of Rev. David Watson.
[26] United Church of Canada Archives, *Wesleyan Missionary Society Reports* 1864-1917.
[27] Loc. cit.
[28] *The First Hundred Years St. Paul's Anglican Church 1872-1972.*
[29] Archives, Anglican Diocese of Toronto, notes on the Deanery of Victoria, compiled by Rev. Canon R.W. Allen, October 1945.

Hallelujah! Praise the Lord!

John "Buidhe" McRae told the story about a lady who had walked in her bare feet a considerable distance across the difficult terrain of pioneer days to attend a Methodist service one hot Sunday morning. As was the custom, shoes were put on just before reaching the church. Soon after she was seated, the service began. The heat was oppressive and her feet were very cramped within her shoes. Finally she decided to remove her footwear.

The minister preached, the lady wiggled her toes to ease the soreness, and the heat persisted. A little dog ambled through the open doorway unnoticed while the pastor exhorted the rapt congregation to seek salvation. Meanwhile, the lady with the sore toes, though attentive to the sermon, contined to wiggle her toes. All of a sudden the dog noted the motion and moved toward the lady's feet; yet she did not see him. When the dog grabbed one large toe, she let out one loud yell: "Oh, my God!"

"Hallelujah! Praise the Lord! Another soul's been saved!" shouted the preacher.

THE FIRST SCHOOL IN S.S. No. 3 situated on the present Hugh Sheehy farm.

Chapter 6

AND THEN THERE WERE SCHOOLS

Although not all of the settlers were literate, most of the people inhabiting Thorah in its early years could indeed read and write. Perhaps no European country put such emphasis on education for the masses, as did Scotland, motherland of the majority of Thorah's early settlers. In 1696 the Scottish Parliament had legislated that a school should be set up in every parish that did not yet have one,[1] and even though some parishes had no schools by the Nineteenth Century, most, in fact, had very good ones. The high respect that Scottish people, and especially the Church of Scotland, held for learning was certain to influence education in Thorah.

With illiteracy in the Township standing at a mere 3.6% of the population in 1861,[2] and the majority of the illiterate people beyond school age even in the 1820's, there seems little reason to believe that education was neglected to any great extent even in those years when clearing the forest, establishing homes, and struggling to provide the bare necessities, must have monopolized the settlers' time and energies. Yet, before the establishment of schools as we know them, most children must have been taught the rudiments of reading and writing if not at home, then surely in a neighbour's log house.

Some disagreement has existed about the first school to be set up in Thorah. Some people have declared that a school situated on a hill on the Peterborough Road, a little east and a half mile south of the more recent Riverview School, was Thorah's first place of learning. Others have claimed that the earliest school in the Township was Sodom School, whose name, hardly appropriate in a place of learning where moral training was considered to be almost as important as academic discipline, was later changed to Eden. A superintendent's report of 1859 indicates that in School Section Number Four, the Beaverton area, the first school was opened in 1835, nine years before any other in the Township.

In the 1840's log school houses were erected in sections later known as

[1] Young, Douglas, *Scotland*, London, Cassell & Co. Ltd., 1971, page 97.
[2] 1861 Census of Thorah Township.

Riverview, Galloway's or Swamp, Egypt, and Eden.[3] However, there was no guarantee that qualified teachers could be hired with the result that schools were kept open rather irregularly.

To cover the cost of teachers' salaries in the 1840's, a provincial grant made up 25.8%,[4] a similar amount came from the County[5] and the remainder was met by the parents of the scholars. Ryerson's Education Act of 1850 gave the boards of trustees of each common school the power to decide whether the school would be free. Eden School took the lead in abolishing tuition fees for students.[6] However, in 1871 an amendment to the Education Act guaranteed free education to all children in Ontario. In 1867 money for the upkeep of schools was received from the Clergy Reserve Fund, amounting to $34.34 per school in Thorah.[7]

In 1847 the teachers' salaries for the four schools in Thorah totaled 80 pounds.[8] Salaries varied from school to school; in 1850 School Section No. 4 (Beaverton) was paying the teacher £75 while Egypt's schoolmaster earned £36 that year.[9]

Mr. James Morrison, grandfather of Mr. Bert Switzer, recalled that he and the teacher, Mr. Duncan Calder, great-grandfather of Calvin Calder, Beaverton lawyer, were the only ones at the school in S.S. #3 (later Galloway's or Swamp) able to speak English.[10] The advantage of a teacher fluent in both Gaelic and English can easily be seen. The students, of course, learned the language of their newly-adopted country while many of the older family members never became fluent in English.

Although the 1842 Census reveals a majority of male scholars, 30 as opposed to 13 females, by 1850 the boys attending Thorah schools numbered 110, the girls 102.[11] Male teachers also predominated in the beginning. David Ross was Beaverton's first schoolmaster,[12] but lady teachers appeared during the 1860's.[13] In fact, one Helen Cameron, who taught at Riverview in 1863, appears to be Thorah's first schoolmistress.[14]

[3] Annual Report of Local Superintendent of Thorah Schools, 1851.
[4] Johnson, Leo A., *History of the County of Ontario, 1615-1875*, Whitby, Corporation of the County of Ontario, 1973, page 160.
[5] Loc. cit.
[6] Superintendent's Report of 1858. Eden School is the only free school; Sections 3, 4 and 5 were partly free and #1 was not in operation.
[7] Superintendent's Report, 1867.
[8] Johnson, op. cit. Page 160.
[9] Superintendent's Report of 1850.
[10] *Beaverton Express*, Sept. 13, 1962.
[11] Annual Report of Local Superintendent, 1850.
[12] Farewell, J.E., *Ontario County*.
[13] Annual Reports of Local Superintendent, 1863, 1864, 1866.
[14] Superintendent's Report, 1863.

It seems that teachers changed positions often, but two gentlemen, Duncan Arbuthnot, who taught for several years at Eden, and John Stanfield, who was responsible for the education of many Beaverton children, remained in these positions for some time.

In the early years a higher proportion of the children of school age attended classes in the rural areas than in Beaverton, with 47 of the 52 children aged five to sixteen living in School Section #2 enrolled in classes in 1850, while in Beaverton only 39 of the 85 school-aged children were on the school register.[15]

Attendance was, of course, quite irregular with only four of the 83 students on Egypt's roll attending at least 150 days in the 1855-56 school year. In Beaverton, 29 of the 145 pupils were in attendance at least 150 days.[16]

The first schools were rather crude structures, often with dirt floors. Planks, attached to the outside walls, served as desks while seats were large timbers set on legs. Later, double desks and benches were used. A big box stove in the centre of the room replaced the earlier fireplace and kept those sitting nearby more than warm, burning hot in some cases, but did little to counteract the drafts felt by those seated near the walls.

RIVERVIEW SCHOOL, S.S. No. 1: The second school in the section, this building was veneered with brick in 1902 and destroyed by fire in 1925.

[15] Ibid., 1850.
[16] Ibid., 1855.

Three millers served as school trustees in Beaverton in 1853: Duncan Calder and George Proctor, whose mills have already been mentioned, as well as William McCaskill who, along with his brother, had operated a grist mill at Cannington. In fact, McCaskill's Mills was that village's original name. About 1848 McCaskill settled in Thorah on lot 10 concession 6, the farm which in more recent times was the Callaghan home.

Beaverton's log school built in 1844, at least the second in use there, was a mere 20 feet by 18 feet.[17] With 48 children on the register in 1852,[18] it can be seen that if attendance were very regular, overcrowding must have been a severe problem. Egypt School was somewhat larger, at 26 feet by 22 feet.[19] According to the Superintendent's Report of 1850 none of the schools had playgrounds; yet in the Report of the following year it was stated that only Beaverton was without a yard for the children to play.

It is generally agreed that Beaverton's first school was at the corner of King Street and Mara Road where the Taylor apartment house is situated. However, there is evidence to suggest that an early school was on the site of the A.P. Cockburn house, later the Houston home on Mara Road.[20]

For many years the Reverend David Watson served as Superintendent of Common Schools in Thorah. Charles Robinson, who also served his community as reeve, justice of the peace, and postmaster, Dr. Peter Davidson, a Beaverton physician, and Rev. J.C. Wilson, a Methodist clergyman, also filled this position for brief terms. For his efforts the superintendent received an annual salary of $20 in 1858.[21] While the superintendents' reports indicated no analysis of the quality of teaching carried on, this being the Board's responsibility, there was close attention paid to the textbooks in use in the schools. In the early days, the Beaverton School surpassed the others in the number of texts being used; those for reading, arithmetic, and grammar were available in all of Thorah's five schools.

With large numbers of pupils on the rolls, several grade levels to be taught, and these complicated by irregular attendance, it was no wonder that maintaining discipline was often difficult. Since the "spare the rod and spoil the child" philosophy was almost universally accepted in the

[17] Ibid., 1851.
[18] Ibid., 1852.
[19] Ibid., 1851.
[20] *Beaverton Express*, Aug. 26, 1897.
[21] Superintendent's Report, 1858.

home and community, the switch or gad was used to keep the scholars in line. There are accounts of schoolmasters in those early days even drawing blood as the switches curled around bare legs and feet, but, no doubt most teachers were less harsh and trimmings were usually given in a more humane fashion. In some cases, the children, boys most often, were sent out to cut their own switches. By nicking them, the boys could be assured that with the first crack the gads would break. Other lads about to be strapped rubbed their hands with resin to deaden the pain.

Rote learning predominated in the early years and the pupils' ability to memorize was well cultivated. Small wonder it is that many of our grandparents could repeat stanza after stanza of poetry, or recite the names of all the counties and county towns in the province.

Just as frame or brick houses eventually took the place of the pioneers' first log dwellings, the original school houses, too, were replaced with improved structures. The year 1859 saw the opening of two frame schools in the township. In S.S. #3 the new building was erected some distance west of the original log structure which stood on the hill on what is now the Hugh Sheehy farm. Situated on the lower terrain at the corner of the fifth line and the sideroad, the new school became known as the Swamp School as some were moved to exclaim, "Oh, you're building your school down in the swamp!"

EDEN SCHOOL, built in 1867 and bricked in 1892, was S.S. No. 2's second schoolhouse and was used until 1962.

THE NORTH STREET SCHOOL, probably Beaverton's third schoolhouse, was built in 1859 and was used until 1883. Later, it was used as a carriage shop storeroom by Mr. Jas. Birchard. Alexander Muir, writer of "The Maple Leaf Forever," taught at this school.

In Beaverton the school on North Street was opened and although the Superintendent's Report of 1859 records 136 pupils, only one teacher, John R. Ross, taught a full curriculum. It was at this school that Alexander Muir, composer of The Maple Leaf Forever, gave his students frequent breaks from their studies to sing and march about the room carrying the Union Jack.

In 1867 the Eden Section built a new frame school at the cost of $603.50.[22]

Grammar schools, established in the Province for the education of children of the elite with emphasis on the learning of Latin and Greek, were more generously subsidized by the Government than were common schools. It seems, however, that plans to set up a grammar school at Beaverton in the mid 1860's never got off the ground. In 1864 the Ontario County Council named Rev. David Watson, Rev. John McLachlan, Dr. Peter Davidson, Charles Robinson, Kenneth Cameron, and Andrew McNab[23] as a board of trustees, but early in 1865 the Standing Committee on Education called for the repeal of the bylaw appointing this board "in consequence of the non-operation of the Grammar School in Beaverton."[24]

[22] Ibid., 1867.
[23] Farewell, op. cit.
[24] *Oshawa Vindicator*, Feb. 8, 1865, County Council news.

GALLOWAY'S, or SWAMP SCHOOL. The third in S.S. No. 3, this building was erected in 1877, was used until 1962, and still stands.

EGYPT SCHOOL, S.S. No. 5. Erected in 1862 to replace the original log school destroyed by fire in 1861, this building was bricked in 1900 and used until 1962.

THE BAY STREET SCHOOL, with four classrooms, was completed by Thomas Treleaven late in 1883 and used for the next forty years. With only the lower storey remaining, it is now the meeting-place of the Masonic Lodge. Josiah Givens was the principal for many years.

As early as 1864[25] there was one ladies' school in Beaverton; this was operated by the Misses Cameron.

Much classroom equipment taken for granted in this century was in short supply in the mid 1800's. Blackboards, in use in all of the Township schools except S.S. #3, a few large maps, and a globe used in the Eden School made up the visual aids in Thorah in 1859.[26] As Dr. Watson wrote in his Report of 1856, "Education is rather backward among us." Even ten years later, Thorah schools could boast no "magic lanterns or other scientific amusements for the pupils."[27]

Helpful as visual aids were, and still are, in training the young, the quality of education was undoubtedly determined largely by the abilities and dedication of the teachers. Surely Thorah schools had their share of effective instruction, and while no institutions of higher learning existed within the Township, many Thorah natives who went on to higher education elsewhere, could attribute much of their success to one or another of the teachers who guided their young minds through the rudiments of reading, writing and arithmetic and instilled in them a love of learning.

[25] *Mitchell's Canada Business Directory*, 1864-65.
[26] Superintendent's Report, 1859.
[27] Ibid., 1856.

Chapter 7

OF MEN AND ROADS

It is wrong to assume that the election of the first Thorah Council in 1850 marked the beginning of the participation of local inhabitants in the affairs of their township. A few men at least had been involved in local affairs for nearly twenty years, and a large number for nine or ten years.

Until 1841 the annual town meetings in Thorah were restricted to appointing local officials to serve under the control of the magistrates, and to the rather minor determination of the height of a legal fence, and what livestock may run at large.[1] Appointments were made for assessors, tax collectors, clerks, fenceviewers, constables etc. The year 1832 may have been the time of the first town meeting in Thorah with the appointment of Donald Calder as constable. He served for that year only.[2] Throughout the 1830's Archibald McBain and Kenneth Cameron served in this capacity with McBain continuing until at least the 1850's.[3] As the years passed other local men served as constables. Some of these were Charles Robinson, John Anderson, John Murray, Thomas Glasford and Philip Brown.[4] John MacKay distinguished himself as clerk for the township for 22 years beginning about 1836.[5]

In 1841 the Home District Council assumed the municipal function previously performed by the Court of the Quarter Session, leaving the magistrates with only their judicial powers.[6] At this time the annual township meetings were empowered to elect a local representative to this new body. However, only the wealthiest men could be candidates for this position because they had to be in possession of land valued at over 300 pounds.[7] Consequently Col. Cameron, a well-to-do man, became the first

[1] Johnson, Leo A., *History of the County of Ontario, 1615-1875*. page 174.
[2] Public Archives of Ontario, M.S. 251 Reel #2, Vol. 5, Page 60, Minutes of the Quarter Sessions of the Peace for the Home District. May 22, 1832.
[3] Ibid., Vol. 6, May 10, 1833, May 6, 1834, et. al.
[4] Ibid., Vol. 7, July 7, 1838, April 3, 1845, et. al.
[5] PAO, M.S. 348 Reel #1, Thorah Council Minutes, Feb. 15, 1858.
[6] PAO, M.S. 251. Minutes of the Quarter Sessions of the Peace for the Home District. Introduction to Reel 1.
[7] Johnson, op. cit. page 173.

representative, and served two three-year terms.[8] Late in the 1840's George Proctor Sr. was Thorah's representative at District Council.[9]

Certainly, by 1841, statute road labour was being expended on Thorah roads, and may have been used earlier.[10] This, of course, meant the appointment of pathmasters to supervise the work, and involved nearly all of the local men in the crucial task of road maintenance. It becomes clear that there would have been no lack of experience or knowledge of local problems at the time of the creation of local council.

The passing of the Baldwin Municipal Act of 1849 brought to Thorah autonomy in strictly local affairs. Possibly just as importantly, this new legislation extended the franchise to freeholders assessed at forty shillings or more, giving many more men a voice in township affairs.[11]

That roads were an all important life line of the township was demonstrated at the second meeting of Thorah Council on Feb. 18, 1850.[12] At that time all of the more passable roads within the township were divided into road divisions for the purpose of performing statute labour. Under this scheme each and every property owner within the township was required by law to perform work on the roads. Generally the number of days work required was determined by the assessed value of the land owned. Thorah seems to have expanded on this, possibly due to a lack of manpower, and required of "every male inhabitant . . . of the age of twenty one years and upwards . . . the performance of two days statute labour".[13] Each man did work in the road division in which he lived. Appointed to each road division was an overseer of highways or pathmaster. Pathmasters were appointed on a rotational basis from among the men liable for statute labour in each division. The pathmaster "called his men out" whenever he deemed it necessary or on instructions from Township Council.[14] The road work was done in strict accordance with a bylaw that detailed the shape and dimensions of the road surface.[15] Failure to perform one's required statute labour could result in the sale of personal property to recover the value of work not performed at the rate of five

[8] Beers, J.H. & Co. *Historical Atlas of the County of Ontario*. 1877. Page 12.
[9] Loc. cit.
[10] PAO, R.G. 1 C-IV. Concession 2 Lot 15.
[11] Johnson, Op. Cit. page 176.
[12] PAO, M.S. 348 Reel #1, Thorah Council Minutes. Feb. 18, 1850.
[13] PAO, M.S. 348 Reel #1, Thorah Township Bylaws #6, 1850.
[14] PAO, M.U. 2139 Mss. Misc. Coll. 1960 #2, Letter from John Spence, Laurel, Ontario, outlining the way in which statute labour was performed . . . in rural areas. Aug. 24, 1960.
[15] PAO, M.S. 348, Thorah Township Council Minutes. April 21, 1851.

shillings per day.[16]

Not all road work was accomplished by means of statute labour. If all available road labour had been exhausted or the improvement required was extensive, a member of council, or sometimes just a trustworthy man, would be appointed commissioner of that project. His task was to advertise for tenders, select the contractor, supervise the work, inspect it upon completion, and ensure that the contractor was paid.[17] Council minutes show scores of men, farmers in particular, who did contract work for the township. Men paid for work on Thorah roads at the July 2, 1958 Council meeting included John Anderson, James McHattie, Duncan Carmichael, Angus Currie, Robert Morrison, Daniel McBride, Angus Cameron, Charles Galloway, and Angus McDougall.[18]

Over Seers of Highways (township roads) appointed by Thorah Council, February 18, 1850:

Road Division #		
	1	Alexander Campbell, mason
	2	Donald Stewart
	3	Donald McIntosh
	4	Charles Little
	5	William Wallis & William Murray
	6	Gilbert McTaggart
	7	William Ross
	8	Donald Cameron
	9	Alexander McRae
	10	Alexander McMillan
	11	John McCuaig
	12	John Anderson
	13	Joseph Furness (sic)
	14	Edward Morrison
	15	David White
	16	James Leith
	17	Duncan Harvey
	18	John Campbell

[16] PAO, M.S. 348, Thorah Council Bylaws #6, 1850.
[17] PAO, M.U. 2139 Mss. Misc. Coll. 1960 #2.
[18] PAO, M.S. 348 Reel #1. July 2, 1858.

The roads were an unending source of aggravation to council. The fact that the township had a relatively small population meant that there was both a shortage of manpower, and a general lack of township revenues to be spent under road commissioners. It is true that grants were received from the county and the province for this purpose, but these amounts did not go far. It would be safe to describe improvements in the roads as slow. Year after year road labour would be expended before much progress had been made. Roads at that time were constructed on top of the native topsoils. A season's work may have been done on a section of road and a layer of gravel laid, but if the rains came and the road bed was of clay, horses' hooves and wagon wheels could quickly churn the gravel into the clay and destroy a year's work.

The roads appeared to suffer from man-made problems as well. Council minutes make frequent mention of farmers' fences obstructing road allowances. At the township meeting of Oct. 24, 1859 it was recorded that James White's fence was "on and across the 7th Concession". In 1852 Council was compelled to pass a bylaw to prohibit the "removal of stone, timber and gravel" from the roads of the township.[19] The previous year George Proctor was requested to remove "an old wall of an intended edifice which stands in the middle of the road". This obstruction was at the eastern limits of the present village.[20]

One special problem that faced Council related to the Lake Shore Road north of Beaverton in the 8th Concession, where it follows the railway tracks today. It seems that from time to time portions of this road would disappear into the lake. In 1858 the road was moved slightly eastward, but the lake must have been as unrelenting as usual, for in 1860 money was allotted to construct a breakwater here.[21] The

THORAH COUNCIL, January 16, 1854

Councillors

Ward	Councillor
Ward 1	Alexander Campbell
Ward 2	George Smith
Ward 3	James Galloway
Ward 4	Neil McDougall
Ward 5	John Bruce

[19] PAO, M.S. 348, Thorah Council Bylaws #26, 1852.
[20] Ibid., Thorah Minutes, May 8, 1851.
[21] Ibid., Sept. 22, 1860.

"... to plank the muddy, dirty, streets of Beaverton ..."
Thorah Council By-Law #33, 1852.

problem was never really solved until the road was located on the east side of the railway tracks many years later.

Bridges, too, required constant attention. Council minutes of Sept. 16, 1850 reported the bridge at the mill in Beaverton as being "in a very dilapidated state and highly dangerous to the travelling public." Alex Calder replaced this bridge by tender the following year and the "materials of which the old bridge was composed were sold by auction."[22] Calder replaced a number of bridges including the one "at Col. Cameron's" north of town.[23] James Morrison contracted in 1853 for the rebuilding of McCuaig's Bridge just east of Beaverton immediately west of the present traffic lights.[24]

The centre road, in Thorah, lies on the boundary between lot 10 and lot 11 from the front of the first Concession to Gamebridge, and is very nearly followed by Highway #12 today. Compared with other roads, it came into existence rather late, with the exception of that part between the 8th Concession and the site of Gamebridge, which was in use in the 1830's. Talk of a central road came quickly on the heels of the separation of Ontario County from York and Peel Counties in 1854.[25] Not only was it designed to give political unity to the fledgling county but also to provide a larger hinterland for the town of Whitby which had been selected as county seat.

Thorah Council supported this scheme from the start and was even on record as supporting it four years earlier.[26] The choice of a central line disregarded the geography of the county, and required it to cross many swamps between Whitby and Thorah. Good progress was made in building a useful road in the south of the County but it was very slow in arriving in Thorah. Council was naturally impatient and in 1857 petitioned the County "for aid to open the portion of the road ... from the rear of the 7th Concession to the front of the 1st of Thorah". They claimed that much of the road was under construction and that it "would greatly facilitate the transmission of staple commodities of parts of this county and of the county of Simcoe to the market of our County Town and the

[22] Ibid., June 2, 1851 and Jan. 20, 1852.
[23] Ibid., Dec. 28, 1852.
[24] Ibid., Nov. 19, 1853.
[25] Ibid., July 1, 1856.
[26] Ibid., Jan. 20, 1850.

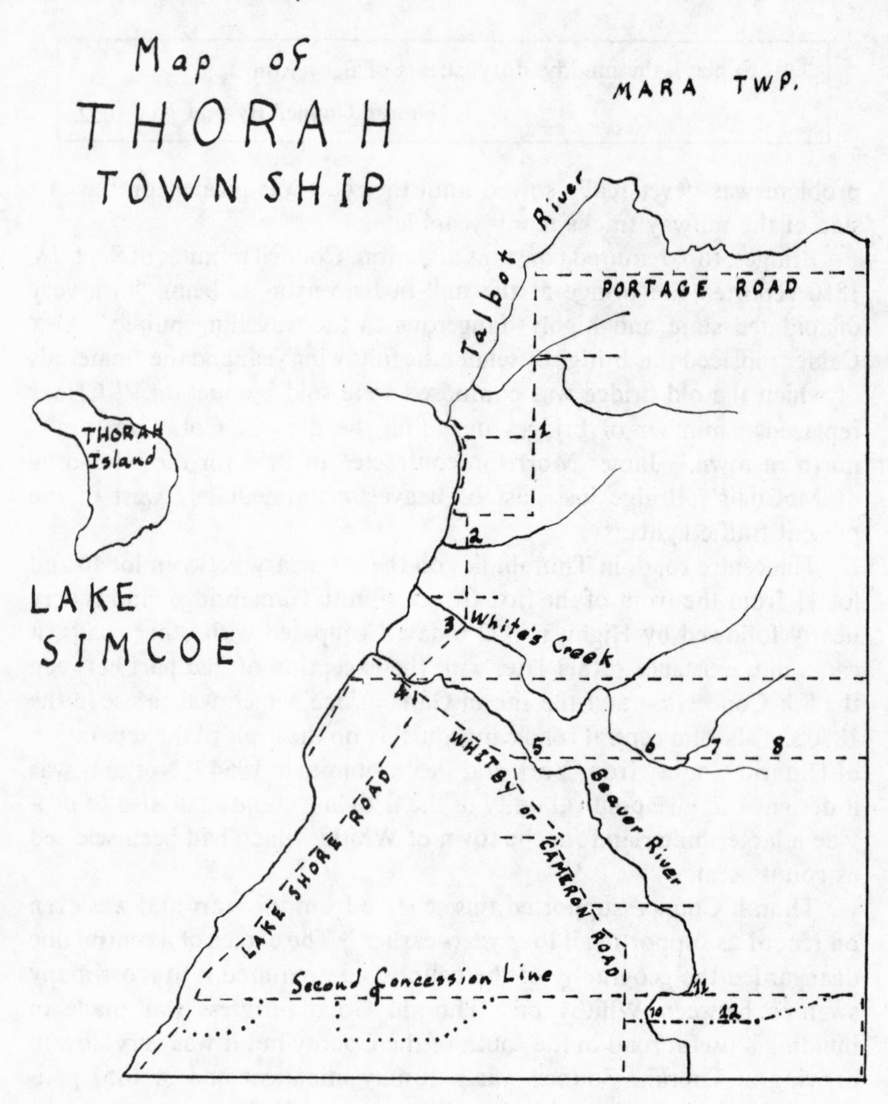

THORAH TOWNSHIP COUNCIL, June 23, 1857
"Work to be made on Victoria Street to make it passable."

KEY TO MAP OF THORAH TOWNSHIP

- - - - Road divisions as laid out at the second Meeting of Thorah Council on February 18, 1850.

-.-.-.- The most easterly detour in the second Concession line as surveyed by Arad Smalley in 1830. It was in use from 1830 to 1873.

..... Detour in second concession line by Arad Smalley in 1830. Period of use is undetermined.

1. Site of S.S. #5 or "Egypt" School.
2. Col. Cameron's Bridge.
3. McCaskill's Bridge.
4. Beaverton, the site of S.S. #4 School.
5. McCuaig's Bridge.
6. McRae's Bridge.
7. Later site of "Swamp" School, S.S. #3.
8. First location of S.S. #3 School.
9. Location of S.S. #2 or "Eden" School.
10. McBain's Bridge.
11. Later site of Riverview or S.S. #1.
12. First location of S.S. #1 School.

reception thereof of such articles of merchandise as may be required for home consumption".[27] No doubt these dreams were shared by the astute businessmen of Whitby as well.

These dreams were a little premature, however. Four years later on May 25, 1861, Thorah Council again petitioned County Council "for some help to open the centre road from the 7th Concession to the townline of Brock." The revealing part of the petition read: "Your petitioners request you will grant further aid in opening it up from the Talbot River to the Townline of Brock and that they would also beg to state that the road already opened is not logged up and unless some further aid be granted the money already expended will be in a great measure lost."[28] These words paint a picture of a road that had never been made passable. The young trees were reclaiming the roadway while the remains of the felled trees lay about.

At this time some action may have been taken, but there was not the desired result. In December 1862 a letter from Peter Burnet, a surveyor, read; "I have surveyed the allowance for the road . . . I found . . . the north half of the first concession, about 60 rods of the south half of the second concession, and about 70 rods of the north half of the third concession open and fit for travel."[29] Obviously this would have been a very difficult

[27] Ibid., June 5, 1857.
[28] Ibid., May 25, 1861.
[29] Ibid., Dec. 27, 1862.

THORAH TOWNSHIP COUNCIL, Second Meeting,
February 18, 1850

Appointed as Tax Collector		— Mr. Thomas Glasford
Assessor and Enumerator		— Mr. Duncan Calder
Auditor		— Mr. James Ellis
Auditor		— Mr. Alexander Calder
Poundkeepers	Ward 1	— Mr. Neil McFee
	Ward 2	— Mr. Duncan McRae
	Ward 3	— Mr. Donald McRae Sen.
	Ward 4	— Mr. Artemus Thompson Sen.
	Ward 5	— Mr. Robert Murray
Fence Viewers		— Mr. John Cameron
		— Mr. Henry Hodgson
		— Mr. William McCaskill
		— Mr. Henry White

road to use. Driving along Highway #12 today one realizes that the great obstacle was the long low section north of the 2nd Concession line. This swamp was the one that required the southward detour in that line thirty years earlier.[30] Although there was a man-made drain, leading to the Beaver River, constructed in 1860, no doubt in preparation for this new road, it may not yet have done its job.[31] Without regular cultivation, and even though drained today, this area makes a good home for willows. The rich black soil on the lower end of the former Cecil Moore farm testifies to the original swamp nature of this area.

At that point in time, possibly because of a change in councillors, Thorah lost its patience with the situation. In January 1863 Council adopted a motion to petition County Council to the effect "That to attempt to open the side line between lots 10 and 11 in the 1st, 2nd, and 3rd concession . . . would be a waste of public money and injurious to the interests of this section of North Ontario." They did not mention the swamp but claimed that this line was so close to the Cameron Road that it was unnecessary, that the line should be abandoned for one on lot 12,

[30] PAO, M.S. 251 Reel #2, Vol 6. Minutes of the Quarter Sessions of the Peace for the Home District.
[31] PAO, M.S. 348 Reel #1. Thorah Council Minutes, June 23, 1860.

and "that it will injure our rising village of Beaverton and prevent our having a home market . . . and by doing so be detrimental to the interests of the agricultural community."[32] These were strong words, and may have echoed the thoughts of many local men who saw greater things for Beaverton and Thorah. Initially a good road from Thorah to Lake Ontario would have seemed certain to bring prosperity to Thorah. Later it must have become obvious that the wealth would be at Whitby, not at Thorah and Beaverton.

There must have been a raging controversy regarding this issue. Col. Cameron may have been speaking for many when he "condemned the return of certain members of Council of 1862, and township officers for voting and petitioning against the Centre Road."[33] This was not the only occasion on which Col. Cameron brought harsh words to bear against the actions of Council. The debate may have continued for some time, but by the early 1870's we can assume the controversy was over, since large sums of money were being spent on the Centre Road as it had been originally surveyed. The arrival of the railway may have been the cause of the end of hostilities. Without a doubt, the arrival of the railway at Beaverton would have removed much of the commercial value of the Centre Road.

The railway had other effects. It brought about the end of the stagecoach era for Beaverton. Yes, Beaverton once had daily stage service from Whitby with connections at Manilla for Lindsay. Perhaps as early as 1848, and certainly by 1851, one could arrive at Beaverton by stage and, if necessary, make connections with the lake boats for destinations such as Barrie or Orillia. Can the reader imagine himself or herself watching the Thorah countryside roll by from the window of a stagecoach as it pitched and swayed along the Cameron road to Beaverton?

One possible stop for the stage was the Greenbush Hotel. This tavern stood at the corner of the Brock-Thorah townline and the Cameron Road and was by no accident halfway between Beaverton and Cannington,

THORAH TOWNSHIP COUNCIL, July 1, 1856.

"Moved that in the event of there being a special meeting of the County Council called for the purpose of reconsidering the gravel road scheme, this council do recommend their Reeve to support only one line of road which would be most central and beneficial for the general interests of the county at large."

[32] Ibid., Jan. 19, 1863.
[33] Loc. cit.

THORAH TOWNSHIP COUNCIL, January 21, 1867

Charles Henry Davidson,	Reeve
Donald Ross	Councillor
Neil Gordon	Councillor
George Proctor	Councillor
John Cameron	Councillor

"Accounts presented; Police trustees of Beaverton for removing carcasses of horse and cow from the Beaver River, $1.50. Council felt that it was up to the parties who owned or caused the said carcasses to be deposited in the river to pay."

Minutes of Thorah Council
Oct. 28, 1871.

From minutes of the Court of the Quarter Sessions of the Peace for the Home District, April 14, 1847: Constables for Township: Philip Brown, John Anderson, John Murray Jr., Thomas Glasford, Archibald McBain.

thus a good location to rest or change teams. No doubt the passengers needed frequent stops as well. The origins of the Greenbush are undetermined, but it was operating in the 1860's, first by W. McArthur and later by Alex McKenzie.[34] The combined effects of the railway and the centre road closed this hotel and stopped the stages. In 1879 the Cameron Road was closed from the 5th Concession line to the 4th Concession line.[35] Four years later it was closed as far south as the front of the 2nd Concession.[36] All that remains of that once vital road is that part across the 1st Concession and Simcoe St. in Beaverton as far as the 5th Concession line.

[34] Churchill, A.G., *Poetical Dictionary*, 1860. PAO, R.G. 21 Assessment, Thorah Township 1865.

[35] PAO, M.S. 348 Reel #1, Thorah Council Minutes, June 21, 1879.

[36] Ibid., Thorah Bylaws #7, 1883.

Chapter 8
THE TOWN HALLS

The old Town Hall was located on the north side of Simcoe Street East where Wright's Hardware Store now stands. The property on which it stood was purchased in 1844 and the wooden building was erected two years later in 1846. The cost of the building was $800.00. The population of the village at that time was only 700.

Grace McElroy, great granddaughter of the first clerk John McKay, said she was told he built the Stone Jail and also had a hand in building the Town Hall. McKay (1789-1873) resigned in 1858 after having served his community for twenty-two years. We must presume, therefore, that there had been a previous building dating about 1836 which had served as a municipal headquarters. It was probably a log cabin.

The Town Hall was painted white in later years. It had wide seven-inch by half-inch thick horizontal board siding. Its size was approximately 25 x 30 feet with an attached wooden tower. The Municipal Council building was owned by Thorah Township but because of the lack of secure storage for documents the first clerk used to carry them home with him each night, to his farm about three miles distant, and lock them in the top drawer of a chest of drawers brought with him from Scotland.

The building was located close to the street and had a central doorway and a bell tower on the east side. The interior consisted of one large room at the front and two small rooms at the rear. The Council Chamber covered more than half the floor space with an eight-inch raised and railed area near the back which was used as a witness stand. There were long benches arranged in the large chamber for spectators. Mr. Cephas Doherty recalls having attended a court session as a boy and having observed such a proceeding. At the rear of the building, with doors opening onto the railed area, were offices for each of the township and municipal clerks. The hall was also used as a community hall for meetings and entertainment at which time the raised platform became a stage. In later years, entertainment was carried out at Alexandria Hall in the Hamilton Hotel.

The first Township meeting was held in Beaverton on the 21st of January, 1850, with councillors Alexander Braik representing Ward 1; Charles Robinson, Ward 2; George Proctor, Ward 3; Donald Cameron, Ward 4. Kenneth Cameron was Reeve. They were far-sighted and visionary men who thought beyond their immediate vicinity to encompass the province as a whole. This is illustrated by the following extract: "At the first meeting a petition to the Government was adopted urging the completion of a great public highway from Port Whitby to Sturgeon Bay on Lake Huron."

When Beaverton became an incorporated village on June 5th, 1884, a new council was formed consisting of: Reeve George F. Bruce and Councillors John Leslie, Jas. Ritchie, Charles T. Young, H. Westcott and Clerk, George Smith Jr. P.L.S.

In 1887 D.A. Cole received Council's permission to erect a barber shop on the corner of the Town Hall lot below the tower. As rental he agreed to ring the bell for seven years.

Perhaps due to the building's small size and the community's new importance as an incorporated village, there began to be talk about the need for a new town hall. In 1887 a joint committee of the two corporations was to receive a report on a new municipal building. In the mean-

OLD TOWN HALL & STEEL TOWER

NEW TOWN HALL erected 1910

time the old bell tower was in a dangerous condition and the clerk was instructed to either remove it or have it repaired. The bell seemed to be a problem, and of no use to the Township. The Council agreed in 1894 to renounce all claim to it for a sum of $20.00. The Beaverton Council inserted a clause in the lease stating that the renter of the ground occupied by the barber shop should ring the bell at the required times. The wooden tower met its doom in 1894 as the Municipal Records note that tenders were to be called for the purchase and removal of the tower. Five years later a contract was awarded to Ontario Wind Engine and Pump Co. of Toronto for a forty-foot steel bell tower with the old bell to be erected in the tower.

The new tower was a four-legged skeleton frame erected directly in front of the doorway to the municipal building. It had a cottage style roof to shelter the bell and a dangling rope attached.

In the Spring of 1900 a fire broke out, causing great excitement for the townsfolk. It destroyed many old records and caused the bell to crack. The bell was recast at the Beaverton Foundry in late June of that year on a Saturday, and raised to the tower on Monday. Alas, the result was disappointing as the tone was thin and poor. Mr. Harry Sturmer was hired in 1906 to ring the bell four times a day at 7 a.m., 12 noon, 1 p.m., and 6 p.m. at a salary of $30.00 per annum.

A period of thirty-three years had passed from the time in 1877 when it had been first discussed until the corner stone of the new Town Hall was laid in 1910. It was situated across the street from the old one, on the corner of Osborne and Simcoe Streets on property owned by Alexander Hamilton. Mr. Cephas Doherty recalls that a dance was held to celebrate the official opening in 1911.

During the two years the old Town Hall remained unoccupied it was used only for a group of young boys as a gymnasium. Mr. Playfair Brown, a boxing promoter in Toronto, kindly donated his services as instructor.

Willard T.S. Glassford purchased the old building from the two communities in 1913 and moved it back from its original position in order to erect his new brick hardware store. In 1948 he sold the property and business to William Wright.

A few years later as business expanded, Mr. Wright needed additional space so incorporated the old Town Hall with the new brick store. He knocked down the wall between the two buildings and removed the stage railings and partitions of the former Town Hall. Rather than see them destroyed, Mr. Ian Murray rescued the railings and later donated them to the Beaver River Museum where they were erected in 1983 at the

Thorah Council:

Reeve:	GEORGE F. BRUCE
Deputy Reeve:	CHARLES THOMPSON
Councillors:	WILLIAM WESTCOTT
	ALEX MCRAE
	JAMES DONNELL

Woodville Advocate, January 6, 1880

One of our constables has been at a loss to know how he was allowed mileage of 75 miles when he took a prisoner to Whitby while the Reeves were allowed 120 miles. The matter has since been explained to his satisfaction.

Beaverton Express, August 21, 1879.

top of the back stairway of the Log Cabin.

The old Stone Jail at the back of the property remained as it had always been until Mr. Wright decided to use it as a garage and had a larger door made for this purpose. In the mid 1970's it was rented to Mr. & Mrs. Byron Eaken as an art gallery.

The new Town Hall has had some changes in its seventy-four years of existence. In 1950 the firehall was moved from the west side of the building to the southward-facing wing formerly used as a farmers' market. The new fire engine was a taller and wider vehicle than the former Model T. Ford and required a larger area to store it. The firehall remained at the market hall until 1980 when it was moved to new quarters on Bay Street on the ground previously used by the curling rink. The Golden Friendship Club has occupied the old market hall since 1981 as their meeting place and drop-in centre.

> "Report and account of Peter Walls, road commissioner, re removing telegraph posts and closing part of the Cameron Road in the 4th concession."
>
> Thorah Township Council, October 2, 1880

> For the past two weeks the roads have been in a frightful condition being filled level with the fences and in some places drifted eight and ten feet high, making travelling on the roads almost an impossibility.
>
> Now these log and rail fences are the cause of all this as every farmer will admit and they will also admit a wire fence along the road would do away with the trouble.
>
> *Beaverton Express* March 4, 1887.

REFERENCES

— Municipal Records

— Abstracts of lots 14 and 15 north side Simcoe St. W. Records at Town Hall

— Farewell, J.E. *County of Ontario*, 1907. Chronicle Press Whitby

— *Beaverton Express*

— Reminiscences of Cephas Doherty, Wm. Gillespie, Kay Wilkins, Wm. Wright, Grace McElroy.

— *County of Ontario Directory 1869-70* for date of old Town Hall. Conner and Colston Toronto.

THE POST OFFICE

The village was called Mill Town until about 1830, when the name was changed to Beaverton. In 1835 Colonel Kenneth Cameron established a post office in his home just north of the village. It remained there for 18 months. It was then moved to Mr. James Ellis' log house on the bank of the Beaver River. The Ellis house still stands on the edge of what is now Centennial Park, just west of the Beaver River Museum brick house. Mr. Ellis was the first village Post Master.

In the 1840's the Post Office was moved to the site on the north side of Simcoe Street where the old I.G.A. store was located. From this location it was once again moved to what had been Mr. Alex Cameron's hardware store in the Proctor Block 1850(c.).

The locked post office boxes were installed on April 17, 1884.[1]

In 1902, Mr. Wellington Harrison was Post Master and at the same time was also Teller in the Standard Bank. Mr. Ben Madill was the Bank Manager at that time. This dual employment of Mr. Harrison's went on for ten years. When Mr. Madill retired, Mr. Harrison also left the Bank to become full time Post Master.

Among the men who have served as Post Masters are the following: Col. Cameron, James Ellis, Robert Harris, Wellington Harrison, Clark Calder, Mr. Alexander, and William Smith. Mr. Smith retired in June of 1983. Mrs. Doris Speedie, who had worked with Mr. Smith was appointed Cannington Post Mistress on September 8, 1982; however she returned to become Beaverton Post Mistress on November 7, 1983.

Mr. Frank Gardner was one of the Post Office caretakers. He took on the responsibility of raising and lowering the flag each day as he said "The sun should never set on a raised flag."[2]

When the Standard Bank moved to its new building in 1922, the Post Office took over the vacated premises in the Proctor Block. This building was the second Proctor building on this site. When this Proctor building was torn down the Post Office had to move temporarily until the present building was completed in 1939 on the same site.

[1] *Woodville Advocate.*
[2] Grace McElroy.
Beaverton Express.
Beaverton Express, The Supplement.
Ritchie, Mary Houston, *A Township on the Lake.*

ELLIS HOUSE — Simcoe Street West Location of original Beaverton Village Post office.

Wrecking the PROCTOR building to make way for the present POST OFFICE. courtesy Calvin Calder

Beaverton (Semi-Staff) (NAME OF OFFICE) — Victoria Ont. (ELECTORAL DISTRICT AND PROVINCE)

LOK 1M0 GR 6 PO 1391-1

DATE OF ESTABLISHMENT— Prior to 1844 OFFICE CLOSED—

OFFICE RE-OPENED—

Office # 330310 330310

ENG. | PR. | RURAL | SUB. | PO

CH. | HX. | ST. J. | QUE. | MONT. | OTT. | TOR. | LON. | N. BAY | WPG. | MJ. | SAS. | CAL. | EDM. | VAN.

CHANGES IN NAME

FORMER NAME ...... DATE OF CHANGE ......

NAME OF POSTMASTER	MILITARY STATUS	DATE OF BIRTH	DATE OF APPOINTMENT	DATE OF VACANCY
Donald Cameron	Shown as P. Mr.		1844	26-10-1856
Charles Robinson			1-10-1856	2-4-1861
Thomas Creighton			1-5-1861	12-10-1861
Donald Cameron			1-11-1861	12-9-1874
James Cameron			1-11-1874	27-5-91
Jas. W. Harrison			1-8-91	12-4-1937
Donald Clarke Calder			14-4-1937	acting
Donald Clarke Calder			21-2-38	8-6-58
Mrs. Nora Munro			16-5-58	acting
Robert George Alexander		1-9-1927	4-12-58	5/11/63
Mrs. Nora Munro		28-7-14	8-5-63	acting
Mr. William Boynton Smithers		14-5-21	1-8-63	2/8/83
Mrs. Deborah Shearer			3-8-83	acting
Mrs. Doris Speedie			7-11-83	

O.B. 39–2M–15-10-56

Chapter 9

MORE THAN A MILL-SITE

With roads opening up, movement among the settlers became less difficult. To take their wheat to the grist mill, to transport logs to the sawmill, to pick up a few necessities at Cameron's store would take the Thorah pioneers to the small settlement which today is called Beaverton.

When Arad Smalley investigated settlement in Thorah in 1830, he noted only two houses in the area that is now within the village: Donald Calder's and that of Samuel Farnsworth situated somewhere on the south half of lot 15, concession 6, probably near the river or on the lake shore.

Even by 1846 it was said that Beaverton contained only a "half dozen houses."[1] The 1851 Assessment Roll suggests that there were at least two dozen families living there then. By 1859 the number of households seems to have increased to at least seventy.[2] It is evident that the late 1840's and the 1850's were times of rapid urban growth.

The grist mills, Calder's and the Proctor mill east on the Beaver River, drew settlers from all over this Township and even from surrounding communities. As farm products increased, so too, did the mills' work expand, requiring, of course, workers such as John Cobbeldick and Richard Brinscombe[3] who, along with their families, took up residence nearby.

Beaverton was the stage terminal. Although there apparently was no wharf there in 1846, the steamer, Beaver, having to stop some distance from shore,[4] evidence suggests that there was one by 1854. The post office, established as early as 1835, brought residents from all parts of the Township to the growing settlement of Beaverton.

All roads led to Beaverton and even people in the southern part of Mara undoubtedly patronized the growing community near the mouth of the Beaver, for by 1851 there existed a tannery, two grist mills, a saw mill, and a carding and fulling mill.[5]

When the pioneers' needs for the essentials were met, there was a

[1] Smith, W.H., *Smith's Gazetteer*, Toronto, H. & W. Rowsell, 1846.
[2] Thorah Assessment Roll for 1859.
[3] 1851 Census, 1852 Assessment Roll.
[4] Smith, op. cit.
[5] *Canada Directory*, 1851-52, Lovell.

TYPES OF THORAH HOMES*

	1851	1861
Stone	2	4
Brick	1	4
Frame	23	67
Log	97	263
Shanties	59	—

*Census data

In 1851 only one brick house — that of the Bethunes, and at present the home of Mr. and Mrs. Ross Baillie — had been built. Within the next decade, three others appeared: the Gunn home which has only one corner now standing; the James White home which was later the Alsop farmhouse; and the Church of Scotland manse which, built in 1855, was the home of the family of Rev. David Watson.

Two stone houses, those of George Proctor and James McHattie, were noted in the 1851 Census. By 1861 there were two others, one belonging to John Anderson, the tanner, and still standing on Simcoe Street West, and the other the home of the "Stonehouse" Camerons (a name to distinguish this family from the many others of this surname) and long gone from lot 12 concession 7.

One of the first stone houses in Thorah, George Proctor's Home, stood east of the present Village. Later the home of the Dougal Gillespie family, it was destroyed by fire early in this century. Today Jim Warren's home is on the property.

growing demand for some of the "better things in life." A fine large frame house would require the skills of a joiner or carpenter; brick as chosen for Simcoe Lodge, the Bethune home, invited the skills of a brick-maker in the 1840's. Surely most well-established households needed some new chairs with nicely turned legs made at Beaverton by Alexander Calder. Why should not the commodities offered by the transient peddlers who travelled the roads be available in Beaverton all the time?

With some of the villagers presenting to Council in 1851 a petition that "horned cattle not be allowed to run at large in the village,"[6] and Donald Calder petitioning Council for sidewalks in 1852,[7] it can be seen that attempts were being made to change Beaverton's image.

In the early years, tradesmen were scattered throughout the Township. Many of these men had taken up land, an economic mainstay when income from their trades was undoubtedly meagre. Angus Grant, stone-cutter and mason, settled in concession three on the lake shore. Angus McInnis and his two sons, John and Alex, carried on their trade of shoe-making in lot 3 concession 5. Two coopers, Duncan McIntyre and William Morrison lived in the third and second concessions respectively. Serving the north part of the Township from his home in the ninth concession, was John McEachern, a weaver.

A well-known maker of spinning wheels was Laughlin McNeill who lived at lot 8 concession 11, the farm presently owned by George McCuaig, on the Portage Road east of Gamebridge. It is said that one woman walked fourteen miles to get a spinning wheel which she carried the same distance home.

As Beaverton grew, establishing itself as the main centre of the Township, tradesmen and businessmen saw the advantages of being located there.

Two village artisans, Hugh Cathcart and George Elder, wove yarn into cloth which was, in turn, fashioned into clothing. Early tailors included John Cameron who operated a store in the village in the 1850's,[8] Andrew McNabb who by 1860 was running a general store as well as making clothes,[9] and James Campbell. Many young women took up dressmaking, one of the few occupations which single females chose to pursue in the early years.

The Ellis carding and fulling mill must have filled a long-felt want in Beaverton. Situated downriver from the grist and saw mills, it was

[6]Thorah Council Minutes, 1851.
[7]Ibid., 1852.
[8]Thorah Assessment Rolls, 1852, 1859.
[9]Ibid., 1859; 1861 Census.

powered by steam. By 1860 at the Ellis mill 10,000 pounds of wool were carded and 6,000 yards of full cloth were produced annually.[10] Ten years later nine men were employed at the mill.[11] By that time, James Ellis's son Godfrey had taken over the business which had been founded by his father but operated for a period of time by Ronald Sillars.

The Beaverton 34th Volunteer Regiment 1870 (c.). The building at the left margin is likely the present Stedman's store. The centre building is possibly a shop built by James Campbell, an early tailor, who purchased the property from the Calders in 1849. By the early 1870's it was John Anderson's grocery, feed and seed store. From 1875-1878 it was Alex Montgomery's General Store. Later Alex Cameron opened business here. The building was demolished in 1893 to make room for a new building.

The building at the right margin, in the early 1870's, would have been Thomas Jefferies' Jewelery Store.

[10] 1861 Census for Thorah.
[11] Ibid., 1871.

In 1852[12] John Anderson bought property below the Beaverton grist mill where he set up a tannery which was operated by water power. In 1860 he processed 600 hides using 20 cords of hemlock.[13] Anderson sold boots and shoes and, of course, leather for shoemakers and saddlers. Within the next decade the operation had been converted to steam power and Anderson's son, James, had taken charge. The Andersons lived across the street in the stone house now occupied by Lloyd Johnson and his family.

Four important industrial establishments stood side by side along the Beaver, each dependent on the river for power: the Ellis mill, the tannery, the grist mill and the saw mill.

"Lace boots and slippers are made in the shop, Long boots and short boots and boots with fine top": thus were the products of Alex Cameron's workmanship described by A.G. Churchill in his *Poetical Dictionary* of 1860. Cameron started up in business in 1858[14] although it seems that he was carrying on his trade in the community before that time.[15] In 1864 he went into partnership with George F. Bruce dealing in dry goods and groceries until 1881.[16]

BEAVERTON

At Beaverton River, on Simcoe Lake shore
Post office, two churches, and also six stores,
One teacher, one doctor, one lawyer for all
One wharf at the harbour, town pound, and town hall,
Steam boat and propeller, three schooners that sail,
And stages bring passengers, light freight and mail,
Shoemakers and bakers, and carpenters build,
Bricklayers and painters, enamel and guild,
Do turning, and planing, and carding of wool,
Do grinding and sawing, they tan and they full,
Waggon Makers, and blacksmiths and tailors abound,
Coopers and butchers, and farmers all round.
In summer it's lovely to view the road lake,
The groves and the islands, and fishes they take.

— A.G. Churchill,
Poetical Dictionary, 1860.

[12] Index to Abstract Land Deeds.
[13] 1861 Census.
[14] *Beaverton Express*, Christmas Edition, 1882.
[15] 1851 Census of Thorah.
[16] *Beaverton Express*, Christmas Edition, 1882.

Another Beaverton shoemaker, John Cathcart, son of Hugh Cathcart the weaver, devised the "Cathcart's Rule for Cutting Boots and Shoes" for which he received a patent in 1861.[17] Well-known in the 1850's for the making of boots and shoes were John Adams, Phillip Keefer, and Gilbert McEwen whom some of our more senior residents remember. Others who used the products of Anderson's Tannery were the saddlers and harnessmakers. It would seem that Robert McHenry and John McArthur were the earliest to practise this trade in Beaverton. McArthur also made trunks.

The general store, of course, sold everything from stove-pipes to ladies' bonnets, from nails to salt, from medicine to leather boots, from rifle caps to tea. By 1851 four of these stores in Beaverton were accommodating the needs of the people in the surrounding area. George Proctor, whose store was where the present post office is situated, Malcolm Morrison, Donald Cameron, and J. Grierson and Co. who also ran the Beaverton Mills at that time, all operated general stores.[18] Usually storekeepers of this era were men with some capital behind them as credit often had to be extended to farmers who had little income throughout the year, and could pay their debts only after their grain or other farm products were sold, most often in the fall season.

Of course, at this time, and indeed, for years later, trade rather than cash sales was the way much business was carried on. The farmwife would appear with some eggs or a few pounds of butter and would take in return any of the goods the store provided and her household required: perhaps some tea, molasses, pepper, or maybe some tobacco for the man of the house, patent medicine, perfume, or matches, a precious commodity at the time.

About seven merchants were in business by 1859.[19] Among them were Charles H. Davidson who built the block which was destroyed by fire in 1979, and his partner William Gordon, as well as Aeneas Cameron, Archibald Campbell, "A general importer well-stocked in his line, Domestic and foreign each side of the brine,"[20] and Andrew McNabb, all of whom were well-known in Beaverton for a number of years.

Not only was the general store a market for some farm products, a bank of sorts, and a provider of almost every line of merchandise, it was a place where neighbours and acquaintances met, passed the time of day,

[17] *List of Canadian Patents from the Beginning of the Patent Office*, June 1824 to the 31st of August 1872.
[18] *Canada Directory* 1851-52, Lovell.
[19] 1859 Assessment Roll.
[20] Churchill, A.G., *Poetical Dictionary*, 1860.

discussed the weather, crops, and high rate of taxes, and no doubt passed along the gossip of the community. It was the meeting place of story-tellers and self-appointed politicians who solved all the important issues of the day from their places around the pot-bellied stove.

Beaverton's important position within the Township was, of course, becoming more evident as time went on. Unlike most townships of that era, Thorah had no other small communities centred around a church, school, and country store with the exception of Gamebridge which, located on the Talbot River, the boundary between Thorah and Mara, would see most of its development after the coming of the railway.

While many activities of a more localized nature were carried on in school houses throughout Thorah, others encompassing the whole Township were centred in Beaverton. As early as 1853 a fair was held on the grounds north of Main Street. The Agricultural Society, organized in January of that year during a meeting at Murray's Inn, named Charles Robinson as president. As well as classes for agricultural exhibits, prizes were awarded for winning manufactures such as boots and shoes, blankets, sets of harness, ploughs, and other farm implements.

The year 1853 also saw the establishment of a library and reading room in the court house situated where Wright's Hardware is today. The librarian was John McKay, Township clerk. By 1859 there were some 500 volumes in this collection.

The years 1857-1859 witnessed a general depression in Upper Canada. The early 1860's also, it seems were regarded as a time of slower growth. As the *Orillia Expositor* of 1868 stated, "For some time it" (Beaverton) "seemed to be at a standstill and did not improve much, but lately it has been different." Census data pertaining solely to Beaverton is not available, but the population increase in the Township, including the

Since 1853, when the Thorah Branch Agricultural Society was formed, fairs have been held in Beaverton with many changes and improvements taking place throughout the years. Plowing matches were sponsored by the Agricultural Society for some time. In 1872 land, in the amount of 2½ acres near where the Osborne Plaza is today, was purchased from Mr. Calder for $160. Two years later, the Drill Shed was built by the Department of National Defence on this site.

In 1915, the fair was held on the present grounds which were leased from Mr. A.C. McKenzie at a nominal rent by the Beaverton Agricultural Society. The race track was laid out, the Drill Shed was moved, and new cattle and horse barns were erected. A few years later, the grandstand was added.

THE BEAVERTON FAIR GROUNDS
on Osborne Street.

> The village green, later occupied by the Methodist Church, which is now Victory Tabernacle, and the neighbouring premises, was often the scene of a great gathering of Scotsmen in the early days. Laughlin McNeill, a wood turner and accomplished piper from the Portage Road, provided the music; and dancing and highland sport "were indulged in with great zest for some days."
>
> Obituary of Mr. McNeill,
> *Beaverton Express*, August 6, 1909

Village, from 1861 to 1871 is not as large as in the prior or subsequent decades. Nevertheless, there were developments which showed that Beaverton was moving ahead during the 1860's. Professional men appeared on the scene. Lawyers such as H.E. O'Dell, W.J. McCleary, and Norman Paterson set up offices. Physicians and a veterinary surgeon were in practice. Burdeen and Tweed and M.L. Carlisle (probably the first owner of Beaverton's Medical Hall) were the chemists of the 1860's. Mr. C.C. Keeler sold insurance, and Silas Beebe, formerly an edge tool maker in the Village, started a photography business.

Before the end of the decade the railroad would arrive in Beaverton, yet as early as 1854 a meeting between the municipal council and the Port Hope and Peterborough Railway Company had been arranged. No doubt the prospect of a rail line to Beaverton gave much encouragement to aspiring businessmen. Certainly, a letter written by Henry White, surveyor, to Mr. Bains, land commissioner, in 1855, in relation to the lots he held in Beaverton suggests that he was optimistic about the Village's growth.

As transportation into this formerly isolated community improved, the people saw self-sufficiency as decreasingly necessary and certainly less than attractive. Not only were some women refusing to do all their own baking, (Heaven forbid, some were purchasing goodies from Mr. P.D. McArthur's bakery!) but households were demanding goods brought in from other parts of the country or even from abroad.

The first stages in the growth of a town clearly behind them, many people of Beaverton and Thorah were now concentrating on the improvement of the quality of life, not only in material things, but also in the social, recreational, and intellectual realm.

The Orange Lodge built their hall in 1865[21] where the Express office now is situated. The year 1868 saw the organization of a St. Andrew's Society. In the same year a cricket club was formed.

As the Beaverton correspondent of the aforementioned Orillia paper remarked in 1868, "Our village is bound to go ahead."

THORAH TOWNSHIP COUNCIL, January 17, 1859.

"The following transmitted to the Commissioner of Crown Lands: The memorial of the Municipal Corporation of the township of Thorah . . . that the townships of Carden, Dalton, Draper, and Macaulay in the recently surveyed district lying to the north-east of this township are rapidly filling with settlers and will conduce much to the interest and convenience of those people were a Crown Lands Agency established at Beaverton (The natural outlet and place of business of those townships) where settlers and intending settiers could get information respecting the land on the spot. . . ."

At Beaverton, Lake Simcoe on Wednesday morning the Beaver River overflowed its banks covering the flats and carrying a schooner out against the ice in the lake. It was feared that the bridge and mill dam in the village would be destroyed.

On the Mail route between Lindsay and Beaverton the road is covered with water in many places to the depth of 2 or 3 feet.

Canadian Post March 24, 1865

[21] Conner & Colston, *County of Ontario Directory*, Toronto, Hunter, Ross & Co.

PRODUCTS OF CLAY

Much of Thorah's soil has left the Township in the form of brick, tile, and pottery. "Traces left by Indians suggest that the Thorah Pottery Works was the scene of Indians' pottery fields."* It very well may be that the aboriginal people, at one time or another, created earthen vessels from all of the areas where good clay existed.

It is said that some of the bricks for Simcoe Lodge, the first brick structure in the Township, were made on the grounds of that home while others came from the southeast corner of lot 13 concession 7. An early pottery, located on Elizabeth Street, was purchased by William Taylor and Arthur Dodge in 1871. In 1869 Mr. Walls made bricks for St. Paul's Anglican Church from his clay deposits in the north part of lot 11 concession 4.** Nearby was the Thorah Pottery operated by George Drake on lot 10 concession 5. In 1871 Drake employed six workers and in 1876 he was unable to supply the demand for brick. After he sold this brick yard and pottery to William Taylor in 1885, Drake purchased the Walls site.***

The local newspaper reported that in 1887 the local brickyards had shipped close to 1,000,000 bricks for rebuilding at Gravenhurst after a disastrous fire. The business became so important that a railway siding was constructed into the Taylor yard.

Another pottery well-known in Beaverton was that of James Bemister on Simcoe Street, now the site of the Odd Fellows' and Rebekahs' Hall.

The last years of the Nineteenth and early part of the Twentieth Century saw many changes in ownership of these brick and pottery works. Such names as R. McCallum, D.A. Smith, John Wilford, Andrew Snelgrove, Fred Teer, William Barclay,*** and Stephen Furniss were connected with this industry.

* * * * *

Tweedsmuir History, clipping from *Beaverton Express*, 1898.

***Orillia Expositor*, March 26, 1869.

***Information given by Mr. Henry Jost, who is probably the only surviving workman at the brick works operated by Snelgrove, Teer, and Barclay. All purchase dates taken from Index to Abstract Land Deeds.

Chapter 10

THE HORSE AND BUGGY DAYS

An old oil painting entitled "The Village Blacksmith" depicts a powerful young man wearing breeches and leather apron with raised right arm wielding an iron hammer as he labours to shoe a horse. Two young children stand in the reflected orange glow of the forge fire while they watch with awe as the sparks fly. Such a scene would have been typical of any village smithy had it included a group of men relaxing from their toil as they gossiped, yarned and whiled the time away in the warmth and friendship of the open-doored smithy.

Blacksmith shops were a necessity in a rural community and large shops stocked harness and gear for horses. Some smiths were also skilled ironmongers and adept at repairing all types of farm equipment. Mr. Morrison Colville recalled that the iron tires of wagon wheels and later threshing machines would loosen after about one month's wear and they would be driven into White's Creek to swell the wood to fit the tires.

Mr. James Gordon was Beaverton's first blacksmith and catered to the first settlers of Thorah Township.[1]

The second smith was probably James McHattie from Scotland, who arrived in town with his wife and eight small children in 1841. Later two other children were born in Beaverton.[2] Undoubtedly it was a log building in which he set up his forge where he made tools, repaired farm equipment and shod horses.

His affairs must have prospered for between 1847 and 1851 he built a large, two storey stone house of severe appearance on the old Cameron Road, now Simcoe Street East. In the Scottish manner, the main floor was raised high above the ground to accommodate the full basement. In those days when most of the homes were shacks or log cabins, such a house would have seemed a mansion. The exterior was plastered over many years ago hiding the ancient stonework. Today it is the home of Miss Margaret McEachern.

By 1861, McHattie and his son-in-law James Bates were working together and in September of that year built a large new blacksmith shop with Bates working as the blacksmith.[3]

[1] *Beaverton Express,* March 27, 1896. Obituary of Mrs. Gordon.
[2] Alsop, H.A., *Some Came from Darnaway,* Beaverton, 1983, page 81.
[3] Ibid., page 82.

James McHattie's youngest son William followed his father in blacksmithing and began his business in a log building at the rear of his home on Osborne Street and continued in operation until about 1901. This frame house was built to fit into the pie-shaped lot where John and Osborne streets meet. This oddly-shaped building called "split-the-wind," was a village landmark for many years until it was torn down in 1968 or 1969 and the property used for a village garden space behind the town hall.

Another early blacksmith in Beaverton was Archibald McKinnon. Later in the 19th century George Bertram operated a blacksmith shop which he erected in 1875.[4]

We know Anson Birchard was in the blacksmith trade in 1859,[5] and he was mentioned in 1865 in the minutes of Thorah Township as having his tender accepted for supplying twelve new scrapers. In 1861 Anson bought the property where the library now stands. His son James Birchard carried on the smithy, forming the partnership of Birchard and Clarke in the Iron Block in 1895 but in the same year a fire broke out in the block and Birchard was one of the few establishments saved.[6] In 1902 he began erecting a large frame building immediately west of the smithy for use as a showroom for farm equipment.[7] Morrison Colville recalls that Birchard was sometimes called Buckanee. He became an important village man being a sportsman, weighmaster and also Reeve despite his strange nickname.

When the library was built on part of the Old Iron Block property in 1912, Birchard moved his shop to the lane running behind the library. By 1913 Arthur Gale worked for Birchard as a blacksmith but when World War I broke out, Gale joined the Artillery in April 1914. He returned to Beaverton in 1919 and the partnership of Birchard and Gale was formed. Their work consisted of blacksmithing and general repairs. They were agents for Cockshut farm machinery as well as general agents for buggies, wagons, lumber and cream separators.

Later Arthur Gale bought the shop when Birchard retired and continued in business for some years. His business consisted mainly of iron work as there was little horse-shoeing done by that time. An example of his work can be seen in the hand-wrought handrails of the Beaverton Presbyterian Church. In the 1960's he sold the smithy to Jim Arnold who only remained in operation for a few years.

[4] Beaverton Express, Dec. 9, 1887.
[5] Assessment Rolls for Thorah Township, 1859.
[6] Beaverton Express, Mar. 22, 1895.
[7] Ibid., August 7, 1902.

Three other blacksmiths are also known to have been in operation during the 1900's: Ned Rowcliffe; Henry C. Howard; later on, William Clark ran his shop on Osborne Street where Harvey's Family Fair is now located.

Blacksmiths, of course always had their place in the shops of carriage and wagon makers, important men in early days, providing, as they did, the only means of locomotion available. Of these, the most famous was Peter McMillan.

Born in Islay, Scotland, in 1824, he arrived in Beaverton in 1852[8] and established his carriage making and blacksmith shop in the building by the river at the intersection of Main Street. There he continued his work-shop for many years and gained a high reputation for his honesty and integrity. He employed one man and hand-crafted his work using pine, ash and oak lumber. It is estimated the factory was erected in the late 1840's and at one time was a distillery brewing a potent whiskey. This old landmark was demolished in 1906.[9]

Two of his seven children, the twins Peter and Duncan (born 1859), later joined the firm and the name of the company changed to Peter McMillan & Sons. In 1888 they bought the property from James Todd which they had occupied since 1882.[10] It was situated at the corner of Main and Mara Streets, where the theatre now stands. Later a large barn for drying lumber was erected.

Many types of carriages were made including phaetons, buggies — open and covered-wagons, sleighs and jump seats. Their business thrived as was shown by the announcement in the newspaper in 1887 "No less than 5 top buggies and a lumber wagon have left their shop this week". Barter was used to a great extent as they advertised they would give "a buggy in exchange for a good milch cow."[11]

In 1888 the brothers built a large 50 x 164 feet frame skating rink beside their factory near the Beaver River. An old-time "raising" was held and in a few hours the great building was up.

In 1872[12] James Snelgrove arrived in Beaverton from Dummer, Ontario and set up a wagon shop, sash, door and planing mill as well as a blacksmith shop at the corner of Bay and Osborne Streets where Tanner's Service Station now stands. He ran a thriving business which operated to capacity. His patented clothes reel for outside use was

[8] Ibid., Sept. 16, 1897. Obituary of Mr. McMillan.
[9] Ibid., Mar. 15, 1906.
[10] Ibid., Special Christmas Edition, 1882.
[11] Ibid., Apr. 29, 1887.
[12] Ibid., Jan. 19, 1899. (Snelgrove's advertisement)

PETER & DUNCAN McMILLAN

advertised to be "the best thing going for its simplicity and durability."[13] He also advertised a buggy with a thousand-mile axle.[14]

The planing mill produced shingles, moulding, sash and doors, while the Steam Carriage Factory was completely furnished to turn out any kind of vehicle in the trade. The blacksmith shop paid special attention to horse shoeing but did all sorts of work in that line. In January of 1879 the Carriage Shop caught fire from a spark from the smoke stack falling on the roof but the fire was promptly extinguished.[15] Fortunately little damage was done.

In the late 90's, with manufacturing becoming more sophisticated, his operation became known as Snelgrove's Steam Carriage Works and Planing Factory. With business doing very well, Snelgrove undertook the building of his new home, a double one, opposite his factory on Osborne

[13] Ibid., Jan. 12, 1894.
[14] Ibid., Apr. 4, 1901.
[15] Ibid., Jan. 23, 1879.

Street.

Mr. Snelgrove remained in business for forty years, a respected man and ardent Methodist temperance worker. He died on November 15, 1913. When his operation closed, the machinery was purchased by Mr. Thomas Doherty who ran a saw mill on Mara Road south of the Grand Trunk railway station. Later Doherty's two sons joined the firm and continued doing woodworking and cabinet making. A fire in 1958 destroyed the building.

One of the remaining examples of Snelgrove's work is the frame building now occupied by the Beaverton Express.

During the years that James Snelgrove was in operation, David Roberts, carriage maker, Duncan McCuaig and John Cameron, wagon makers were also in business; the latter also sold farm equipment.

As the Village of Beaverton had grown to a sizeable community by the late 19th and early 20th centuries, public transportation for both passengers and freight was a necessity, and skilled artisans were needed to make and repair trappings for horses.

We know that Jas. Hunter operated a Livery Stable in 1884 located at the end of the Mara Road bridge[16] and that Robert and Alexander Turner ran a rival business with a Saddlery and Livery Station in the late 1800's.

Although automobiles had made their appearance in town by the early 1900's their numbers were few. It is unlikely that liveries operated cars at that time. Jas. Lytle advertised his operations as the "Beaverton Livery" in 1902 and Stephen West his as "Express and Cartage" in 1914. Dan Cameron was also in competition at that time as he bought the cartage business and also the residence on Bay Street of M. Joseph Nealon in 1913.[17]

A new harness making and repair shop opened in 1914 and was run by John T. Sparks.[18] Four years later, R. Magee sold his "Express and Cartage" business to George McRae.[19] Business in town seemed to be booming!

By the 1920's automobiles had definitely come to stay, although in rural communities horses were still widely used as is illustrated by two advertisements in the Express for 1925: one an "Express and Cartage" of Murdoch McRae's and the other for "Auto Repairs and Sales of Star and Durant cars"[20] at Yule and Taylor's Bay Street garage.

[16] Ibid., July 10, 1884.
[17] Ibid., May 1, 1913.
[18] Ibid., Nov. 5, 1914.
[19] Ibid., Sept. 12, 1918.
[20] Ibid., July 9, 1925.

Peter, one of the McMillan twins, famed for their lacrosse prowess, was an able gymnastic performer with illuminated Indian Clubs. Lighted candles would be placed inside the brightly painted translucent clubs, the lights would be lowered or extinguished, and the ensuing gyrations and twisting spins would make a colourful exhibition.

Harry Furniss recalls seeing Peter McMillan do this demonstration at a village reception for Preston Emes who returned, wounded, from World War I in 1916.

INDIGENT SCOTSMEN

In 1868 the St. Andrew's Society was started for the purpose of helping Scotsmen who had fallen on hard times. It was open only to men born in Scotland, their sons or grandsons. Annual fees were 50¢ each. By 1880 it had disbanded — probably because there were no indigent Scotsmen! One of the features of the Society was a St. Andrew's Day dinner held Nov. 30 at one of the local hotels.

Chapter 11

ACCOMMODATING PEOPLE

The undependable state of the roads, and the distances between pioneer homes made travel slow and difficult. The miles of bush and mud offered little protection from the rain, snow and bitter winter winds. A warm hearth and a friendly smile were not only a convenience, but could be a life saving necessity. For this reason, few early inhabitants of Thorah ever locked their doors or turned weary travellers away. The more enterprising and well situated dweller might have seen some promise in accommodating wayfarers, and in this manner Thorah's first inn may have come into being. This early innkeeper may have intended to farm, but found he was disinclined to such an occupation, or have been a farmer who, because of several poor crops, was forced to supplement his income in order to support his family. Whatever the reason, his door was open to the weary, the cold, and the hungry. Here the gossip was current, advice to the new settler practical, and the whiskey cheap.

Such establishments could abuse their position as servant to the traveller. For this reason, and as a source of income for the magistrates, such businesses came to be licenced. Three enterprising Scotsmen were the first licenced tavern owners in Thorah. In 1835 the magistrates licenced Christopher McRae, Finnan McDonald and Thomas McDonald for the sum of three pounds.[1] With these licences came regulations, which although they were changed from year to year, usually required that "the bar or tap room was to be kept shut the whole of the Lord's Day, Christmas, and Good Friday."[2] There were also limits placed on the quantity drunk and the length of time spent tippling, and stipulations about who could drink at a tavern.[3] An innkeeper was expected to be in "possession of a dwelling house containing at least three bedrooms beyond those required for the use of the family and to have at the time of application at least three good beds over and above those required for the use of the family and be possessed of a good stable capable of stabling at least two pair of horses."[4]

[1] Public Archives of Ontario, M.S. 251, Reel 2, Vol. 6, Page 95. Minutes of the Court of the Quarter Sessions of the Peace for the Home District. Jan. 5, 1835.

[2] Ibid., Dec. 24, 1836.

[3] Loc. cit.

[4] Loc. cit.

These regulations placed a lower limit on the size of licenced establishments and thus effectively limited the number of locations for which licences may have been granted.

There are indications of a number of inns throughout the township which served the travelling public but are not recorded as licenced establishments. The names John Murray, Donald McRae and Frederick Fraser can all be associated with early inns. In the case of Murray and McRae, the term "inn" was used as a distinguishing name to prevent confusion regarding two men of the same name.[5] Whereas Fraser appears on the assessment roll,[6] Christopher McRae, the first resident to apply for a tavern licence, retained it for only one year.[7] His tavern probably stood on lot 9 Concession 2 the traditional site of the McRae Hotel.[8] The fact that the McRae Hotel still lives in memory adds substance to the possibility that it operated for many years. Widow Stewart may have operated a casual inn along this same well-travelled route, if Samuel Richardson's diary is any indication.[9] Considering the fact that unlicenced inns leave little evidence of their existence, it seems possible that they may have been as numerous as the licenced variety.

It may have been difficult to obtain and keep a tavern licence in the 1840's. It must have been true that the tavern keeper had to be on good terms with the township constable, and the occasional generosity and correct political outlook would have ensured his friendship. At special sessions of Court in York, it was customary for both the petitioners for the tavern licences and the constables from each township to be present.[10] Few words from the constable would have been required to have a licence revoked or a petition denied. By this mechanism, licenced tavern keepers were kept on the straight and narrow. From 1837, the year of the rebellion, in addition to a previously required proof of character, applicants had to swear an oath of loyalty to obtain a licence.[11] On June 2, 1842, the magistrates concluded that "no licence. . . . will be renewed. . . . unless they (the tavern owners) shall have accommodations of superior description and are of unquestionable character of sobriety and general good conduct."

[5]Minute Book of the Maintenance Committee of St. Andrew's Presbyterian Church. July 10, 1865.

[6]PAO, R.G. 21, Assessment of Thorah Township, 1859.

[7]PAO, M.S. 251, Reel 2, Minutes of the Court of the Quarter Sessions of the Peace for the Home District.

[8]Interview with Bill Bursby, Feb. 24, 1978.

[9]PAO, R.G. -1 CB -1 Box 9, Diary of Samuel Richardson, 1844.

[10]PAO, M.S. 251, Reel 2, Vol. 6, Minutes of the Court of the Quarter Sessions of the Peace for the Home District. Oct. 17, 1848.

[11]Ibid., Dec. 17, 1837.

With these points in mind, one need not feel ashamed of an ancestor who operated an inn or tavern.[12]

Besides catering to the general travelling public, early inns and taverns provided a valuable service to itinerant pedlars. These men filled a need in days when stores were either non-existent or the toil of pioneer families made trips to a distant store infrequent or inconvenient. With horse packs brimming with bolts of cloth, fine threads, salt, sugar and many other essentials, pedlars made the rounds of their circuits, returning again to each locality after several weeks or months. These men of the road had no home but that of the customer or that of the local innkeeper. After a long day, a pedlar could put up his feet and swap stories with the tavern owner or other travellers. During the conversation he might even learn of a new customer with hard cash to spend so that he would not have to accept goods as payment, which were the usual fare.

As Beaverton began to take shape in the late 1840's, licences were granted for taverns that were verifiably within the confines of the present village. On the south side of Simcoe Street, the present site of the McRae Block, now housing the Sears office, was a tavern licenced to Alex Cameron for 1849 and 1850.[13] Donald McInnis operated a hotel at the west end of the present town hall lot from March 1848 to 1850.[14] Donald Campbell's tavern was described as being at the junction of the Whitby Road and the Lakeshore road in 1850.[15] He may have been renting a building on the site of the new I.G.A. James McHattie, a blacksmith at the eastern boundary of town, held a tavern licence for 1849 and 1850.[16]

When a stage coach came to a halt in Beaverton in the early 1850's, the disembarking passenger would have found himself standing in front of a hotel operated by John Boynton.[17] An Englishman, Boynton was then operating the hotel owned by Alex Cameron, on the south side of Simcoe Street.[18] He remained licenced until 1853 when he appears to have moved on.[19] If in 1853 our traveller had happened to walk east to the present junction of Simcoe and Osborne Streets, he would have found Hugh Murray, and his recent bride, Margaret, busily attending to

[12] Ibid., June 2, 1842.

[13] Ibid., Dec. 21, 1848 and Dec. 3, 1849. Registry Office, Whitby, Abstract to Land Titles, Beaverton.

[14] Ibid., Mar. 9, 1848 and Registry Office, Whitby, Abstracts to Land Titles, Beaverton.

[15] PAO, M.S. 348, Reel 1, Municipal Minutes, Thorah Township. Feb. 18, 1850.

[16] PAO, M.S. 251, Reel 2, Vol. 6, Minutes of the Court of the Quarter Sessions of the Peace for the Home District. Dec. 21, 1848 and Dec. 3, 1849.

[17] Lovell, John, *The Canada Directory,* 1851.

[18] Census 1851, Ontario County, Thorah Township. Assessment 1851 and 1852, Thorah Township.

[19] PAO, M.S. 348, Reel 1, Municipal Minutes, Thorah Township. Mar. 7, 1853.

customers at the Murray Inn.[20] Murray bought the hotel property previously owned by Donald McInnis. Though he owned this land until 1868 he leased it to other innkeepers after 1854 and may have taken up farming.[21]

It was at the time that Murray and Boynton were in business, that Thorah Council became responsible for licencing and regulating local taverns, and they enacted a few new bylaws regarding Houses of Public Entertainment, as they preferred to call hotels or taverns. At that time hotel owners were required to post a bond of 100 pounds, and the two securities to each bond had to post the sum of fifty pounds.[22] This was required to ensure good behaviour on the part of each licencee. Each hotelkeeper was required to have "a good and comfortable house containing at least one sitting room and four bedrooms. . ." Along with other regulations, they were not allowed to permit the playing of "nine pins, bagatelle, cards, dice, draughts, nittles, shooting matches, raffles, lotteries, wheel of fortune. . . or any game at which money could be won or lost."[22]

One tavern inspector was appointed from each ward. In 1853 the inspectors were Alex Campbell, Norman Leslie, Donald McFadyen, Andrew McNabb, and Charles Waistcoatt (now spelled Westcott).[23] These men were empowered to "enquire into the life, character, and behaviour of the applicant" for licence and ascertain "that he or she is sober, honest and diligent, and a good and loyal subject."[24]

Even as roads and travel improved, inns and hotels remained important businesses. The hotelkeeper was employed to maintain fresh teams of horses for the stage lines, as well as accommodate the travellers who used the stage. Travelling salesmen could obtain overnight lodging while conducting business in the area. The innkeeper's knowledge of the local people would be a definite asset to any salesman. Here he could hire a horse for calls out of town. Another service provided to the salesman was the sample room, where a salesman could display his wares on large tables usually kept for that purpose. Local merchants would be given ample opportunity to inspect the samples before completing a deal for a large order to stock their stores. One such sample room was constructed for Angus McKinnon as an addition to his hotel in 1876.[25]

[20] Loc. cit. Registry Office, Whitby, Abstract Land Titles, Beaverton. PAO, G.S. 6397, Parish Records of John MacMurchy. Hugh married Margaret Martin on Apr. 6, 1853.
[21] Assessment 1859, Thorah Township.
[22] PAO, M.S. 348, Reel 1, Bylaws, Thorah Township. Bylaw 18, 1853.
[23] Ibid., Jan. 17, 1853.
[24] Ibid., Bylaws 18, 1853.
[25] *The Northern Light,* Orillia, Jan. 20, 1876.

Lectures on Temperance. . . . . at Beaverton by A. Farewell and R. Hardner.

Oshawa Vindicator, January 29, 1862.

In 1853, while Boynton was still leasing his hotel, an enterprising man from Brock Township purchased it from Alex Cameron.[26] David Glover, then 35 years of age, took up the licence the following February, and thus began what was to be a nearly thirty-year association with Beaverton's business section.[27] That same year he purchased the lot immediately east of the hotel; possibly he purchased the stables that Boynton had rented in conjunction with the hotel.[28] The Glover hotel provided the usual services including catering to local organizations[29] Glover continued to use this name until possibly 1868, when for some reason he changed the name to "The Revere House".[30] This was the name of another hotel operated from 1865 to 1867 by William Parkin possibly on property owned by Donald Cameron, a local merchant.[31]

In 1869 Glover sold the new Revere House to Duncan McNabb who operated it until 1872.[32] McNabb was given the honour, one day in 1870, of a visit from John Ramsay of Islay.[33] Ramsay was on an inspection tour of Ontario to discover the results of the emigration of many of his former tenants from Islay to Eldon and Thorah. McNabb sold out to John Montgomery who leased his hotel first to William Fountain and lastly to P. Flynn.[34] On February 6, 1877, a fire started in a nearby store, and put an end to this early hotel.[35]

After selling his hotel to Duncan McNabb, Glover remained out of the business only two or three years. On October 13, 1871 he bought, what was advertised as a recently constructed hotel, from John Cameron.[36]

[26] Registry Office, Whitby, Land Registration, Deed 48763, Mar. 7, 1853.
[27] PAO, M.S. 348, Reel 1 Thorah Council Minutes. Feb. 15, 1854.
[28] Registry Office, Whitby, Abstracts to Land Titles, Thorah.
[29] Churchill, A.G., *Poetical Dictionary.* 1860.
[30] *Orillia Expositor,* Orillia. Dec. 11, 1868.
[31] *Canadian Post,* Mar. 17, 1865. PAO, M.S. 348, Reel 1, Thorah Council Minutes, July 9, 1864 and Mar. 2, 1867.
[32] Registry Office, Whitby, Abstracts to Land Titles, Thorah Township.
[33] Ramsay, Freda, *Sir John Ramsay of Kildalton.*
[34] Registry Office, Whitby, Abstracts to Land Titles. PAO, M.S. 348, Reel 1, Thorah Council Minutes. Feb. 26, 1875. Beers, J.H. & Co. *Historical Atlas of the County of Ontario,* 1877. Cumming reprint. Also, PAO, R.G. 21, Assessment of Thorah Township, 1873.
[35] *The Northern Light,* Orillia, Feb. 7, 1877.
[36] *Whitby Chronicle,* May 20, 1869. Registry Office, Whitby, Abstracts to Land Titles, Thorah Township.

This property, which may have been the site of earlier taverns, is where we find the new I.G.A. today. Glover repeated his previous action, that of purchasing an adjacent lot. This time he added lot 55 north of Bay Street to his new hotel property, and by doing so gave the hotel access to another street.[37] His intentions may have been to build what became one of Beaverton's more unusual features. This was the site of the drive sheds, estimated to have been 300 feet in length, that older residents can recall serving the Ontario House Hotel. For an annual charge a farmer could rent a stall to tie his horse whenever he came to town.[38] The hotel that Glover purchased in 1871 was, no doubt, the very structure that many can recall standing at the south west corner of Osborne and Simcoe Streets. This building followed the contour of the intersection so exactly that there was only room for a narrow sidewalk between it and the street surface.[39] Angus McKinnon first leased this hotel in 1876 and later purchased it, only to lease it in turn to Henry Musgrove, for a year.[40] The year 1883 found McKinnon selling to John Kennedy of Gamebridge.[41]

The stage stopover for Beaverton in the early 1860's was Workman's Hotel.[42] In January 1862 William Workman first applied for his tavern licence.[43] In March of the same year he purchased the property, on which his hotel stood, from Lachlin Campbell.[44] Tragedy struck on June 11, when William died at the age of 32.[45] His death was not the only misfortune to befall his wife, Mary. They had lost a child in 1860, and a son aged one and a half years in 1861. A daughter Williametta died, just two months after her father.[46] A brother of Mary's, David Fleming, who may have been helping her run the hotel, died the following April.[47] These deaths may possibly be attributed to typhoid fever which seems to have been prevalent at the time.

Seemingly unhindered by her losses, Mary carried on the operation of the hotel. Sometime in the next four years a young man came to work for her. In 1866 they were married and the Workman Hotel became the Hamilton House under the management of her new husband, Alex

[37] Loc. cit.
[38] Interview with Fred Veale, Mar. 8, 1978.
[39] Loc. cit.
[40] *Beaverton Express,* Mar. 18, 1882.
[41] Registry Office, Whitby, Abstracts to Land Titles, Thorah Township.
[42] *Canadian Post,* Lindsay, Oct. 17, 1861.
[43] PAO, M.S. 348, Reel 1, Thorah Council Minutes. Jan. 20, 1862.
[44] Registry Office, Whitby, Abstracts to Land Titles, Thorah Township.
[45] Cemetery Committee of Beaverton Thorah Eldon Historical Society, Tombstone transcriptions of the oldest part of the Old Stone Church Cemetery, 1979. Stone #0-A20.
[46] Loc. cit.
[47] Loc. cit.

> "Moved that whereas it is reported that parties in the township are selling liquor without license. The inspector is hereby notified to endeavour to obtain evidence against the said parties so that they may be prosecuted according to law."
>
> Thorah Council, July 9, 1864.

> "Petition of John Gunn to prohibit the sale of Spirituous and fermented liquor in stores."
>
> Thorah Council, December 9, 1871.

Hamilton.[48] The building at that time bore no resemblance to the fine structure we see now. Business must have been good, for the main part of the present structure appears to have been built in 1870.[49] The following August, Hamilton bought the lot adjoining to the west, and 1875 saw the erection of Alexandria Hall on part of this lot. *The Whitby Chronicle* of May 6, 1875 reported; "The walls of Mr. Hamilton's new stores are going up rapidly and he expects to open his music hall by a grand concert on Dominion Day."[50]

Oddly, Hamilton transferred his hotel licence to Armstrong and Canning in October of the same year.[51] In November he entered into farming, as most of Beaverton's hotel owners seemed prone to do, by purchasing lot 10 Concession 10, the southeast quadrant of Gamebridge.[52] Though the 1881 census finds him at Gamebridge and apparently farming, he was anything but retired.[53] He seemed anxious to push forward his business career by various ventures. In 1882 he bought the site of the Revere House, which had burned five years previously. He sold lot 3 to John McRae, who at that time built the McRae Block that still stands next to the Red & White store.[54] Newspaper reports of the time intimated that Hamilton intended to build on the remaining lot. But he moved a building to the site instead.[55] The chosen structure was the old Shortiss Hotel that had stood at the corner of Albert and Main Streets. While in

[48] Britnell, W.E., *County Marriage Registers of Ontario, Canada, 1858-1869* Vol. 2, *Index to Ontario County*, 1979.
[49] Registry Office, Whitby, Abstract Index to Land Titles, Thorah Township.
[50] *Whitby Chronicle*, May 6, 1875.
[51] PAO, MS. 348, Reel 1, Thorah Council Minutes, Oct. 16, 1875.
[52] Registry Office, Whitby, Abstracts to Land Registration, Thorah Township.
[53] Census of Thorah Township, 1881.
[54] Registry Office, Whitby, Abstract Index to Land Titles, Thorah Township.
[55] *Beaverton Express*, Sept. 1, 1882.

passage to its new home, this building may have raised the ire of the inhabitants by blocking the street, at least partly, for more than a month. The *Beaverton Express* of November 3, 1882 stated; "The old hotel is on the way to its new site next to J.J. Glover's harness shop where we learn it is intended to convert it into two stores."[56] December 15 finds "the old hotel now in course of removal a decided nuisance on the road."[57] Moving large buildings is not something confined to our more mechanized age. The Shortiss hotel was probably moved, as were other even larger buildings, on large smooth rollers. The building was raised and placed on large squared timbers, which rested on the rollers. The building was moved by means of a large capstan securely anchored to the ground. Using a heavy draw rope the structure was winched up to the capstan, which was then moved to a new location. The process was repeated until the new site was at hand. A crew was kept busy removing rollers from the rear and placing them in front of the building.[58]

Hamilton opened the old hotel as two stores for rent. A sharp businessman, he owned several town properties as investments which he usually rented out to poorer businessmen. His hotel was first leased to Armstrong and Canning, later to William Watson, then to Farquhar McRae and in the 1890's to W. McIntyre.[59] His store properties experienced similar changes in tenants.

Talk of the arrival of the railway in the late 1860's brought a boom to Beaverton; everyone hoped to make his fortune. It was at this time that Hugh and Margaret Murray returned to the hotel business. Happily, Mrs. Murray had inherited a large town property from David Ross,[60] the teacher. On this lot, and with money derived from the sale of their old hotel property, they built a fine new hotel, which they called the "Railway Hotel".[61] This new venture did not last long. The Murrays were only licenced for two years and it was not long before the building became a private residence.

Murray's hotel coincided with the arrival of the first railway to town.

[56] Ibid., Nov. 3, 1882.
[57] Ibid., Dec. 15, 1882.
[58] Interview with Fred Veale, Mar. 8, 1978.
[59] *Beaverton Express*, July, 8, 1880, May 6, 1883.
[60] Registry Office, Whitby, Instrument 23805, Will of David Ross.
[61] The site of the present Wayside Apartments.

CRICKET

Cricket? OH! that's a game they play in England. Did you know they played cricket in Beaverton?

On April 13, 1883, the *Orillia Packet* reported "The Beaverton Cricket club had their annual meeting at the Ontario Hotel. Over 40 members have inscribed their names and feel confident of showing a good season."

Cricket had started long before the village was incorporated. The *Orillia Expositor* of July 17, 1868 reported "At a meeting at the Hamilton House a few evenings since — young men made a move to get up a cricket club."

Orillia seemed to be their regular opponent.

Sometimes they won.

The *Northern Light of Orillia,* Sept. 16, 1870 reported: "A cricket match was held Tuesday between Beaverton and Orillia. Beaverton won by 53 runs."

So they rejoiced.

After the game, all repaired to the Hamilton House for an excellent dinner, then adjourned to a large sitting room for conversation, music, songs, toasts and speeches.

Sometimes they lost.

The *Northern Light* of Sept. 18, 1872 reported "The annual match between the Orillia and Beaverton clubs was played on the grounds of the latter club yesterday and resulted in a victory for Orillia by nine wickets. There was no victory dinner . . .

Cephas Doherty in 1983 recalled that about 1900 the Beaverton team had a tinsmith named Andrew Murray as wicket keeper. His hard and horny hands served him well, as he had to catch the hard leather bound ball, bowled overhand with the speed of an express train.

The McMillan twins also played cricket, as did Joe Givens, the teacher and Alex Dobson, the miller.

From minutes of the Court of Quarter Sessions of the Peace for the Home District, January 5, 1849: "Ordered that representation be made to the District Council . . . that the respective town meetings should in no case be held in taverns . . . if so then no liquor be sold . . ."

Midland Railway engine 17 turned over in turntable pit, Beaverton. Courtesy of the Public Archives of Canada.

Chapter 12

ROMANCE OF THE RAILS

Thorah Township was surveyed in 1820 and settlement began four years later. Natural highways, the rivers and lakes, no longer met the needs of the settlers. If material progress was to be achieved, it was necessary to improve methods of communication. Every community wanted a railway without delay, so distance must be bridged regardless of labour or cost.

Investigation showed that the best way to join Lake Ontario and the upper lakes was to build toward Georgian Bay.[1] By 1853 trains were running to Barrie. Two years later the steamer "J.C. Morrison" was launched on Lake Simcoe by the Northern Railway, and made daily trips to Orillia and Beaverton.[2]

Progress in the Township of Thorah was slow but steady. By 1850 the small settlement of Beaverton "was still a struggling hamlet. . . . it contained a grist mill, a saw mill, two distilleries, two asheries and a tannery."[3] The Port Hope and Lindsay Railway had promised to extend its line to Beaverton but had failed to do so. At this time the availability of a railway was only a dream.

When the Toronto and Nipissing Railway began selling bonds and asking for grants in the area, competition was feared. As a result the name "Beaverton" was added to the name of the Railway in 1854 and construction began.[4] Man power was recruited from England to help with the work. Among those who came to Beaverton were the Shorter and Tarbox families. Mr. Cephas Doherty tells of his grandfather, Mr. Henry Shorter, and his family from London arriving in Beaverton on May the twenty-fourth, 1870. In 1869 the Township gave the Port Hope and Lindsay Railway a bond of $50,000 with interest at three per cent per annum in perpetuity. Beaverton was to be the northern terminus.[5]

Enthusiasm ran high when the first train arrived in Beaverton on Christmas Eve, 1870.[6] Mr. Joseph Buller was the first station agent. The local folks were sure Beaverton would now be a great inland port. A dock

[1] Middleton, J.E., *The Romance of Ontario,* Toronto, W.J. Gage. 1938, page 174.
[2] Ritchie, Mary Houston, *A Township on the Lake,* page 67.
[3] Johnson, Leo A., *History of the County of Ontario 1615-1875*, page 143.
[4] Heels, Charles H., *Railroad Recollections,* page 1.
[5] Johnson, op. cit., page 309.
[6] Gill, Dave, History 230, *The Impact of the Railroad on Beaverton and Area.*

MIDLAND RAILWAY OF CANADA.

No. 6. **TIME TABLE,** No. 6.

TAKES EFFECT ON MONDAY, MAY 27th, 1872.

TRAINS MOVING NORTH.

Miles	Stations.	No. 1 Beaverton Mail.	No. 3 Lakefield Mail.	No. 5 Beaverton Mix'd	No. 7 Lakefield Mixed.	No. 9 Way Freight.
66	† Beaverton, Arr.	12.30 P.M.	....	8.00 P.M	....	....
58	† Woodville,	12.10	....	7.30d / 7.18a	....	....
54	* Oakwood,	11.53	....	7.00	....	....
49	* Cambray,	11.41	....	6.42	....	....
43	† Lindsay,	11.25d / 11.20a	....	6.20d / 6.00a	....	8.40 A.M
38	* Kelly's,	11.08	....	5.38	....	8.20
33	† Omemee,	10.58	....	5.20	....	8.05
28	† Franklin,	10.43	....	**4.55**d / **4.35**a	....	7.42
26	* Brunswick,	10.38	....	4.27	....	7.35
24	† Bethany,	**10.33**	....	4.20	....	7.27
40	† Lakefield,	....	12.40 P.M.	....	7.00 P.M	....
31	† Peterboro',	....	12.00d / 11.40a	....	6.20d / 6.00a	....
24	* Fraserville,	....	11.16	....	5.36	....
18	† Millbrook,	10.15d / 10.10a	**11.00**d / **10.50**a	**3.50**d / **3.30**a	**5.20**d / **5.02**a	**7.00**d / **6.50**a
14	* Summit,	9.58	10.35	3.12	4.45	6.30
10	† Campbell's,	9.46	10.18	**2.50**	**4.25**d / **4.10**a	6.10
9	* Perrytown,	9.43	10.14	2.45	4.05	6.03
5	* Quay's,	9.35	10.04	2.35	3.55	5.52
0	† Port Hope, Dep.	9.20 A.M.	9.45 A.M	2.15 P.M	3.35 P.M	5.30 A.M.

TRAINS MOVING SOUTH.

Miles	Stations.	No. 2 Beaverton Mail.	No. 4 Lakefield Mail.	No. 6 Beaverton Mix'd	No. 8 Lakefield Mixed.	No. 10 Way Freight.
0	† Beaverton, Dep.	3.00 P.M.	....	7.00 A.M.	....	....
8	† Woodville,	3.25	....	7.30a / 7.42d	....	....
12	* Oakwood,	3.37	....	8.00	....	....
17	* Cambray,	3.49	....	8.18	....	....
23	† Lindsay,	4.05a / 4.10d	....	8.40a / 9.00d	....	11.40 A.M
28	* Kelly's,	4.22	....	9.22	....	12.02
33	† Omemee,	4.35	....	9.40	....	12.20
38	† Franklin,	**4.47**	....	10.00	....	12.43
40	* Brunswick,	4.52	....	10.08	....	12.52
42	† Bethany,	4.57	....	**10.15**a / **10.33**d	....	1.10
0	† Lakefield,	....	1.50 P.M.	....	5.20 A.M.	....
9	† Peterboro',	....	2.30a / 3.00d	....	5.55a / 6.10d	....
16	* Fraserville,	....	3.24	....	6.32	....
48	† Millbrook,	**5.15**a / **5.20**d	**3.40**a / **3.50**d	**10.55**a / **11.15**d	**6.50**a / **7.00**d	1.35a / 1.55d
52	* Summit,	5.30	4.04	11.33	7.17	2.15
56	† Campbell's,	5.43	**4.22**	11.53	7.37	**2.35**a / **2.50**d
57	* Perrytown,	5.46	4.26	11.58	7.42	2.55
61	* Quay's,	5.54	4.36	12.08	7.53	3.06
66	† Port Hope, Arr.	6.10 P.M.	4.55 P.M	12.30 P.M	8.15 A.M	3.30 P.M.

* Platform Stations, Trains stop on Signal only. † Telegraph Stations. Heavy Figures denote Train Crossings. The figures set opposite the Stations indicate the leaving time of Trains.
All Trains must start promptly on time. [illegible]

was constructed at the foot of Victoria Avenue and two sawmills were erected nearby. The first reeve of the village, Mr. G.F. Bruce, had a cargo of grain ready to go on the first train. Soon, some 18 to 20 carloads of lumber were leaving here daily. These trains were pulled by woodburning locomotives which were decked with wide, screened smoke stacks. As they soon filled with cinders the firemen had to strike the stacks with long poles so the cinders could be shaken down and the draft improved. In spite of this they were able to make from thirty-five to forty miles an hour. Sometimes the farmers' rail fences would suffer when an emergency arose and more wood was needed.[7]

Many people came to Beaverton speculating on a prosperous future. Several fine homes were erected including the John Proctor house on the corner of Simcoe and Mill Street which was demolished in order to make room for the new Canadian Imperial Bank of Commerce. The George Proctor house still stands on the corner of Simcoe and John Street and has remained in the family for many years. On Mara Road Captain C.H. Davidson built the fine home which was later occupied by the Hodgson and McKenzie families and is today owned by Dr. L. Rosen. For 15 years

[7] Middleton, op. cit., page 175.

the Port Hope, Lindsay, Beaverton Railway proved to be one of the most prosperous of all Canadian short lines.[8]

When railway promoters could not secure a monopoly of the lumber trade around Lake Simcoe, they concentrated on the Mid-West grain trade. In order to do this they obtained from the provincial government a right of way to Georgian Bay. Grain could then be carried from Midland to Port Hope a distance of 66 miles. In December, 1869, the Railway was renamed the Midland Railway of Canada. Residents now realized if the extension to Midland took place, Beaverton would be only a whistle stop on the line. As they felt the Railway had broken their promise to make Beaverton a terminus they passed a motion which almost resulted in the $50,000 bond being withdrawn. This bond remained in force until November 4, 1965.[9]

The net revenue of the Midland Railway the first year was $113,227,019,[10] but when the source of timber became more distant profits became smaller. When the Midland absorbed the Toronto Nipissing Line in 1881 and converted to standard gauge track, a direct service to Toronto via Lorneville was provided.

The directors were more interested in a line which would make them wealthy than making Beaverton a port. Although Beaverton remained a small town, the railway brought about higher prices for farm produce. Toronto was now the business centre instead of Whitby. People became more interested in public affairs as isolated communities merged into a provincial spirit. Politicians were able to travel to distant parts of their ridings. Pedlars were replaced by commercial travellers. In spite of these advantages the railway exploited communities, destroyed forests and gave little.

The Midland always faced competition from the Hamilton and North Western Railways and the Northern Railway of Canada. In 1883 the Midland amalgamated with the Grand Trunk Railway of Canada.[11] Due partly to the slump after World War I, the Grand Trunk was taken over by the Canadian National Railway system on January 30, 1932.[12]

In 1931 the Beaverton Council received word of a possible reduction in train service due to lightness of traffic between Midland and Blackwater Junction.[13] This they unalterably opposed but to no avail. The following

[8] Heels, op. cit., page 2.
[9] Graham, George, Clerk Administer, Township of Brock.
[10] Trout, J.M. & Edw., *The Railways of Canada, 1871,* page 169.
[11] Heels, op. cit., page 29.
[12] Mika, Nick and Helma, Toronto, McGraw-Hill Ryerson, *Railways of Canada.* 1978, page 65.
[13] Minutes of Beaverton Council Meeting, Nov. 4, 1931.

OLD GRAND TRUNK STATION

One of Lytle's Livery buses is seen waiting beside the Canadian Northern station to meet the incoming steam train.

A prosperous future was predicted for Beaverton when the Port Hope, Lindsay Railway was extended here. Several fine homes were built including this one, the home of Captain C.H. Davidson.

year the board of Railroad Commissioners had permission to remove the station agent at Beaverton East and leave an assistant there. Mr. Thomas Dickson was the last agent, serving until 1960 when the station was closed. Beaverton East station was demolished and the tracks were removed in 1965.

When the Canadian Northern Railway extended its line from Western Canada in 1902, a line was built from Toronto to Sudbury via Parry Sound in order to have traffic feeders for the transcontinental line.[14] This gave Beaverton a second railway and Mr. John Nicholson was the first station agent here. The Beaverton Express of November 22, 1906, states: "A large number of persons assembled at the station of the Canadian Northern Railway Monday to witness the arrival of the first regular passenger trains from Toronto and Parry Sound respectively. Prompt on time 10:59, No. 1 steamed in with a handsome train attached." Ex-Reeve Treleaven was the first person to buy a ticket from Beaverton to Toronto over the new line.

During the first week eight horses were killed on the track between Beaverton and Gamebridge. Two of the horses which belonged to Mr. W.A. Barrett encountered the train at the White's Creek bridge. A mile away six fine animals, the property of Messrs. T. Windatt and Philip Veale, broke from their pasture, crossed the cattle guards, and were struck by the train. (*Beaverton Express,* Nov. 22, 1906.)

Two passenger trains locally referred to as the "Winnipeg" passed through Beaverton each day, the west bound one arriving in the early evening. While the locomotive took on water from a tank on the north side of Victoria Avenue, the passengers enjoyed a meal served by Mr. A.S. Harrison and staff at his lunch counter in the station.

When the "Winnipeg" was rerouted to the other side of Lake Simcoe, it was replaced by an electric train known as "Sparkplug" or "Sparkie." It consisted of two cars, one for baggage, the other for passengers. Originally "Sparkie" left Beaverton early in the day and returned in the evening. A building to house "Sparkie" and where its batteries were recharged over night was built on the South side of Victoria Avenue. Mr. Richard Lund was the conductor.

On January 30, 1923, the Canadian Northern was taken over by the government of Canada, renamed, and became part of the Canadian National Railway system.[15] It is still one of the main Northern routes from

[14] Middleton, op. cit., page 178.
[15] Mika, op. cit. page 131.

Toronto. When Mr. A. Evans who had been station agent for many years retired, he was replaced by Mr. Merle Smith who became the last agent. Mr. Harvie Miller was a relieving operator.

With the feverish building of the railways, highways were neglected. As a result automobiles were few and everyone travelled by train. Excursions by special trains at reduced fares were popular for picnics and sporting events. The station was the centre of activity. When the evening train arrived at Beaverton East where Mr. Jack McLeod was agent for years, there was always a group to welcome it. Lytle's livery met all trains and picked up the mail bag and passengers. The luggage, express and freight were ably delivered through the years by such men as Steve West and his brother Bob, Murdoch McRae, Barney Reilly, Mark Harris and George McRae to mention a few. While the mail was being sorted by W. Harrison, Lulu Scott, Jack MacDonald or C. Calder, outside a crowd would assemble. The older folks met to talk over the news of the day and the young people to get together for the evening.

Each year many young men from Beaverton area would go West on the harvesters' excursion to help with the Western harvest which was later than here. A special train equiped with colonist cars would transport the workers for a low fare which they could recover after working for the required time. With the introduction of the combines no stooking was necessary, so less man power was needed and the excursions discontinued.

Dreams of a great inland port faded but instead of lumber and grain the railway brought a new industry to Beaverton. People were quick to recognize the beauty of Lake Simcoe and the surrounding country side. Cottages were built and an excellent summer hotel, Victoria Park, was erected and operated by Mr. and Mrs. George Veale. Tourism had arrived. Businessmen now turned to serving the new industry which now is as popular in Winter as in Summer.

Even with two railways the expansion Beaverton expected did not come about. Since this is a choice agricultural area, it is not destined to expand at the rate expected in the eighteen seventies.

After World War II, diesel engines replaced steam and the sights and sounds of steam became but a memory. Gone are the days when the people of Beaverton enjoyed excellent passenger service. Quiet are the station platforms where town folks gathered together for tearful departures and joyous reunions. Long gone, alas, is the excitement and romance of this magnificent historical era.

Chapter 13

FIRES AND FURNACES

When Wm. G. Smith began his foundry in Beaverton in 1871 it was one of the very few such concerns operating north of Toronto. The countrywide sale of its products helped spread the name of Beaverton far beyond its rural boundaries.

Wm. Smith was born in Montrose, Scotland in 1834 and operated his successful foundry here for many years before his death in 1921. His first frame building was situated at the corner of Mill and Church Streets. To finance the erection of this factory, Smith borrowed $1,000.00 from Alexander Hamilton. Within a year he had repaid the sum in full. Two pictures of his father are in the possession of Don Smith, the youngest son of his third wife, and show the founder at two different stages in life. The first one is a painting by Bill (St. Thomas) Smith, W.G.'s eldest son, portraying in the Victorian manner, a man of stern and rigid mien sporting a flowing brown beard. The second, a snapshot taken much later in his life, reveals a charmingly intimate glimpse of a gaily smiling man with a wispy white beard and a merry twinkle in his eye.

Although the foundry prospered, three of the early frame buildings were destroyed by fire. The second wooden factory was completed by 1881 and was named "Beaverton Foundry, Machine Shop and Saw Mill." It employed six men during the 1880's, including Colin Campbell who operated the saw mill and woodworking facilities. An extensive catalogue of farm machinery was produced in the shop including reapers and mowers, plough points, sulky rakes and the "Peerless" fanning mill. Trade was often conducted by barter for old iron, lumber or fire wood. Local business rivalry was great and in the late 1880's envious nearby foundrymen would spread libelous tales about Smith and his operation.

Havoc raged one July evening in 1888 when fire broke out. For the second time Smith's foundry was destroyed. The loss of $15,000 was great for those times and as no insurance company would insure wooden foundry buildings run by steam, the owner had to accept the loss.[1] Smith was in Britain that summer and on his return found that various residents of the village had rallied to his assistance and promised money to help with a new building. The factory had employed from 10 to 20 "hands" for

[1] *Beaverton Express,* July 27, 1888.

seventeen years and nearby towns such as Cannington were angling for him to rebuild in their villages. However, it appears that the amounts of money promised were larger than those received, so Smith thought he would abandon his plans for a large brick building and settle for a wooden one. Yet the third factory, the Phoenix Foundry, was of brick after all, and was built on Mill Street between Simcoe and Bay, one block north of the first two foundries. This building included a foundry and machine shop but no saw mill, as the lumber trade had moved north into the Muskoka area.

During the 1880's through the 90's, competiton from the large industries to the south such as the Massey, McCormick and Harris Companies became increasingly pervasive. The Beaverton foundry adjusted to the challenge and still thrived by building machinery for the production of peat. As Alex Dobson held patents for its manufacture, he and William formed a partnership called "The Foundry and Machine Company" and turned out farm implements, several makes of ploughs including riding and gang ploughs, scufflers, turnip drills and root pulpers. William was the mechanical manager and the firm employed 20 men.

By 1902, the firm had accepted the agency for McCormick equipment. That year became the busiest ever.

In 1913 William Smith sold the business to James Reid,[2] who in turn sold it to George Minorgan and sons.[3] In 1918 A.C. McKenzie took over the foundry.

In the old building beside the Mill on Simcoe Street West where James Duncan and Sidney Parsons had run a tannery, the brothers, Fred and George Smith, carried on business welding, moulding, and repairing. They made parts for farm machinery, plough points, castings for implements, and pumps. Fred was widely respected for the meticulous care he took with all his work and his youngest brother Don recalls an incident typical of this. A man brought a '410' gun to Fred and asked if he could repair it. "No," he said, "I can't."

"That's what they told me in town," the man replied.

Riled at this, Fred took it back, worked on it a while and soon had it working. He had been well trained under an able tutor, having worked with his father for many years in the machine shop.

[2] Ibid., June 19, 1913; also Index to Abstract Land Deeds.
[3] Ibid., January 29, 1914; also Index to Abstract Land Deeds.
Fleming, Rae. Article written for *Beaverton Express* Supplement 1978. Smith, Don. Memoirs.

Fred Smith outside his house leaning on the wrought iron fence made at his foundry.

A third fire broke out in the foundry on September 15, 1920. A new core oven overheated causing a fire in the casting house, badly gutting the structure, and causing great delays in filling orders. An era ended on April 15, 1921, with the death of Wm. Smith at the age of 87 years.

When A.C. McKenzie bought the business, it assumed the name of The Beaverton Toy Company Ltd., although it continued making the same farm equipment as formerly, as well as toys. In the planing mill at Osborne and Bay Streets formerly owned by Snelgrove, its woodworking department made house trim, door sashes, and screen windows. The wooden toys were cut out there and assembled and decorated on Mill Street. The foundry toys included cast iron banks, mechanical horses, wagons, fire wagons etc. with stamped designs. Children were hired to paste paper covers on the wooden toys. Advertisements showed a beaver holding a Union Jack bearing the inscription "A Beaverton toy brings each child joy." Some 119 different toys were produced. Such toys as Cuban Cart, Pacing Bob, and Butterfly Push Toy met widespread acceptance, even being exported to Europe. In January of 1918 the

Hark the herald angels sing

Smith's pumps are just the thing.

Peace on earth and mercy mild

A man can pump them and so can a child.

Wm. A. Smith passed this printed card to prospective customers.

RELIEF OF LADYSMITH

To our grandparents, the Relief of Ladysmith on February 28, 1900 signified the arrival of reinforcements to the badly beleagured garrison of British troops at Ladysmith, Natal, very shortly followed by collapse of the remaining Boer resistance, and the end of the Boer War. Relief of Lady Smith had a very personal meaning to the "Foundry" Smith family in Beaverton. That was the day that Donald Smith was born, giving "relief to 'Lady Smith,' his mother.

TOY FACTORY

WM. SMITH

superintendent of the plant, James Smith (no relation to W. Smith), wrote that the company was one of the most prosperous toy factories in Canada. Although A.C. McKenzie died in 1919 in Winnipeg, the business continued to prosper until 1920 after which Wm. Shapiro ran it for a short while. By the 30's, the property on Mill Street was vacant.

When World War Two broke out, A.C. McKenzie's son Cameron together with the Smith brothers, Fred and George, combined to make war materials in the old stone tannery building. At the end of the war Cameron McKenzie and George Smith became partners, renting the old Bay Street school from the Masons to manufacture wire products such as sweater and sock stretchers, towel racks, refrigerator racks, shopping carts and milk crates. In 1948 the partnership was dissolved and Cam. McKenzie continued to do business under the name Beaverton Specialty Co. In 1950 the roof of the old school was so damaged by fire that McKenzie built a new factory on the site of his father's toy factory. McKenzie continued to manage the business along with two Toronto men until his death in 1963.

MILL & FOUNDRY

CANADA'S FIRST GREAT MARINE ARTIST

"The first great marine painter Canada has produced," was the way *The Globe* described William St. Thomas Smith (1862-1947) in 1912. Receiving his elementary education at Beaverton, William Smith was guided by this Village's most famous teacher, Alexander Muir, at the North Street School. Smith went on to study at the Ontario College of Art. Son of William Smith, long-time Beaverton foundry-owner, St. Thomas took his pseudonym from the Ontario city where he located in 1888.*

Much of Smith's work was accomplished on the other side of the Atlantic, an ocean he crossed about 38 times. Considerable time was spent on the Orkney Islands, although Italy, the South Pacific Islands, and the foggy Newfoundland coasts were subjects of his paintings too. He was a Fellow of the Royal College of Art and was associated with the Group of Seven.**

His eldest daughter, Erie, Mrs. Ramsey, was a talented portrait artist.

* R. Hamilton, *Prominent Men of Canada 1931-32,* Montreal, National Publishing Co., p. 502.

** Donald J. Smith, brother of St. Thomas.

Chapter 14

THE CHURCHES — MID YEARS

With the first churches built, growth was steady, for the most part. In 1871, Albert C. Wilson, missionary of the Whitby District of the Wesleyan Methodist Mission Society, reported: "The work of Christ was never more encouraging." and in 1872: "We have started five Sunday Schools."[1]

People loved their churches and churchgoing. In the early days shoes were costly. Men and women might walk barefoot from homes miles away, carrying their shoes, which would then be put on when they came in sight of the church.[2] Mrs. Rachel McMillen walked 14 miles from the 8th concession in Eldon to Rev. David Watson's induction in 1853, and was present at least once a year thereafter.[3]

The hour-long service of today would never have been accepted in our forefather's days. Services at the Old Stone Church, then called St. Andrew's, included an hour long sermon in English, next an hour long sermon in Gaelic, followed by Sabbath School for all ages. Service ended by 4.00 p.m. In later years, when a visiting preacher was available, he would preach in English in the church, and Dr. Watson would preach a Gaelic sermon in the drive shed.[4]

Communion in the Old Stone Church was a once-a-year celebration, held usually in June.

The first day was Fast Day. Anybody seen working in the fields on that day was in fear of ostracism! Saturday was Preparation day, when eligible communicants received the precious pewter tokens which entitled them to receive communion on Sunday, Communion Day. The book racks of the front four pews, when tilted up, became continuous tables which, covered with spotless white cloths, held the communion elements. The sombre activity of Communion Sunday was followed by a final day, Monday, of Thanksgiving.[5] In later years, communion was celebrated twice a year, but was of shorter duration.

Money was scarce in the early days. The record of 1866 from St. Andrews stated "the sum raised annually is altogether inadequate for the

[1] United Church of Canada Archives, *Wesleyan Missionary Society Reports 1864-1917.*
[2] *The Toronto Evening Telegram,* September 21, 1907.
[3] *History of the Presbyterian Church at Beaverton.*
[4] *Sketch of Church Life in Beaverton 1929.*
[5] Loc. cit.

ST. PAUL'S ANGLICAN CHURCH before steeple and parish hall were built.

minister's proper support."[6] Dr. Watson's stipend was chiefly from pew rents.[7] Some of his income came from the operation of the 100 acre farm on which church, manse and cemetery were placed.[8] In 1872-3 the Methodist minister's salary was deficient.[9] At the Anglican Harvest Festival of 1884, receipts were $1.50 in envelopes, $9.00 loose.[10]

By the time one or two generations had lived in the Beaverton area, the need was felt for larger or more attractive church buildings. The Roman Catholics replaced their original log building with a frame structure. By 1909 they expanded again, building the present brick church on Simcoe St. and a rectory.

Their other churches in Vroomanton and Virginia became missions of Beaverton parish.[11]

Presbyterians too, found the need to expand. The Free Church congregation moved across the river, and under the pastorate of Rev.

[6] Minute Book St. Andrew's Church 1866.
[7] *Sketch of Church Life in Beaverton 1929.*
[8] Loc. cit.
[9] United Church of Canada Archives, *Wesleyan Missionary Society Reports* 1864-1917.
[10] Record of services St. Paul's Anglican Church 1880-1980.
[11] *History of Roman Catholicism in Georgina Township,* 1963.

METHODIST CHURCH.

John McNab, built Knox Church on Osborne St., opening it in 1877.[12] For fifty years it stood on the north west corner of Church and Osborne Sts. immediately opposite the Anglican Church.

With the development of Beaverton as a commercial centre and consequent population growth the need for building a Church of Scotland in the village arose. In 1877, by a vote of 256 to 8, it was decided to proceed with the construction.

In 1879 the building now called St. Andrew's United Church, was opened.[13] It was decided that the original church (the Old Stone Church, always difficult to heat in winter) should be used during the summer months only.

Because regular schooling had been interrupted in favour of farm chores in the early settlers' days, many of the children of those times had grown up lacking in education. As a result, many of the people in Dr. Watson's congregation were illiterate. Well educated himself, and a one time teacher, Dr. Watson held adult evening classes in basic literacy.

[12] *History of the Presbyterian Church at Beaverton.*
[13] *Sketch of Church Life in Beaverton 1929.*

Because of his teaching experience, he served as a school inspector, going into local schools to ensure that adequate teaching programs were being carried out.[14] A true leader of his flock, Dr. Watson ensured that widows and their families received support from fellow parishioners.[15]

THE LOYAL TRUE BLUES

The skirl of the fife and drum will bring back memories as the Orange Lodges of Ontario North parade through Beaverton on July 14, 1984.

The local Orange Lodge, number 129, did not receive its charter until June 13, 1892, but there is a long history of local Orange Lodge meetings. Before their church was built in 1871, the Anglicans met for services in the Orange Lodge clubrooms on Victoria Avenue. Over the years, three disastrous fires burned out their clubrooms, including all their records.

The Orange Lodge has contributed much to community life. In a May 1908, *Beaverton Express* we read "Beaverton Orangemen will test the new canal as an excursion route and Monday, May 24 will run an excursion by the streamer 'Geneva' to Fenelon Falls, leaving the wharf at Beaverton at 8.00 a.m. The fare for the round trip is 75¢ and from Kirkfield 50¢".

MURRAY LODGE - ANCIENT, FREE AND ACCEPTED MASONS (A.F. & A.M.)

Scarcely a year younger than the village, Beaverton's Masonic lodge started on Feb. 19, 1885. Its first master was Alexander P. Cockburn, the federal M.P. Its first member was Robert P. Turner. The first Masonic ball was held in 1886 at the Hamilton House.

Though not connected directly with any church, it embraces general Christian beliefs. Once a year, the Masons attend one of the local churches in full regalia. There were 110 worshippers at a Masonic service in the Anglican church on Aug. 28, 1910.

All Masons aspire to reach the 33rd degree achieved through many devoted years of Masonic service. Locally, one can progress only to three degrees, after which he must affiliate with the Scottish Rite in Barrie, for further degree work.

The 125 local members meet once a month in their hall, the former school at the corner of Bay and York Streets.

[14] Conversation with Miss Mary Fowler, great grand-daughter of Rev. David Watson.
[15] Loc. cit.

Chapter 15

AN AUGUST DAY IN '84

"Ceit, cait a bheil thu à dol an dràsda?"[1] Her insistence on the straight course brings me out of my day dream. It always seems to me that half the common sense, in these parts at least, belongs to the horses. She knew I was headed for town and kept the straight course even though I was trying to turn her up Bill's lane.[2] In my reminiscent stupor I was going the old way to town along the Cameron Road. It's true it would still be shorter than taking the Centre Road. I mustn't tell the wife. She'll only say I'm getting dotty in my old age. She's said it a lot lately and I'm worried it's coming true.

When Kate knows the way to town all I've left to do is ponder the way things have changed in Thorah in my lifetime. Years ago the fields were just a few acres surrounded by huge forests. Now fields are everywhere and in some parts there's hardly a tree to be seen. I reaped many acres of wheat, first with a sickle and then with a scythe and cradle. A few years ago the better-to-do farmers bought those mowers and reapers. Now self-binders are the rage.[3] I thought I might have one but Christy talked me out of it. She said it would make me lazy. Even pumping water might be a thing of the past. I heard the other day that the Gunns north of Beaverton have put up some gadget to raise water.[4] Mmmmm, must pay a visit some

[1] MacLearen, James, *MacLaren's Gaelic Self-Taught,* Reprint of Fourth Edition, Gairm, 1978. Page 15. Translates as: "Kate, where are you going now!" An anonymous farmer has been created for this chapter. Through his eyes, words and thoughts it is hoped that the reader can gain some knowledge of Thorah and Beaverton as they were one hundred years ago. The typical inhabitant was either of Scottish origin or a first generation Canadian of Scottish descent. Since the majority of these were Highlanders, Gaelic would have been the predominant language. Many of the original Highland settlers could speak Gaelic only and depended on others for communciations requiring English. Their children, however, tended to be fluent in both Gaelic and English, being exposed to one at home and the other at school. Of course English has completely displaced Gaelic, but use of the Gaelic in every day greetings on the street was still in use well after the turn of the 20th century. It is with these points in mind that a few Gaelic sentences are included to illustrate a man who can converse in both the old and the new language.

[2] Beers, J.H. & Co., *Historical Atlas of the County of Ontario, 1877.* Cumming reprint 1972. Page 52. William Skinner lived at Lot 8 Concession 2. His house was very close to the Cameron Road. When this part of the Cameron Road was closed in 1883, part would have been left as his private lane.

[3] *Beaverton Express,* August 1, 1884.

[4] Loc. cit.

day to see for myself. I think they call them windmills or something.

Things just keep changing. Just a few years ago the St. Andrew's people raised a new church in Beaverton. I guess putting it in town ensures that none of Rev. Watson's flock fall asleep from exhaustion during the service. Another thing too, that lovely tall spire would give some of us Presbyterians, at least, a head start for Heaven. Not to be out done, the Free Church People have their equally spacious church up on Osborne St. Some of the Presbyterians in Ontario have made up and reunited. But there's no forgiving or forgetting in Thorah yet. I bet I'll be dead before there is.

The once tiny hamlet of Beaverton has grown a lot in the last thirty years. More than likely the railway brought it on. Even talk of the railway sent some otherwise cautious citizens on rampages of land speculation, years before the tracks ever approached town.[5] Funny though, a lot of those new town lots still remain vacant with the owners finding no prospective buyers.

Now Beaverton's grown up, Reeve Alex McRae presented Alex Hamilton's petition to County Council and finally they've got the go-ahead for the first council in the New Year.[6] I guess all those businessmen just figured that old Thorah was holding them back. Must admit though, there are no hard feelings, anywhere, that I know of. Now the talk is that Beaverton might become the county town of some new county, namely the County of Lorne.[7] The story goes that Thorah, Mara, Rama, Eldon and even Orillia would be in the new county. Guess there's always been the dreams; some come true and some just don't. We'll have to wait and see. Lately there have been attempts made to lure tourists to Beaverton. Alex Hamilton even opened up sort of a park at the lake and named it Ethel Park after his daughter.[8] Mr. Barber fixed up a number of his boats and raised a pavilion.[9] I heard that over 1000 people were at Barber's grove one week in July.[10] The country is so settled now that people travel a long way just to have a rest. Seems strange to me.

The sound of a train whistle returns me to reality. I discover I'm just east of McHattie's old home and heading into town. The whistle sounded from north of the river. I'm bewildered why the train would be so far off

[5] Public Archives of Ontario, Land Records. Letter — H. White to Commissioner J. Bains. Feb. 3, 1855.
[6] *Beaverton Express,* June 13, 1884.
[7] Ibid., Aug. 8, 1884.
[8] *Woodville Advocate,* May 17, 1883.
[9] Loc. cit.
[10] *Beaverton Express,* July 25, 1884.

schedule. Oh, it's the "Checkers Special" headed for Peterborough.[11] Our boys are duty-bound to give those Irishmen a good lesson on how to play lacrosse. The train looks filled to capacity with Checkers' supporters willing to pay a dollar a head to see the boys play.[12] I've heard that some of the employers are not too pleased with the time some of the men take off.[13] The glory that Beaverton reaps must not be paying the bills too well.

Away from the train my eyes fall to the site of the old Proctor Mill by the river.[14] Frightful how the water levels have fallen, leaving less for the mills to run on. The mill has been abandoned for just a few years yet I can scarcely believe its state of ruin. Old George Proctor has been dead four years now[15] and his son, John, now runs the fine mill at the bridge in town.[16] John like all the Proctors has a fine business sense and is into a number of ventures including farming.[17] Just lately he has raised a large new barn on his farm by the lake.[18] Last year he put new equipment in the mill. The farmers like the product so well that they are coming from greater distances than usual.[19]

West of McHattie's old place is Maj. Paterson's home.[20] He sells insurance and has money to loan.[21] Next is Archie McInnis' house. Archie and his son John are carpenters about town.[22]

On the hill south of McInnis' is Tom Treleaven's home.[23] Tom is the contractor who built the new Beaverton School on Bay Street last year.[24] At the end of the new sidewalks[25] on the north side of the street is Ronald

[11] Ibid., Aug. 8, 1884.
[12] Loc. cit.
[13] Ibid., May 23, 1884.
[14] Beers, J.H. & Co., Op. cit. Page 52.
[15] Transcriptions; Stone Church Cemetery, by Cemetery Committee of the B.T.E. Historical Soc. Inc., 1979.
[16] PAO, R.G. 21, Assessment, Thorah Township, 1884.
[17] Beers, J.H. & Co., Op. cit. Page 52 and Loc. cit.
[18] *Beaverton Express,* Aug. 1, 1884.
[19] *Woodville Advocate,* Nov. 23, 1883.
[20] PAO, R.G. 21 Assessment, Thorah Township 1884; also a telephone interview with Mrs. Grace McElroy, Jan. 2, 1984. The present home of Kathleen Duncan. 627 Simcoe St.
[21] *The Beaver.* A monthly Magazine for the Missions of Beaverton and Point Mara, St. Paul's Church. Jan. 1884.
[22] PAO, R.G. 21, Assessment of Thorah, 1884. Also interview with Mrs. Grace McElroy, Jan. 2, 1984. This house then stood very near the site of the present Catholic Church. It now stands further east at 613 Simcoe St.
[23] PAO, R.G. 21, Assessment of Thorah Township, 1884. Later was the home of the "Booie" or "Buigh" McRaes. Presently, Dave McCall's home.
[24] *Woodville Advocate,* Dec. 13, 1883.
[25] *Beaverton Express,* Oct. 27, 1882.

Sillars' home.[26] He came to this country from Campbelltown in Kintyre[27] and brought his trade of weaving[28] with him. He has the distinction of being one of our local poets as well as being musically inclined.[29]

Next to St. Andrew's, some of Ed Tisdale's children romp and play in the yard.[30] There's Rev. Watson coming down the steps of the church.

"Good afternoon, Baldy" as he waves me down for a chat. Wonder if he remembers I missed last sabbath.

"Aye, 'tis a fine day, Reverend Sir. All those red sunsets keep callin' for more fine weather."

"That's correct Baldy, but do you know the reason for those beautiful sunsets?"

I thought for several seconds for some connection between sunsets and not getting to church. Finally defeated, all I could say was "Can't say I do."

"They're the result of the dust thrown up by a great volcanic eruption in the south seas last year. Nearly the whole island of Krakatua disappeared in the explosion."[31]

Being baffled on two counts, "Well Bless me, ya don't say", was all I could utter. After a short chat we parted.

"Tha e' na dhuine eolach."[32] He's been trying to spread some culture around this township for years. Back in the spring I brought Christy to town to hear him lecture at the church. Since 'Water' was the topic[33] I thought I'd slip down town and socialize the time away. Rev. Watson must have added a lot to swimming, washing and drinking because the wife babbled without end for two days about the fine properties of the stuff.

Across the street, judging from the smoke, the Bemisters are starting up the fires in the kilns.[34] Next to the potteries, and down the hill is Bill

[26] PAO, R.G. 21, Assessment of Thorah Township, 1884.

[27] Transcriptions, Stone Church Cemetery. Stone 0-H9.

[28] PAO, R.G. 21, Assessment of Thorah Township, 1884.

[29] Telephone interview with Mrs. Grace McElroy, Jan. 2, 1984. Story has it that he was also musically inclined and was a great friend of Alexander Muir while Muir taught in Beaverton.

[30] PAO, R.R. 21, Assessment Thorah Township, 1884 and also PAO, Census of Thorah, 1881. Presently, home of Mrs. Violet Currie, 535 Simcoe St. Next east of Ed Tisdale in 1884 was Christopher McRae a retired gentleman aged 77.

[31] *Beaverton Express,* July 11, 1884.

[32] MacLearen, op. cit. Page 34. Translates as; "He's an intelligent man."

[33] *Beaverton Express,* Mar. 7, 1884.

[34] PAO, R.G. 21, Assessment of Thorah Township, 1884. Site of later DeGuerre's Bakery, now Rebekah Hall. East of Bemister's lived in 1884, William Gilbertson a carpenter, in possibly the same house now occupied by Gordon Hall, 526 Simcoe St.

Turner's comfortable house.[35] Bill's a cooper and lives shoulder to shoulder with many local notables. Two of his sons, Robert and Sandy, are harness makers in the town and daughter Mary Jane is a dressmaker.[36] Across from Bill's is John Leslie's house. John is in partnership with John Harrison and they have a store under Alexandria Hall.[37] Next is Alex McDougall a retired farmer,[38] and then Jimmie Cameron another respected merchant[39] who, until recently, was in partnership with Henry Westcott in the hardware business.[40] South across the street, is David Williamson's home then Alex Cameron's, Beaverton's elder storekeeper, who has a very handsome home.[41] On the north side are several vacant lots, then Donald Campbell's house, then Daniel Tucker's, another local cooper.[42]

At the corner of Simcoe and John Streets stands George Proctor's huge white brick mansion,[43] which was built about nine years ago.[44] It certainly gives one the notion that George has money. George and the wife are in the North-West this summer. Possibly he's scouting the land for more money-making propositions.[45]

Across the corner comes the familiar ring of hammer and anvil from Jim Birchard's blacksmith shop. It must be 25 years ago that, as near as I can remember Anson, Jim's father, started his shop on that very corner. Anson's family were Quakers who settled in Mariposa. About that same time, June 1860 I think, he married Catherine Fraser. She was Presbyterian and he a Methodist. Because of the lack of Methodist services at that time here, he became a Presbyterian. It's been nearly a year since Anson passed on, leaving Jim in charge. Anson didn't exactly live to a ripe old age either. He was friendly, but most of his energy went into his business. Some people say he just plain worked too hard, and so he died at the age of 48 of a heart problem.[46] Jim will have to work hard too, because five of the children are under ten years of age. No doubt brothers Alex and Ronald will be able to help out. Alex, the oldest, is a very smart lad and has taken

[35] Loc. cit.
[36] PAO, Census of Thorah, 1881.
[37] PAO, R.G. 21, Assessment of Thorah Township, 1884.
[38] Loc. cit.
[39] Loc. cit.
[40] PAO, R.G. 21, Assessment of Thorah Township, 1882.
[41] PAO, R.G. 21, Assessment of Thorah Township, 1884.
[42] Loc. cit.
[43] Loc. cit. Presently, the house at 414 Simcoe St.
[44] *Whitby Chronicle,* May 6, 1875.
[45] *Woodville Advocate,* Sept. 18, 1884.
[46] PAO, M.U. 135, Birchard Family Papers 1808-1938. Present location of Beaverton Library. Shop was moved south when library was built.

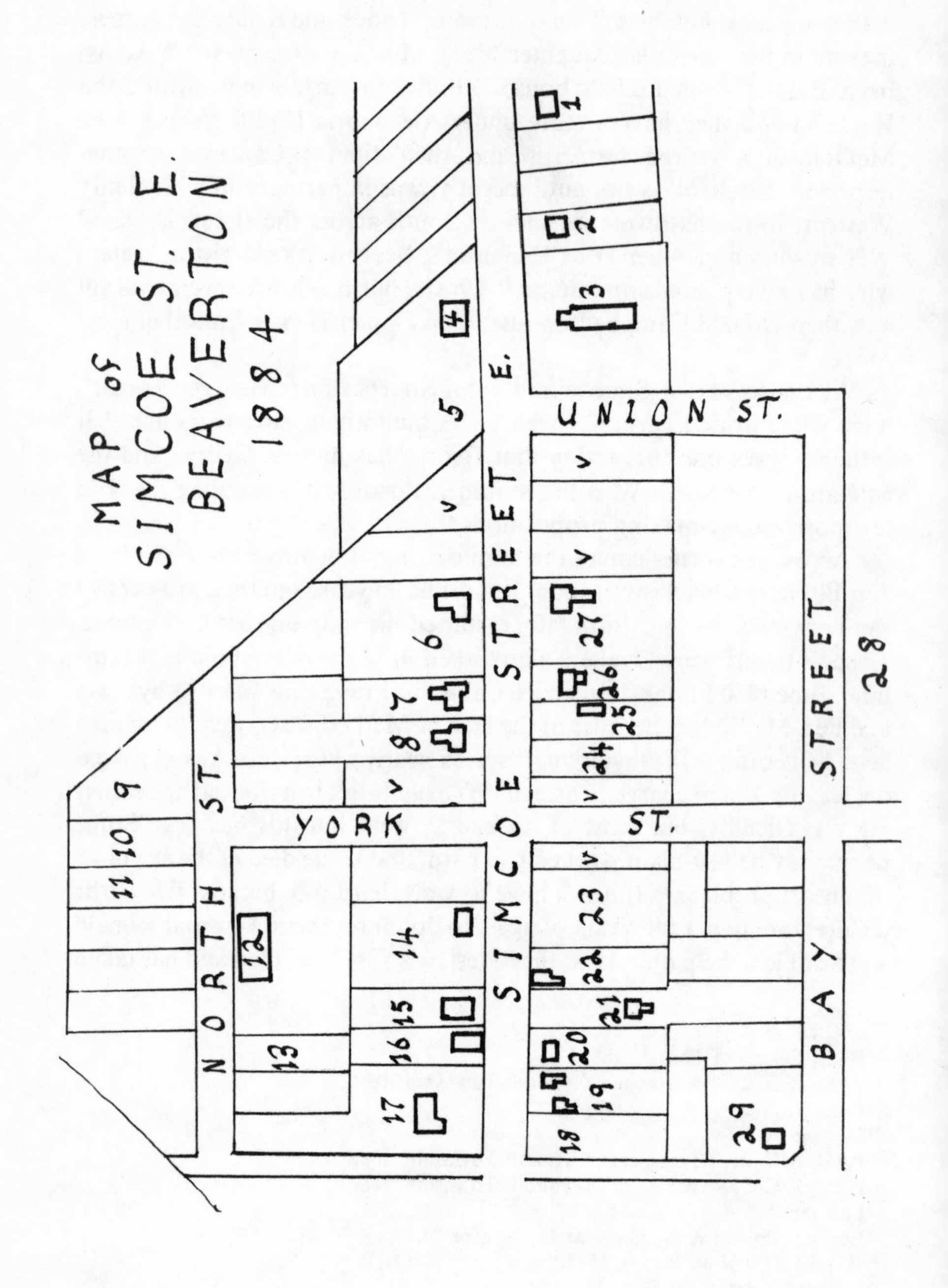
MAP of
SIMCOE ST.
BEAVERTON
1884
SIMCOE STREET E.
UNION ST.
YORK
NORTH ST.
SIMCOE ST.
BAY STREET
1
2
3
4
5
6
7
8
9
10
11
12
13
14
15
16
17
18
19
20
21
22
23
24
25
26
27
28
29

KEY TO SIMCOE STREET EAST 1884

1. Assessed to Christopher McRae, aged 77, retired farmer, from North half of lot 3 Concession 2 Thorah and father of John McRae the merchant.
2. Assessed to Edwin Tisdale as a tenant of Mrs. Stanfield.
3. St. Andrew's Presbyterian Church.
4. Assessed to William Gilbertson, carpenter, aged 67.
5. Assessed to James and Walter Bemister. This was the site of the Bemister Pottery.
6. Assessed to William Turner, cooper, aged 67.
7. Assessed to Alex McDougall, gentleman, aged 66.
8. Assessed to James Cameron, the hardware merchant.
9. Assessed to Robert Ross, farmer, aged 54.
10. Home of Ted Leigh, the town carter.
11. Home of William McRae, labourer, aged 23.
12. The site of the old North Street school. This property had been purchased by the trustees of School Section 4 in 1868. With the opening of the new Bay Street school in 1884, this property was sold to Hugh Stoddart.
13. James Benham, plasterer; and James Cameron, agent; both were assessed as tenants on this lot.
14. Home of Donald Campbell.
15. Assessed to Daniel Tucker, cooper.
16. Home of John Harrison, merchant, aged 35.
17. George R. Proctor's white mansion still stands here as it did in 1884.
18. Assessed to Ewen H. Cameron, apparently a vacant lot. Known to have been flooded for a skating rink in the early 1880's.
19. West half assessed to William Glassford, east half assessed to Alex McRae, aged 62.
20. Assessed to Alex McRae, aged 62 and to Donald McRae, aged 27.
21. Home of Archibald McKinnon, the blacksmith and father of John McKinnon the druggist.
22. Assessed to Charles Lawrence, merchant, aged 21. May have been site of P.D. McArthur's first store, 1862-1867.
23. Possibly the home of Alex Cameron, the merchant, but he also has a lot east of York Street.
24. Also assessed to Alex Cameron, merchant.
25. Home of David Williamson until he moved out west in mid-1884.
26. Assessed to Angus McDougall, farmer, aged 57. Owned by Charles McLean.
27. Home of John Leslie, merchant, aged 35.
28. Site of the Bay Street Public School. The first classes were held here in 1884.
29. Home of Catherine Birchard, widow of Anson. No doubt her son James, the blacksmith lived here too.

easily to teaching, but somehow I think Beaverton will not hold him long.[47]

I was looking forward to a chat with David Williamson, the tailor, who had his shop just west of Birchard's shop.[48] But I've forgotten that he and his family left for the West back in July. It seems that somebody from every family is going West. They can't find their fortunes here, so they move on. Dave's wife died years back,[49] and probably some of the children wanted to try their luck, so he tagged along. They are going to join some other members of the family who live near Regina.[50] It seems strange not to have old Dave to chat with. He's been in business here since 1855.[51]

South on John Street are the Campbell brothers, John C. and Dougald sometimes known as D.A.[52] Both the lads are carpenters and furniture dealers. Jack for the past while has been the local undertaker, and keeps a fancy hearse.[53] He also sells musical instruments and sewing machines. Dougald for a time, at least, was a farm implement agent for Bill Smith[54] who manufactures equipment over on Bay Street, but appears to be back in business with his brother now.[55]

Next to Campbell's shop stands William McHattie's log blacksmith shop and of course the familiar sounds can be clearly heard.[56] McHattie's house is an odd one. It is shaped to fit into the wedge of land where John Street meets Osborne Street.[57] Across the corner is James Snelgrove's Carriage shop.[58] Jim's been making wagons and such for over ten years in Beaverton.[59] Through the door I can make out freshly made wheel rims waiting to have the tires fitted. Outside, one of Jim's men, with a very steady hand, is painting the striping on the wheels of a new buggy. Just as I turn into the back lot of the Ontario House I spy Mrs. Carmichael's

[47] Loc. cit.
[48] PAO, R.G. 21, Assessment of Thorah Township, 1884.
[49] Transcriptions, Old Stone Church Cemetery, Stone O-G8.
[50] *Beaverton Express,* July 11, 1884.
[51] *The Beaver.* A monthly magazine for the Missions of Beaverton and Point Mara, St. Paul's Church, Jan. 1884.
[52] PAO, R.G. 21, Assessment of Thorah Township, 1884.
[53] *The Beaver.* A monthly magazine for the Missions of Beaverton and Point Mara, St. Paul's Church, Jan. 1884.
[54] *Woodville Advocate,* Christmas Issue, 1882.
[55] PAO, R.G. 21, Assessment of Thorah Township, 1884.
[56] Loc. cit.
[57] Known to some as "Split the Wind".
[58] PAO, R.G. 21, Assessment of Thorah Township, 1884. Present location of Tanner's Service Station.
[59] *Beaverton Express,* Jan. 19, 1899.

old roan cow swaying up the street at Smith's foundry.[60] The cantankerous old soul is pulling a length of rope with a peg on the end, as usual. Around the foundry I can make out fanning mills, ploughs and land rollers, just some of the work that Smith's foundry turns out.[61]

Kate seems relieved to be pulled up in the shade of her usual stall in the hotel sheds. I slip in the back door of the Ontario House to visit for a moment with Johnnie Kennedy, one of the owners.[62] John is just returning from the sample room where he has been assisting a travelling merchant from Montreal to arrange his wares for display.[63] Later, some of the local shopkeepers will have an opportunity to inspect the goods and place orders to stock their own shelves with. Our chat wanders from the weather to business, the price of wheat, and, finally, to the newly formed Beaverton Fire Company which he is involved with, along with most of the businessmen.[64] They met back in January in the hopes of providing for themselves and the town better organized fire protection. In February they held a concert to raise funds for equipment and so far things have been going fine. I paid my annual fee for stall rent and left by the north door.[65]

There's a foot-crossing leading from Kennedy's door to that of the Hamilton House.[66] The crossing is of little value at this time of year, but in the spring or during long wet spells, the streets turn into quagmires. Then the crossings allow ladies and finer dressed gents to cross without much fuss. Farquhar McRae has been running Hamilton's fine hotel for a year now.[67] He's a good natured sort and fits in well with the business community. Alex has leased the hotel out for nearly ten years. He seems to prefer to attend to his many other business ventures. He's a busy man. After Taylor and McArthur's petition for village incorporation failed, he took up the cause and was successful.[68] Lately he's been advocating that Beaverton be the site of the proposed county Poor House:[69] that is,

[60] PAO, R.G. 21, Assessment of Thorah Township, 1884. Yes, Mrs. Carmichael had a cow, that it was roan is purely hypothetical. It was common for cows kept in town to wander the streets. Her home, 76 Bay St.

[61] *Beaverton Express,* Jan. 18, 1884. Site of Nillan Industries.

[62] PAO, R.G. 21, Assessment of Thorah Township, 1884. Site of new I.G.A., once the site of Williamson's Garage, later Al Hayward's Esso Station.

[63] *The Northern Light,* Orillia, Jan. 20, 1876. Angus McKinnon added this sample room.

[64] *Beaverton Express,* Jan. 18, 1884.

[65] Interview with Fred Veale, 1978. Fred related that in later years the fee was $3.00 per annum.

[66] PAO, M.S. 348, Reel #1, Thorah Council Minutes, Oct. 14, 1876.

[67] *Beaverton Express,* May 6, 1883. Present site of the Beaverton Hotel. During the 1880's, Farquhar raced horses on the frozen lakes at Beaverton, Orillia, Port Perry etc.

[68] Ibid., Jan. 18, 1884.

[69] Ibid., Jan. 4, 1884.

if it ever gets built anywhere. Alex also led the petition to Thorah Council which resulted in Reeve Alex heading a delegation to Ottawa. The object was to try and get the government to complete the Trent Valley Canal to Lake Simcoe.[70] Hamilton spends a lot of time and effort for the general good of the village. What is good for the village is good for Alex's pocket-book.

Directly across the way is Alexandria Hall, Beaverton's largest indoor gathering place. The Fire Company held their concert up there in the winter.[71] The Checkers held their big do there as well.[72] Even the St. Paul's Busy Bee Society held their bazaar there in the spring.[73] Sherwood, the portrait painter has his studio up there somewhere, I'm told.[74] The Express claims he's painted portraits of Mrs. George Proctor, Mrs. Gordon and others. Below the hall and next west of the hotel is the store run by John Leslie and John Harrison.[75] To attract every Scotsman for miles around they have labelled it the 'Cheapest Store."[76] They have a big stock of clothes, cloth by the yard and sell fancy hats as well.[76] Still under the hall and next to Harrison and Leslie is Jimmie Ritchie's store.[77] He sells everything from boots to chewing tobacco, and has Miss Gunn, a milliner, hired to make fancy hats.[78]

The words "Good Afternoon Baldy" turn my head.

"Aye, Ben, 'tis indeed a fine afternoon." It's Ben Madill the manager of the Black & Co. bank in Proctor's old store east of the townhall.[79]

"Would ya be changing much money lately Ben?" I continued. That makes him pause for a second. "Yes certainly, would you care to borrow some cash at reasonable rates?" Ben always managed to end most sentences with a mysterious lisp, for effect I suppose.[80] Without waiting for my reply, which he already knew, and obviously contemplating some big deal, he marched on, studying the planks in the sidewalk as he went.

Next west of the Ontario House is J.J. Glover's harness shop.[81] Just

[70] Ibid., Jan. 18, 1884.
[71] Ibid., Feb. 15, 1884.
[72] *Woodville Advocate,* Nov. 23, 1883.
[73] *Beaverton Express,* May 2, 1884.
[74] Ibid., Jan. 4, 1884.
[75] PAO, R.G. 21, Assessment of Thorah Township, 1884. One source states that Jim Ritchie's store was here. Presently, Maxine's Fashion and Fabric store.
[76] *Beaverton Express,* Jan. 4, 1884.
[77] PAO, R.G. 21, Assessment of Thorah Township, 1884. Presently, Hartmier's store.
[78] *Beaverton, Express,* Apr. 4, 1884.
[79] Ibid., Jan. 4, 1884. Presently *site of* Post office.
[80] Interview with Donald Smith, Kirkfield, Nov. 30, 1983.
[81] PAO, R.G. 21, Assessment of Thorah Township, 1884. Just east of present Gormley Group Real Estate Office. Later this building was replaced by a brick building housing Williamson's harness shop, which was demolished to make room for a service station.

The HOTEL HAMILTON was built in 1870 on the site of the earlier WORKMAN HOTEL by Alex Hamilton. It is presently operated as the BEAVERTON HOTEL by Mr. and Mrs. Frank McMillan.

lately he has put a new front on his small shop and given it a coat of paint.[82] Jim started business here when his father still ran the Ontario House. In fact he bought that sliver of land from his father.[83] I can see him talking to Ted Leigh at the back of the shop. No doubt Ted is getting a price on new harness. Last week his horse ran away, destroying the wagon and possibly the harness as well.[84] Ted's the town carter and cannot be without his delivery wagon for long.[85] He lives with his mother, Elizabeth,[86] a school teacher, over on North St.[87]

Next to Glover's is the old Shortiss hotel[88] which Alex Hamilton had moved up from near the lake and fixed up as two stores for rent.[89] Hec

[82] *Beaverton Express,* June 13, 1884.
[83] Registry Office, Whitby, Abstract to Land Registration.
[84] *Beaverton Express,* Aug. 1, 1884.
[85] PAO, R.G. 21, Assessment of Thorah Township, 1884.
[86] PAO, Ontario Census of Thorah Township, 1881.
[87] PAO, R.G. 21, Assessment of Thorah Township, 1884.
[88] Ritchie, Mary Houston. *A Township on the Lake,* 1952. Page 51. Presently, The Gormley Group Real Estate office. Previously housed many businesses, including Dan's Cafe.
[89] *Woodville Advocate,* Nov. 3, 1882.

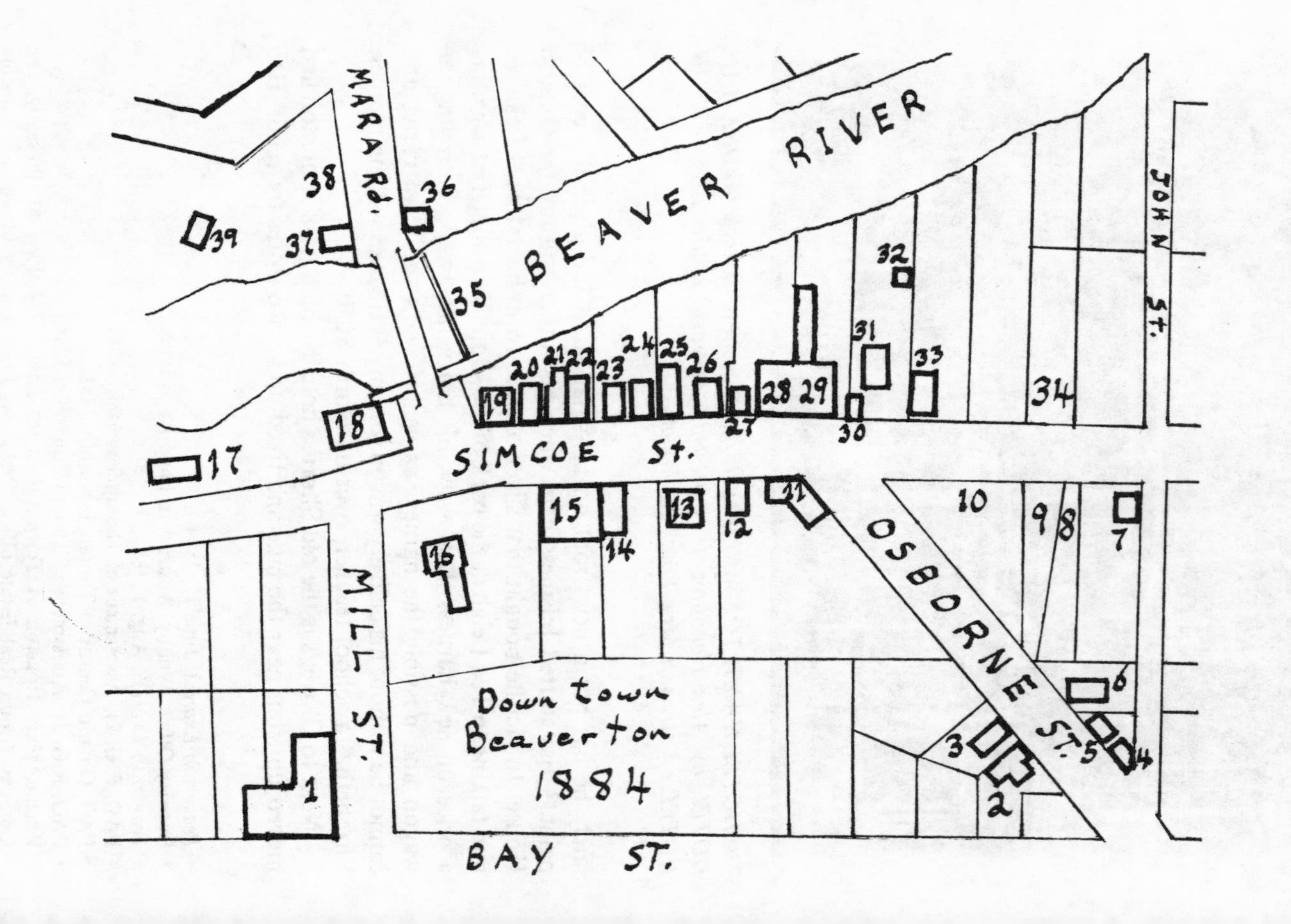
MARA Rd.
BEAVER RIVER
JOHN ST.
SIMCOE ST.
OSBORNE ST.
MILL ST.
BAY ST.
Down town
Beaverton
1884

KEY TO DOWNTOWN BEAVERTON, 1884

1. Site of William Smith's Foundry.
2. Store and residence of John French.
3. Strangely missing from the 1884 assessment. In 1880 this was the site of James Cameron, the tailor's shop. Owned 1868-? by John McArthur a harness maker.
4. The home of William McHattie, the Blacksmith. Until the time of its demolition in the 1960's, it was known as "the split the wind" because of its unusual shape.
5. William McHattie's blacksmith shop. Reported to have been a log structure.
6. Assessed to John C. and Dugald A. Campbell and may have been used as a home at that time.
7. James Birchard's blacksmith shop. This business was founded by his father, Anson, around 1861 on this site.
8. The site of David Williamson's tailor shop. After David moved west in 1884 a Dr. Spooner was a tenant for a time. Later Duncan McRae owned the property. The building was reported to have been rough cast and was destroyed by fire in 1895.
9. Site of a large building owned by "Commissioner" John Cameron. May have been used as a store by his son Alex, who is not to be confused with either Alex the Merchant, or Alex the contractor.
10. The site of Alex Hamilton's "Iron Block".
11. The Ontario House Hotel 1869(c.)-1935(c.).
12. J.J. Glover's harness shop. Williamson's brick harness shop was built here later.
13. Described as "Hamilton's New Block" in 1884. Rented to Hec Logan, the tailor and Henry Westcott, the hardware merchant.
14. John McRae's store. Completed in 1883.
15. The Cameron Brick Block was built during the early 1880's by Alex Cameron, the contractor.
16. The John A. Proctor brick house built about 1875.
17. The Parson & Duncan Tannery.
18. The Proctor Mill built 1873.
19. Described as "Proctor's New Block." Purchased by P.D. McArthur in 1883 and sold to A.D. Morrison in 1894. In 1920 it became the Sterling Bank of Canada. Until recently was the home of the Canadian Imperial Bank of Commerce.
20. Known as the Calder block, this building housed Harry Waller's shoe shop in 1884. Later Henry Westcott had his hardware store here. It was known for many years as Percy Byrne's Jewelry Shop.

21. This building contained two narrow stores. The west half was F.S. Dunningan's Grocery and bakery. In the east half was Donald Ross's store. For many years this building was owned by W.D. Rodman the tailor. This building was converted to one store by L. Hartmier. It was destroyed by fire in 1979.
22. Known as Davidson's new block, this building was occupied by Duncan McNabb in 1884. Later owned by Smith Thompson and later still, by Joe Polito.
23. Present site of Gillespie's Hardware. It was the home of Cameron & Westcott's Hardware 1880-1882. By 1884 it was James Cameron's Hardware and Stove Emporium. It was known for years as the Cameron & Cameron Hardware.
24. In 1884 and for many years after. F.S. King's butcher shop.
25. Now the site of Millar's Store. A store on this site was owned by P.D. McArthur from 1870 to 1873 and again from 1878 to 1889. In 1884 he was renting to John McKinnon the druggist.
26. Now the home of Stedman's. The function of this building cannot be determined as yet with certainty in 1884. May have been the post office.
27. In 1884 this log store was operated by Alex Cameron, merchant. One of its earliest occupants was James Campbell a tailor. From 1875-1878 Alex Montgomery's General Store. In 1893 L.J. Cameron had it demolished and replaced with a brick building which was destroyed by fire in the 1920's.
28. Alexandria Hall was constructed by Hamilton in 1876. Under the hall, James Ritchie and Harrison & Leslie were tenants, in 1884.
29. The Hamilton Hotel.
30. This building may not have existed in 1884. However there are references to a photo gallery by W.E. O'Brien "one door west of the town hall" in 1883. If not for the existence of a building at this location, describing the gallery as "being in the Hamilton House" would be more appropriate. In 1887 D.A. Cole was reported to have been erecting a barber shop on the the townhall lot Was he replacing an old building or building one for the first time here?
31. The townhall.
32. The township "Lock-up".
33. "Proctor's old block."
34. Assessed to George Smith, butcher, in 1884.
35. The mill dam was above the bridge, contrary to the present situation.
36. James Gordon's home,
37. C.T. Young's Woolen Mill.
38. Possible site of Hunter's Livery Stable in 1884. Could also have been across the street.
39. The first McMillan's Blacksmith shop.

Logan has just recently moved his tailoring business in to the east half.[90] I find him sitting cross-legged on a counter near the door and we engage in a chat.[91] He responded to my words without even looking up as he repaired the stitching in a coat. After a time, unfortunately, the conversation turned to politics, and he found time to pour scorn on the Conservative government for giving those Canadian Pacific fellows $30,000,000 more to spend on the railway in the North-West.[92] His voice rose steadily in agitation with the thought, and his stitching accelerated considerably until he had no more to say. If I had ventured opposition however, our conversation could have become long and fiery.

In the other half of the building, Henry Westcott has opened out his new hardware store.[93] He has placed many items on the sidewalk for public display. I step around picks, axes, shovels, trowels, hammers and dozens of other items to get a good look through a window.[94] Inside I can make out lamps, crocks and fancy glassware.[95] From experience, Henry allows no credit and advertises it on the sign over the door which reads; "The Cheap Cash Store, H. Westcott."[96]

Where the first Glover Hotel stood,[97] John McRae built a large brick store just last year.[98] He put large plate glass windows in the front.[99] I'll bet he's hoping that some hooligan won't break them, come Hallowe'en. John's a short quiet man[100] who started in business as a grain buyer for Matthew's in Lindsay, then returned to Beaverton.[101] Farquhar McRae, John's nephew,[102] works as a clerk in the store.[103] He's a much larger[104] and more talkative man than[105] John, but no less respected or liked. I'll slip in for a chew of tobacco.

"Nach eil an la blath"[106] John greets me from his perch on a stool.

[90] *Beaverton Express,* Jan. 4, 1884.
[91] Thompson, E.P., *The Making of the English Working Class,* England, Penguin, 1982 (copyright 1963) page 363.
[92] A man of the Liberal Persuasion.
[93] *Beaverton Express,* Jan. 4, 1884.
[94] Loc. cit.
[95] Loc. cit.
[96] Loc. cit.
[97] Ibid., Sept. 1, 1882.
[98] Ibid., July 26, 1883. Presently housing the Sears' office.
[99] Loc. cit.
[100] Interview with Cephas Doherty, Dec. 3, 1983.
[101] Interview with Donald and Ina McRae, Nov. 26, 1983.
[102] Loc. Cit.
[103] Loc. Cit. No hard evidence that he was actually working here in 1884, but did work here before and after this date.
[104] Loc. cit.
[105] Interview with Cephas Doherty.
[106] MacLearen, op. cit. Page 15. Translates as; "Is the day not warm" or "Warm day isn't it."

"Tha."[107] The chat continued for some time touching on the King, Burke and Co. Circus which was in town on July 22.[108] Much fun was made of their collection of strange creatures, supposedly, of God's creation. And not just the simplest of folk around here parted with their money for the privilege of viewing such oddities as the three-headed lady.[109] Between short interruptions by paying customers, the deplorable state of the wharfs at the lake was discussed.[110] Soon the lake steamers won't be able to dock at all. Without such improvements, popular social excursions on the lake might come to an end.

George Smith, the township clerk,[111] added to our commentaries for a time. He, along with his son, George, under the name of Smith and Smith are local surveyors and drainage engineers.[112] They have their office in the town hall[113] so it is convenient to George Sr.'s duties as clerk.

With much of these debates in my head, I survey Alex Cameron's new store block which is next to McRae's.[114] Alex's been so busy these last few years that he has not had time to quite finish his new white brick building.[115] He's one of the "Stonehouse Camerons" and generally makes a living contracting for only the most difficult jobs in the township, or sawing lumber at his mill northeast of town.[116] A rather likeable sort of man,[117] of average height, he's heavy-set and very strong.[118] Though not very excitable, he always manages to get things done, a trait that is useful when moving houses and such.[119]

And there's John Proctor's great house. It's certainly very nearly as large as brother George's.[120] Across the way is John's mill.[121] Archie Campbell is his miller and has worked in the mill since he was a boy. He

[107] Loc. cit., "It is" or "Yes".
[108] *Beaverton Express,* July 11, 1884.
[109] Loc. cit.
[110] Ibid., June 13, 1884.
[111] Ibid., Jan. 4, 1884.
[112] Loc. cit.
[113] Loc. cit. The building still stands behind Wright's hardware.
[114] PAO, R.G. 21, Assessment of Thorah Township, 1884. Presently, Red & White store and Family Trust Real Estate office. Still known to some as the Brunning Block.
[115] *Beaverton Express,* July 26, 1883; "The Cameron Block is at a standstill." The assessed value in 1884 would lead one to suspect it was very nearly completed but there seems to be little evidence that it was occupied.
[116] Interview with Cephas Doherty.
[117] Loc. cit.
[118] Loc. cit.
[119] Loc. cit.
[120] PAO, R.G. 21, Assessment of Thorah, 1884. Presently the site of the Canadian Imperial Bank of Commerce.
[121] Loc. cit. At north-west corner of Simcoe St. and Mara Rd.

lives on Elizabeth Street by the river.[122]

West of the mill is the tannery operated by Sid Parsons and Jimmie Duncan[123] and further down is Bill Brain's home.[124]

Here comes Alex McRae walking up the street. "Ciamar a tha thu an diugh, Gilleasbuig."[125] He addresses me.

"Tha mi gu math, tapadh leibh."[126]

"Well B-y-e G-o-l-l-y, Baldie,[127] havin't seen yer hide for too long. Might ya be in town on business?" his words drawn out in his characteristic manner.

"Aye, jest might be", I replied without admitting that it was mostly Christy's business. Sandy's been working on Proctor's new barn this summer. We compared notes for some time on the corner, then each went our own way.

The new Proctor block,[128] which was built in the 70's[129] was owned by the Proctors until 1881.[130] John McRae rented part of it until his new store on the south side was finished.[131] A druggist by the name of Bauld was in the other half.[132] When John McKinnon returned to town he bought out Bauld's business but now operates further up the street.[133] Up until last year Doc Grant had his office over the store[134] and so did Doc Johnston,[135] though only for a short time. Now Peter McArthur owns the building[136] and has opened out his new stock after removing from the other building he owns.[137] P.D.'s a baker by trade[138] but seems to prefer being a general merchant.[139] Now he carries groceries, wines and liquors.[140] He's been

[122] PAO, R.G. 21, Assessment of Thorah, 1884. Also Beaverton Express Mar. 29, 1883.
[123] Loc. cit.
[124] Loc. cit. Presently, Beaver Museum, Brick House.
[125] MacKinnon, Roderick, *Gaelic*, Teach Yourself Books, London, 1972 copyright 1971. Translates as; "How are you today, Archie?" Gilleasbuig or Gillespie, for some reason is synonymous with Archibald in Gaelic.
[126] Loc. cit. Translates as; "I'm fine thank you."
[127] Known to most as "Big Alex." He was a brother of Farqhur McRae who worked with John McRae, the storekeeper.
[128] Presently, "Tasty rite" Burgers and John's Pinball Palace. Until recently, the Canadian Imperial Bank of Commerce.
[129] *Beaverton Express*, Oct. 24, 1878.
[130] Registry Office, Whitby Abstracts to Land Titles. Part of lot 1 north of Simcoe St.
[131] *Woodville Advocate*, Oct. 24, 1878.
[132] Ibid., Nov. 14, 1878.
[133] Ibid., Feb. 26, 1880.
[134] PAO, Assessment of Thorah Township, 1884.
[135] Loc. cit. Also *Woodville Advocate*, Mar. 29, 1883.
[136] Registry Office, Whitby, Abstracts to Land Titles.
[137] *Beaverton Express*, Jan. 4, 1884.
[138] Ontario Census, 1881, Ontario County, Thorah Township.
[139] *Woodville Advocate*, Christmas Issue, 1882.
[140] *Beaverton Express*, Jan. 4, 1884.

in business in town since at least 1860, altering the nature of his business to suit the times and the competition.[141]

For a long time I stood looking at the old wooden dam above the bridge, and watched the water choose whether to go over the dam or into the sluiceway that took it to the power machinery in the mill. I can't remember how many dams came before that one. Sooner or later they all rotted somewhat. Then the spring ice would break parts away, and damage the stone filled wooden cribs that supported the middle of the bridge.[142] Nearly every ten years the bridge had to be replaced because of such damage or because it was rotting. Near the north end of the dam is Jim Gordon's house.[143] He's one of the local grain buyers and has a large warehouse at the rail station.[144] Next is the McMillan Carriage shop.[145] Things seem quieter than usual. It's a safe bet that the twins, Peter and Duncan, were on the Checkers Special that I saw earlier. Bill McNichol, their blacksmith,[146] can be seen hammering out some fancy iron work for a buggy.

Across from Gordon's house and at the bank of the river is Charlie Young's Woolen mill.[147] As well as spinning, fulling and weaving, he sells ready-made tweeds and flannels.[148] And there's Jim Hunter's livery.[149] Jim's only been in business there since June. He rents horses and fancy rigs to travelling gents and salesmen as well as providing a fancy team for John A. Campbell's hearse. On the north side of Main St. is "Sweet Cake Smith's" home and bakery.[150] There was a time when every home provided their own baking but now that times are easier it's strange that some just don't have the time.

Across Mara Road is Doc Grant's fine home[151] that was built by the Murrays as a hotel.[152] North of Smith's bakery is Flora McCaskill's

[141] Churchill, A.G., *Poetical Dictionary,* 1860.

[142] Interview with Jack Mitchell, Argyle, Nov. 19, 1983.

[143] PAO, R.G. 21, Assessment of Thorah Township, 1884. Now the site of the Hodge Podge.

[144] Loc. cit. The Grand Trunk Station.

[145] Loc. cit. Now the site of the Strand Theatre.

[146] Loc. cit.

[147] Loc. cit. Also, *Beaverton Express;* Jan. 4, 1884 and Woodville Advocate; Nov. 31, 1881; and Dec. 29, 1881.

[148] *Beaverton Express,* Jan. 18, 1884.

[149] Ibid., July 10, 1884. Hunter's Livery is difficult to locate with certainty.

[150] PAO, R.G. 21, Assessment of Thorah Township, 1884. On the site of Frank Rowe's home, 302 Mara Rd.

[151] Loc. cit. Building became known as the Way Side Inn and was demolished to make room for the Wayside Apartments.

[152] PAO, M.S. 348, Thorah Council Minutes, Dec. 10, 1870. Also Whitby Registry office, Abstracts to Land Titles.

The A.P. COCKBURN HOME.
This house was built by A.P. Cockburn and later purchased by Alex Dobson in the mid '90s. It became the St. Andrew's manse for a few years after the turn of the century during the time of Rev. Best.
Photo courtesy of Grace McElroy

home.[153] Alex Cockburn has a fine white brick house next to Flora's.[154] Sandy's sort of a local celebrity. He's made good with his boats on the Muskoka Lakes[155] and just now is our Member of Parliament.[156] He is a man of foresight and considerable powers of persuasion[157] as well as helpful political and family connections.[158] He married Helen Proctor in 1864.[159] She is a sister of John A. and George R. Proctor of town. The

[153] PAO, R.G. 21, Assessment of Thorah Township, 1884. Presently, home of Annie Johnston, 306 Mara Rd.

[154] Loc. cit. Later owned by Alex Dobson and once the St. Andrew's Manse. Presently, 326 Mara Rd.

[155] *The Canadian Biographical Dictionary and Portrait of Eminent and Self-Made Men,* Ontario Volume, American Biographical Publishing Co. 1880.

[156] Johnson, J.K., *The Canadian Directory of Parliament 1867-1967.*

[157] *Coombe, Geraldine, Muskoka, Past and Present,* McGraw-Hill Ryerson, Toronto, 1976. Page 54.

[158] Coombe, op. cit. Page 55. A.P. borrowed money to start his Muskoka operations from his father-in-law, George Proctor Sr.

[159] Britnell, W.E., *County Marriage Register of Ontario, Canada, 1858-1869.* Volume 2 Index to Ontario County, Generation Press, 1979. Page 66.

The WAY SIDE INN. Built by Hugh and Margaret Murray as the Railway Hotel in 1869. This building was the residence of Dr. Andrew Grant for many years. When the hotel closed in protest to the introduction of local option, this building was opened by the Beaverton Hotel Company to meet the needs of the traveling public.

In 1915 Robert Way purchased the building and named it the Way Side Inn. With the death of his only daughter Florence, the building was demolished in 1976 to make way for the new Senior Citizen's apartments that have been appropriately called the Way Side Apartments.

Rev. Watson married another sister, Elizabeth Jane.[160] Next to A.P.'s is the home of Moses Armstrong, a local sawmill engineer.[161]

North of Grant's home is Hec. Logan's tidy residence.[162] Then there's Old William Neill's home.[163] He's a weaver with a heavy Irish accent, and must be about 70 years of age.[164]

Across from Neill's is the home of James Ritchie, the merchant.[165] He

[160] PAO, G.S. 6397. Parish Registers of Reverend John McMurchy.
[161] PAO, R.G. 21, Assessment of Thorah Township, 1884. Presently, 334 Mara Rd., home of Bill Curley.
[162] Loc. cit. Possibly the site of 333 Mara Rd., home of the late Maude McLeod.
[163] PAO, R.G. 21, Assessment of Thorah Township, 1884.
[164] Ontario Census, 1881, Ontario County, Thorah Township.
[165] PAO, R.G. 21, Assessment of Thorah Township, 1884.

erected that great white brick house just last year.[166] Next to Ritchie's is a new home just being completed for William Daly by some of the local carpenters.[167] Then there's Charlie Davidson's huge white brick mansion that was built just a few years ago.[168] In every sense his home shows the rewards of years of hard work. He's still involved with the farm and rents store property on the main street.[169] He's a good member of the English church.[170] Across the way are a number of much humbler homes. Widow Cowie lives in one. Her son Andrew, like many others, has gone to Michigan to seek his fortune.[171] Wm. Campbell the blacksmith has scarcely more than a shanty for a home.[172] Then there's Widow McGregor, who originally came from Gamebridge.[173] Further up is Widow McDonald's. Flora's lowly home must scarcely protect her from the elements,[174] though most people who have lived long in Thorah have lived in such a home at one time or another.

The Midland Railway's tracks cross Mara Road just north of Flora's. The Township Council certainly has been stewing over the refusal of the Midland directors to make use of the wharf at the lake. Their wrath was almost indescribable when the railway dismantled part of the wharf and removed the tracks leading to it.[175] I guess it was inevitable, though. Council and the people were hopeful of having Beaverton at the end of the track, but were badly disappointed when the railway was run further north. Now the last of the dream of being an important trading town has been crushed. The turntable at the station has been abandoned. No need to turn locomotives now. The stock yard is in poor repair,[176] but rumour has it that a new, larger yard will be built soon. I remember that Johnnie Kennedy told me he was going to have an acoustic telephone installed from the Ontario House to the rail station.[177] When I asked further, he told me he would be able to talk to people at the station from the hotel. I don't know who else he's tried to fool with that strange story.

[166] *Beaverton Express,* June 26, 1919. Also PAO, R.G. 21, Assessment of Thorah Township, 1884. Presently, 346 Mara Rd., Fred Taylor's apartments on the corner of King St. and Mara Rd.
[167] *Beaverton Express,* July 11, 1884. Likely the home of Mr. Gordon Suggitt, 362 Mara Rd.
[168] *The Northern Light,* Orillia, May 4, 1876. Known recently as the McKenzie House.
[169] PAO, R.G. 21, Assessment of Thorah Township, 1884.
[170] Ontario Census, 1881, Ontario County, Thorah Township.
[171] PAO, R.G. 21, Assessment of Thorah Township, 1884.
[172] Loc. cit.
[173] Loc. cit.
[174] Loc. cit. At the site of Becker's store.
[175] *Beaverton Express,* Feb. 15, 1884.
[176] Ibid., Sept. 5, 1884.
[177] Ibid., Nov. 7, 1884.

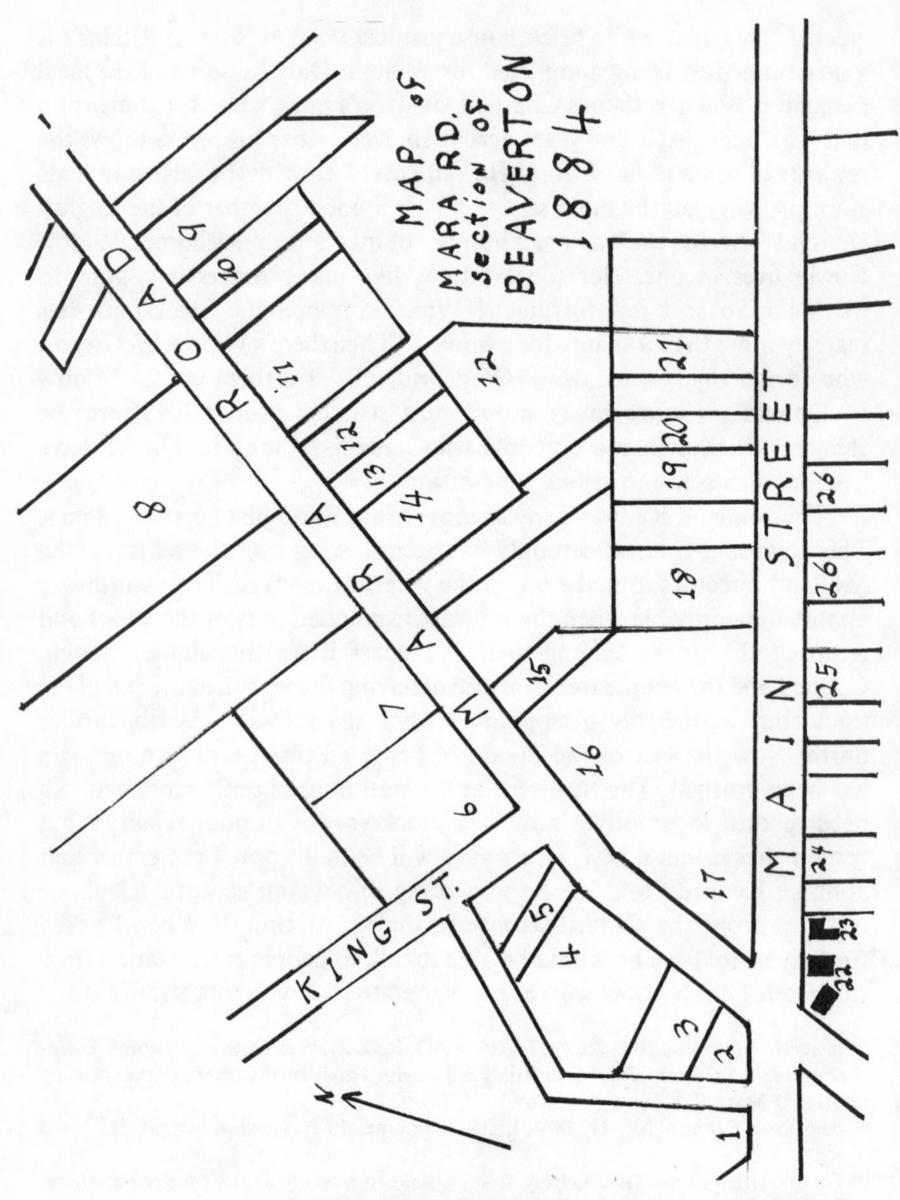

KEY TO MARA ROAD 1884

1. Later site of the Beaverton Express Office.
2. "Sweet Cake" Smith's bakery. Destroyed in the same fire that consumed the Beaverton Express office in the 1890's.
3. Flora McCaskill's home.
4. A.P. Cockburn's home.
5. Home of Moses Armstrong.

6. James Ritchie's home.
7. William Daly's home.
8. C.H. Davidson's house.
9. Site of Flora McDonald's home.
10. Assessed to John Cameron, labourer, aged 52.
11. Mrs. McGregor's house.
12. Home of William Campbell, blacksmith, aged 46.
13. Widow Cowie's home.
14. Assessed to Jane Cameron.
15. Home of William Neil, the weaver. Owned earlier by Alex Gamble who was also a weaver.
16. Possible site of Hec Logan's home in 1884. Later he moved into a new house on the west side of Mara Road.
17. Dr. Andrew Grant's home in 1884. Previously the Murray's Railway Hotel. Much later it was purchased by Robert Way and operated as the Way Side Inn.
18. Home of Daniel Cameron, carpenter, aged 59.
19. Assessed to James McNabb, labourer, aged 33.
20. Home of Ewen H. Cameron.
21. Home of James McMaster, blacksmith, aged 40.
22. The McMillan Blacksmith Shop of 1884.
23. Possibly the home of William McNichol, blacksmith.
24. Home of Joe Elliott.
25. Home of William Waddell, labourer, aged 47.
26. Property assessed to William Taylor, brickmaker.

Annie Warren lives close to the station on Centre St.[178] At the corner of James St. and the 6th Concession, Henry Shorter makes his home.[179] Next north is Joe Wilkinson a railway worker.[180] At the corner of James and Centre is Andrew Hudson, a cooper.[181] At the corner of Franklin and Centre is Robert Adams, the plasterer. East from him is Bill Tarbox and north is David Haley's home.[182] Most of these men came to Beaverton as railway construction workers. Some work for the railway and some have reverted to their old trades.

I can hear the 5 o'clock south-bound train crossing the trestle at White's creek.[183] Isn't that a caution! I've wandered about town all afternoon and done nothing. I'd better get downtown, do my errands and

[178] PAO, R.G. 21, Assessment of Thorah Township, 1884.
[179] Loc. cit. Presently, Van's Bicycle Shop, 524 Main St.
[180] Loc. cit. 532 James St. Possibly the home of B. Wells.
[181] Loc. cit. Possible house at 439 Centre St. Home of Robin Croft.
[182] Loc. cit.
[183] *Beaverton Express,* Nov. 21, 1884.

head home.

From near Logan's home I see Doc Grant, his coat undone, with his bag, walking in haste to Hunter's livery for his horse and buggy. A small cloud of dust follows him east on Main Street. He passes Joe Elliot's,[184] Dan Cameron, the carpenter's, house,[185] William Taylor's lumber yard[186] and Jim McMaster's.[187] Just after the Methodist Church the street leads him from sight.

Realizing that I am standing and staring up Main Street, instead of hurrying uptown, I make haste for the drive sheds. After rounding the corner at P.D. McArthur's I sneak a wee peek in Harry Waller's shoeshop in Calder's Block.[188] He advertises his trade with a golden boot hung over the walk.[189] An Englishman[190] with a heavy old country accent, he is well liked and does a brisk trade. Seems to me he's been in town about ten years.[191] Next is Frank Dunnigan,[192] a baker and grocer.[193] The building houses two narrow stores. The other one is occupied by Donald Ross[194] under the name of the "People's Store."[195] He carries a big stock of overcoats, suits, felt hats, shirts and a few groceries.[196]

In Davidson's brick Block is Duncan McNabb's "Toronto House."[198] Dunc carries much the same as Ross but sells furs too.[199] Some day, when I have more time, I'll slip into Jimmie Cameron's Beaverton "Hardware Store and Stove Emporium."[200] Christy's been itching for one of those fancy new cook stoves that Jim's got in. A little thing like that would go a long way to staying on her good side. Here's Fred King's butcher

[184]PAO, R.G. 21, Assessment of Thorah Township, 1884. Presently, site of Mrs. Helen Cameron's home.

[185]Loc. cit.

[186]Loc. cit. Also *Beaverton Express,* Jan. 4, 1884.

[187]Loc. cit. James McMaster was a blacksmith.

[188]Loc. cit. Later, P.E. Byrne's Jewellery store. Presently Golden Star Restaurant, 306 Simcoe St.

[189]*Beaverton Express,* Oct. 17, 1884.

[190]Ontario Census, 1881, Ontario County, Thorah Township.

[191]*Beaverton Express,* Oct. 17, 1884.

[192]PAO, R.G. 21, Assessment of Thorah Township, 1884.

[193]*Beaverton Express,* Dec. 5, 1884.

[194]PAO, R.G. 21, Assessment of Thorah Township, 1884. These two stores combined by L. Hartmier as one, burned in 1979.

[195]*Beaverton Express,* Mar. 28, 1884.

[196]Loc. cit.

[197]PAO, R.G. 21, Assessment of Thorah Township, 1884.

[198]*Beaverton Express,* Dec. 4, 1884.

[199]Loc. cit.

[200]*Beaverton Express,* July 18, 1884. For many years this was the Cameron & Cameron Hardware. Presently, Gillespie's Hardware.

shop.[201] I'd love to jaw with him for a while but must get home for the chores.

Next to the butcher shop is John McKinnon's drug store that he rents from P.D. McArthur.[202] John's a fine and popular man in town.[203] Sad to say, his wife died a month or so back.[204] Lizzie was the daughter of Rev. Watson and a general favourite of the people of Beaverton.[205] They had only been married a year or so.[206] John's the son of Archibald McKinnon, one of Beaverton's blacksmiths.[207]

After 'Commissioner" Cameron's place[208] is Alex Cameron's store.[209] In that humble old log store[210] he sells boots, crockery, and groceries.[211] Sandy's been doing business in town for nearly thirty years[212] and, like the rest of us, has seen great changes in that length of time. For nearly twenty years he was in partnership with George Bruce, but now operates by himself.[213]

Taking the short cut through the Ontario House, I hitch Kate and turn from Bay Street north onto Osborne. Across the street from McHattie's is John French's grocery store.[214] Strange to say, John is blind,[215] but can walk about the store and point to things on the shelves as if he can see them.[216] Of course his wife helps out. Bob Furniss works for him, peddling

[201] PAO, R.G. 21, Assessment of Thorah Township, 1884. More recently, Stanley's Meat Market and Cleland's Butcher shop.

[202] Loc. cit. The assessment gives McKinnon's location as lot 1 south of Simcoe and a tenant of P.D. McArthur. However, a study of land ownership proves that McArthur never owned lot 1 south Simcoe (which was also the site of John Proctor's large house and owned by him.) McArthur does own part of lot 3 north of Simcoe in 1884. For this reason we can place McKinnon's drug store at the present site of Millar's Shoe Store and Men's Wear.

[203] *Woodville Advocate,* Aug. 10, 1883.

[204] Ibid., July 3, 1884.

[205] Loc. cit.

[206] Loc. cit.

[207] Ontario Census, 1881, Ontario County, Thorah Township. Archibald McKinnon lived on Bay St.

[208] Now houses the Stedman's store. Traditionally a very old building and known to have been the post office, at sometime. The post office was housed in the Cameron & Westcott store here in 1882. Evidence for the status of this building in 1884 has yet to come to light.

[209] PAO, R.G. 21, Assessment of Thorah Township, 1884.

[210] *Beaverton Express,* May 26, 1893. Report of demoliton of log store.

[211] *Woodville Advocate,* Christmas Edition, 1882.

[212] *Beaverton Express,* May 26, 1881

[213] Ibid., June 2, 1881.

[214] PAO, R.G. 21, Assessment of Thorah Township, 1884. At what is now the north end of Sproule's Texaco.

[215] Ontario Census, 1881, Ontario County, Thorah Township.

[216] Interview with Cephas Doherty, Dec. 3, 1983.

goods[217] in the countryside and clerking in the store.[218] North of Dougald Campbell's on the east side of the street is the small frame building that Harry Waller, the boot maker lives in.[219] At the corner on the east side is Alex Hamilton's Iron Block.[220] A shop right at the point of the corner is occupied by Archibald McFadyen.[221] Archie is an agent for various implement companies.[222] He sells sewing machines as well and I can see a poster in the window advertising Manitoba land for sale.[223] East of Archie's are several shops rented out to an ever changing assortment of tradesmen. Presently the only permanent tenants are two shoemakers: Lachlan McDonald and Gilbert McEwen, and Andrew Murray, son of Peter, who is a tinsmith.[224] Robert Turner, a local harness maker, worked out of one of the shops until recently.[225] From time to time, a photographer will open out in one of the shops but they always move on. They must not be able to do a big enough trade in town.

Across from the Iron Block is Ben Madill's bank. His brother, Frank, is a lawyer, and a smart one too. In '81 he got elected to the legislature at the tender age of 21, but last year was defeated.[226] For a time John Reynolds sold furniture next door to Ben.[227] Now Frank has his office there. Across from Birchard's shop is George Smith, the butcher.[228] He buys eggs, poultry, beef and pork from the farmers and in turn sells it to the town folk.

I wake to find Kate standing patiently at the gate in the darkness. While operating the gate to let her pass through, it strikes me that I had forgotten everything that Christy had sent me to town for.

[217] Ontario Census, 1881, Ontario County, Thorah Township.

[218] PAO, R.G. 21, Assessment of Thorah Township, 1884.

[219] Loc. cit. Assessed as a tenant, his business is definitely at lot 1 north of Simcoe, so it is possible this is his residence. There is a possibility that he was assessed for part of the Iron Block rather than his building.

[220] Loc. cit. Also, *Beaverton Express,* Jan. 14, 1887. "Hamilton's Iron Block". Now site of Beaverton Townhall.

[221] Loc. cit. Also *Beaverton Express,* May 23, 1884. "At the corner store opposite the Hamilton House."

[222] *Beaverton Express,* May 23, 1884.

[223] Ibid., Jan. 4, 1884.

[224] PAO, R.G. 21, Assessment of Thorah Township, 1884.

[225] *Beaverton Express,* Sept. 12, 1884.

[226] Johnson, K.J., op. cit. Page 127.

[227] *Woodville Advocate,* Apr. 15, 1882.

[228] PAO, R.G. 21, Assessment of Thorah Township, 1884. Not to be confused with George Smith the township clerk or George Smith the surveyor.

Chapter 16

MEN OF THE PRESS

The newspaper was and continues to be an important social and commercial link with the communities it serves. Its business is to cover national and international news, local news which was as important in early times as it is today, editorials, letters to the editor, sometimes a weekly serial and, of course, lots of advertisements. All of this was presented in a style of writing that was clear, concise and grammatically correct.

In those early years, Beaverton seems to have had difficulty in supporting a press, none surviving more than six months to three or so years. Not until the time that Joseph J. Cave arrived in town from Woodville, previously from Ardtrea near Orillia, did a newspaper ever become a success.[1]

The earliest mention of a paper in Beaverton was in 1855 when William Hillam published the *Packet* for a couple of years.[2] From Beaverton he went to the Uxbridge newspaper field.[3] During his short time in Beaverton, he was made an honorary member of the Thorah Branch Agricultural Society of the County of Ontario.[4] Previously, due to the fact that there was no paper in 1854, Thorah Township Council was forced to advertise a By Law in the *New Era* newspaper of Newmarket about the taking of stock in the Port Hope and Peterboro (sic) Railroad.[5]

However, Beaverton did produce two local sons that did make successful careers in this business. The earliest was Christopher Blackett Robinson, born on November 2, 1837 in Thorah Township, son of Charles Robinson and Ann Gunn, early pioneers.[6] Fifty odd years he devoted to the newspaper business getting his early start at the age of nineteen, as editor of the *Beaverton Post* or *Weekly Post*.[7] At this time, in 1857 a Mr. Harris was publishing this paper with a H.W. Sherman as

[1] *Beaverton Express*, June 23, 1932.
[2] Beers, J.H. & Co., *Historical Atlas of the County of Ontario*, 1877, Cumming reprint 1972. Page 14.
[3] *North Ontario Advocate*, Uxbridge, 1862.
[4] Ritchie, Mary Houston, *A Township on the Lake*, Page 59.
[5] Public Archives of Ontario, M.S. 348, Reel #1, Thorah Township Council Municipal Records. Feb. 15, 1854.
[6] Lindsay Library, *Lindsay Daily Post*, June 12, 1923.
[7] Lindsay Library, *Canada Directory 1857-58* (of Beaverton).

printer. Robinson appears to have purchased this Reform weekly which stayed in Beaverton only until June 1861, when it removed to Lindsay under the banner "*Canadian Post.*"[8] In July of that same year the great fire of Lindsay destroyed the Post's premises preventing its appearance until September 1861. George Cruikshank and Company were the printers and publishers.[9] Robinson, in 1864, was editor and proprietor of the *Whitby Gazette.*[10] From Whitby, back to Lindsay, Robinson re-purchased the *Canadian Post* which he had established only a few years earlier. For two years he stayed in Lindsay; then he ventured to Orillia to establish the *Orillia Expositor* in 1867, with Peter Murray, a Beaverton local, as editor. Murray purchased this paper from Robinson in November of the same year.[11]

By 1869-70, Robinson was still editor and proprietor of the *Canadian Post* which, in 1870 incorporated the *Lindsay Advocate* established in 1854.[12] At some point in 1870, Robinson and his family moved to Toronto where he established the *Canadian Presbyterian* and continued there until 1897.[13] In the year 1900, Robinson moved to Ottawa where he established and carried on publication of the *Dominion Presbyterian* until 1911. He died in Ottawa on June 11, 1923, at the age of 85.

Besides being involved in the newspaper field, this Beaverton personality was a man of many capabilities. He was for a number of years Government Printer for Ontario. He published the *Dominion Oddfellow*, the *Rural Canadian,* the *Canada Law Journal* and *The Week,* a high class literary journal. Robinson also published a large number of books by Canadian writers. Included were several historical works concerning the progress of Canada in the early and middle portions of the ninteenth century. He was president of the Canadian Press Association in 1897, director of the Central Bank of Canada in 1887, a Liberal, a member of the General Assembly, and a strong Presbyterian.

C. Blackett Robinson was married twice, first to Mary Burnside and later to Frances Cameron; he had two sons, C. Blackett Robinson Junior and Thomas Burnside Robinson, and three daughters.

As mentioned earlier, Robinson became involved with Peter Murray, son of Peter Murray the tinsmith of Beaverton, in 1867. After purchasing Robinson's *Orillia Expositor,* Murray sold to Dr. William Ramsay in

[8] Lindsay Library, Introduction to microfilm of Canadian Post, 1879-1883.
[9] Ibid., 1864-1866.
[10] Lindsay Library, *Canadian Post,* Fri. Nov. 18, 1864.
[11] Orillia Library, Introduction to the Orillia Times microfilm Nov. 1905-1907.
[12] Lindsay Library, *Directory-Lindsay, County of Victoria* 1869-70.
[13] Lindsay Library, *Lindsay Daily Post,* June 12, 1923.
[14] Loc. cit.

1869, and moved to Lindsay to found the *Lindsay Expositor*, but it died in infancy.[15] He then gave Beaverton a trial with the *Beaverton Expositor* in 1871.[16] However, shortly thereafter, he went back to Orillia, moving the press of the *Beaverton Expositor* and using the former name — the *Orillia Expositor*.[17] Jefferis(sic) and Company delivered the *Orillia Expositor* to subscribers in Beaverton in 1872. Subscriptions and single copies were obtained at the Beaverton News Depot.[18] The *Expositor* continued to print Beaverton news in 1874 with a circulation in the north riding of Simcoe, Ontario and Victoria and the district of Muskoka.[19] Eventually the paper amalgamated with *Simcoe County Times* and gradually with the *Orillia Times*.[20] By 1879, Murray was still with the *Times* and in 1893 moved to Cleveland, Ohio,[21] accepting a position as manager of the *East End Signal*.[22]

Two brothers from the Omemee area, George Hughes Hale, 1846-1916,[23] and William H. Hale 1848(c.)-1923,[24] published the *Beaverton Packet* in 1867(c.).[25] George as publisher in 1871[26] left Beaverton to join his brother, William, who founded the *Orillia Packet* in November 1870.[27]

Not until January of 1877 did another paper appear in Beaverton. The *Beaverton Bee* was started by James Henderson and William Murray, (possibly a brother to Peter Murray).[28] This press was located at the present site of the Presbyterian Church[29] and lasted only six months.[30] The press was then removed to the Campbell Block in Woodville.[31] The *Canadian Post* of August 10, 1877, reported that "the *Beaverton Bee* has been removed to Woodville. Its valedictory in the last issue was hard on the Beaverton people and they feel indignant. We wish the *Bee* greater success in its new departure." The *Bee* thus became the *Woodville*

[15] Kirkconnell, Watson. *The History of the County of Victoria*, page 133.
[16] Almanac of 1871.
[17] Orillia Library, Introduction to the Orillia Times microfilm 1905-1907.
[18] *Orillia Expositor*, March 20, 1872.
[19] PAO, original newspaper.
[20] Orillia Library, Introduction to the Orillia Times microfilm 1905-07.
[21] Hunter, Andrew *A History of Simcoe County*, 1909, Vol. 1.
[22] PAO, *Beaverton Express*, 1896.
[23] Simcoe County Archives, *Printer & Publisher*, Jan. 1917, The MacLean Publishing Co. Ltd.
[24] *Beaverton Express*, May 17, 1923.
[25] Ibid., May 28, 1897.
[26] Census of Industrial Establishment of Thorah Township.
[27] Orillia Library, Introduction to the Orillia Times microfilm.
[28] Beers, op. cit. Page 14.
[29] Beaverton Library, *Tweedsmuir History*.
[30] Beers, op. cit. Page 14.
[31] *Beaverton Express*, Sept. 1926.

JOSEPH J. CAVE
1900 (c.)
courtesy, Mrs. Maureen Meagher, granddaughter.

Advocate under James Henderson and Joseph J. Cave.[32] However, this partnership dissolved around the middle of 1880. In February 1882, Cave published the first *Beaverton Express,* distributing through an office in McKinnon's store, though printed in Woodville.[33] Later the *Beaverton Express* was printed in the Orange Hall, previously called Robinson's Hall,[34] a three storey frame building on the same site as the present *Beaverton Express* office on Victoria Avenue.[35] With the issue of February 7, 1957, the *Beaverton Express* celebrated its seventy-fifth Anniversary "during which time it has always been carried on by its first owner and proprietor and his descendants, the late Joesph J. Cave. It is the only business in Beaverton which has survived that long period of time in the business world in Beaverton, under the same family ownership . . ."

[32] Kirkconnell, op. cit., Page 41.
[33] *Beaverton Express,* Feb. 15, 1884.
[34] Ibid., Dec. 1868.
[35] Ibid., Feb. 7, 1957.

BEAVERTON EXPRESS Printing Office
1900 (c.)
courtesy, Mrs. Maureen Meagher

In August 1894,[36] a disastrous fire started in the James Smith Bakery just across the lane, where Mr. & Mrs. Frank Rowe's home now stands. The entire corner was completely destroyed: the Bakery, the Express office and a log house on the west side of the printing office, where Ann Gordon the first white girl in Beaverton was born. The forms for the *Express* were almost ready for press when the fire started and were hurriedly locked up and passed out the window from the second storey, and taken to Orillia where the edition was printed, thus preventing any interruption in publication. Temporary quarters were set up in a house where Briars Dairy store house formerly stood.[37]

As well as serving Beaverton, Cave also published the following papers: the *Woodville Advocate* founded in 1877; the *Mara Monitor;* the *Cannington Echo,* founded in 1896; the *Sunderland Mirror;* the *Gazette;*

[36] Ibid., Sept. 21, 1894.
[37] Ibid., Feb. 7, 1957.

"Farquhar McRae's mare, Mayflower, won the free-for-all at Hastings, also the open trot at Fenelon Falls last week."

Beaverton Express, February 10, 1888.

The Express this week for the first time was printed by the magic power of electricity. Our three presses are run by "harnessed lightning". . .

Woodville Advocate May 22, 1896.

Report reaches us that one evening last week a person who should be behind bars just now, stood in the alleyway between the stores of Messrs. Morrison and Westcott making indecent suggestions to every female who passed besides making indecent exposure of his person. The constable should make it his business to enquire into this matter and if possible bring the scoundrel to justice. We would also again suggest that he make those who nightly perch themselves upon both sides of the footway of the bridge move on. It is an annoyance to have to run the gauntlet of the not too refined witticisms of these fellows which the public should not be asked to tolerate.

Beaverton Express May 31, 1896.

and from 1894-1896 the *Ontario and West Victoria Gazette,* a monthly paper devoted to the interests of the home and family.

For upwards of sixty years, Cave had taken a keen and lively interest in all affairs in the County of Ontario. In politics he was of a most independent nature, being at times a strong Liberal, a patron of industry, but mostly a Conservative, and his influence and that of his paper was a deciding factor in many of the stirring elections held in the historic riding of North Ontario.

Cave's independent nature extended beyond his flexible and rational political outlook. He possessed an intellectual honesty that could have cost him many subscribers in any day and age. In Cave's eyes there was no such thing as anonymous scoundrels. Contrary to present day policies, Cave usually printed the name of the offending party. True, this action may be construed as contravening the presumption of innocence, but may have constituted a form of moral crime prevention.

In early years of publication, Cave showed his displeasure with unpaid accounts by publishing a list of those in arrears. The following is "A Black List" as it appeared in the *Woodville Advocate* of Thursday September 15, 1881:

We should be sorry if any names appended are those of men who, from adverse circumstances, have been unable to pay. We do not think however that such is the case as ample time has been given to each party to settle. We shall continue this list until accounts are settled and intend adding others whom we have notified, if not paid before our next. We hope our readers will note the names in this list for their own protection.

Dr. R. Ramsay, Orillia, debt contracted when practising in Beaverton, reputation for paying just debts very bad	$9.25
P.L. Burnet, P.L.S. for printing	$1.00
Beaverton Lacrosse Club of 1879 for Printing Bills	4.00
S.N. Lasher, music teacher dead beat of worst kind, for printing	9.25
Wm. Lee, dead beat, to advertising and subscription	4.00
Wm. Johnson, dead beat, an individual passing for a lawyer to advertising	4.00
R. Pirt, of Argyle, an abusive individual, one of the mean class, who accept a paper for a year and a half and return without paying, to subscription and advertising	3.70

Joseph J. Cave moved his residence to Beaverton in 1885[38] and over the years became a valued citizen. He was involved in municipal politics, and was the first president of the Beaverton Horticultural Society when it was founded in 1922.[39] For some forty-five years he was an active member of the Beaverton Lodge #249 I.O.O.F. of which he was the organizer.[40] In 1909 the library was seeking aid from the Carnegie Institute. Mr. Cave was instrumental in getting a grant of $7,000.[41] He was also active in the town band, which his father had helped to organize and to train. This band presented a very fine dance in the new printing office, after the fire of

> The moonlight excursion under the auspices of the Band on Monday evening was largely attended. The sail to the island was delightful. A pleasant hour was spent dancing in the pavillion to the music of Calignini's famous orchestra.
>
> *Beaverton Express* Aug. 9, 1896.

[38] *Woodville Advocate,* June 12, 1885.
[39] *Beaverton Express,* Aug. 22, 1957.
[40] Ibid., June 23, 1932.
[41] Ibid., 1909.

GORDON V. CAVE
in his World War I uniform
courtesy, Mrs. Maureen Meagher.

"Constable Scott seems determined that the cow by-law shall not be a dead letter in this village and on Saturday impounded several animals found wandering on the streets."

Beaverton Express, May 2, 1901.

The Lock-up accommodated five tramps on Friday night last. All looked very respectable and pleaded scarcity of work as the reason of their necessity. They came from the north in the hope of obtaining work on the Trent Valley Canal.

Beaverton Express March 22, 1896.

1894.[42] The musical talent carried over to the third generation when J.J. Cave's daughter, Miss Irene, became a much loved local music teacher.

Joseph J. Cave married Bridget Murphy and had four sons and three daughters. Two of his sons followed in his footsteps with Harold John editor of the *"Uxbridge Times Journal"* and Gordon Vincent who joined his father's business in 1920 and became editor following the death of his father on June 19, 1932. Gordon continued the business with the help of his brother, Harold, until his death in 1956. Gordon E. Smith of Orillia purchased it in March of 1957.[43]

In 1891, a competitor, the *Beaverton Enterprise* appeared. However, there seems to be little information about when it came and what happened to it. The *Enterprise* advertised itself as being "published every Thursday morning at the office, Iron Block, Simcoe Street. It is devoted to the political, social and moral questions of the day; agricultural and commercial extracts; an epitome of the general and local news of the week together with carefully selected miscellany. J.J. Macartney, Editor and Publisher."[44]

Gordon Smith carried on the tradition established by Cave and his sons. At the Ontario Weekly Newspaper Convention of 1960 it was named as one of the award winning papers.[45] Glenn Stewart, a Beaverton native, having apprenticed under Cave was appointed manager of the *Beaverton Express* in late 1961.[46] The paper was sold in March 1962 to Harry Stemp and William Keyzers of Uxbridge.[47] One of their columnists was the popular Alfred Brodie of Beaverton.[48] In May 1963 the paper was taken over by R. James Wallace of Seaforth. It was staffed by his wife Beulah and brothers-in-law, Carl and Eldon Dennis. Mr. Wallace remarked in his edition of May 9, 1963, ". . . that Beaverton's hearty welcome with a friendly smile, was a deciding factor in making a decision to locate here." In November 1964 the sale of the *Cannington Gleanor* to Wallace, was announced, with Mrs. Margaret (Roberts) Shier as editor.[49] On March 1, 1976 the *Beaverton Express* was sold to Harry Stemp (editor), Bill Keyzers, John Lee (publisher) and Loretta Addison. The *Beaverton Express* is now published in a chain of six other weekly tabloids.

[42] Ritchie, op. cit. Page 71.
[43] *Beaverton Express,* Mar. 1, 1962.
[44] PAO, #12—2, original copy.
[45] *Beaverton Express,* Feb. 11, 1960.
[46] Ibid., Oct. 19, 1961.
[47] Ibid., Mar. 1, 1962.
[48] Ibid., July 26, 1962.
[49] Lambert, I., *Call Them Blessed.*

THE LAKE SIMCOE MONSTER.

Over the years the Lake Simcoe "sea monster" has been seen by Beavertonians on many different occasions "in all its horror-striking reality."

The Nov. 3rd 1881 edition of the Beaverton Express states: "The Lake Simcoe sea-monster has again been seen; this time he is described as being about thirty feet in length, with long fish-shaped tail and four fins or arms with claws, those in front being long and powerful, while the two hind ones were about the length of a man's arm. The head was sharp and pointed, with large prominent eyes placed high up in the forehead like a cow's, and an immense gaping mouth."

This dreadful apparition was again seen in July of 1906 when, according to the Beaverton Express "two Beaverton ladies of unimpeached veracity" while canoeing on the lake, "saw a long serpent-like body making its way between Georgina and Thorah Island."

With such worthy witnesses, who could doubt the existence of such an awe-inspiring creature!

The Express does not often "blow its own horn" but we confess to a feeling of pride in the fact that we have lost but four subscribers from our list of 1895 . . .

Beaverton Express Mar. 13, 1896.

Our village woollen mill is doing some very fine work at present in the manufacture of blankets which for beauty of finish we do not think can be beaten anywhere.

Beaverton Express July 26, 1896.

The Advocate appeared last week printed on orange paper in deference to being published on July 12.

Beaverton Express July 19, 1896.

Vital Statistics for the village of Beaverton for the year 1895: Births 20, Marriages 10, Deaths 19. For Thorah: Births 36, Marriages 4, Deaths 18.

Beaverton Express Jan. 24, 1896.

Chapter 17

CONCERNS FOR HEALTH

During the early years of Beaverton the family doctor was a key figure in the community. Whenever an emergency or a severe illness occurred, the doctor was summoned. No doubt he would react as this Woodville doctor who advertised in the Beaverton Express:

"C.C. Grant. M.D.
Physician, Surgeon and Accoucheur
Responds to calls night or day
Town or country."

As well, the Beaverton doctors would respond to calls from the residents of Thorah Island.

With his essential black bag the doctor was a familiar figure travelling to his calls on foot or in a buggy or Model T car. Frequently he would have a driver for his vehicle in order that he would be able to catch up on his sleep between house calls.

Upon arrival at the patient's home he would greet each member of the waiting family, warm his hands at the stove and then go in to see his patient. Such behaviour reinforced his position as a trusted friend. This strong bond between the doctor and the family was in evidence as the doctor regularly attended funeral services of his former patients.

The broad concerns of the doctors were reflected in their involvment in community affairs. Both Dr. James Galloway and Dr. J. Masson Smith found time to be members of the Beaverton School Board. In fact, Dr. Galloway served as Secretary of the School Board for thirty-five years. An impressive record!

Long service records were built up by Dr. Andrew Grant and Dr. J. Masson Smith as Medical Health Officers for Beaverton. Despite the token salary, of $1.50 for each meeting,[1] Dr. Andrew Grant was Medical Health Officer from 1889 until his death in 1934. His successor was Dr. J. Masson Smith who acted as Medical Health Officer for a period of nineteen years.

The list of doctors who have served Beaverton is long. One of the earliest records was mention of a W.R. Cluness, doctor in the Assessment Roll for 1859. Later, business cards in the *Expositor* (Orillia) of 1875

[1] Beaverton Board of Health Minutes. Feb. 4, 1895.

advertised two doctors practising in Beaverton, Dr. Alex McKay and Dr. J.E. White. The names of other doctors appear in the next decade in assessment rolls and newspaper records. These include Dr. R.C. Fair, Dr. Peter Davison, Dr. W.H. Johnson, Dr. Kidd, Dr. Richard Ough, Dr. Alex Robinson and Dr. Ramsay.

Dr. Andrew Grant, who was born in Eldon, established his practice in Beaverton in 1878. He served the community well, both in his private practice and in his work as Medical Health Officer. On his retirement, Dr. Grant's practice was taken over by Dr. G.W. Ogilvie Dowsley, who also served as coroner.

Another well known doctor was Dr. James Galloway. He was born in Thorah Township, son of William and Ann Galloway. During his study at the University of Toronto he was a silver medallist. He set up practice in Beaverton in 1887.

Dr. J. Masson Smith, who was born in Cannington, came to Beaverton in 1909, planning to spend only a period of five years in the village. Instead, he spent forty-three years in practice in Beaverton, retiring in 1953. His practice was then taken over by a young doctor from Hamilton, Dr. Harold D. Ames, who has continued with his predecessors' long tradition of service.

The badge of the early doctor was a little black bag which he carried on his calls. From the mysterious interior of the bag would come instruments for operations; drugs for relief of pain; bandages, dressings and sutures for wounds and the inevitable stethoscope for "listening in" to the chest.

Although the doctor was usually a lone operator, on occasion he was asked to assist a colleague. Such an event was recorded in the Beaverton Express of April 15, 1880: "On the 6th instant, Dr. McKay of Woodville assisted by Dr. Clark and Dr. McKay of Beaverton removed from Mrs. McDonald of Kirkfield a tumour weighing about thirty pounds. The patient who is sixty years of age and suffering for the last year, is making a rapid recovery."

Maternity cases were seldom sent to hospital. When the doctor was called to a home confinement he was usually assisted by an experienced practical nurse. Such a person was Miss Eliza Shorter, aunt of Cephas Doherty. It has been said that in later years, Miss Shorter from her long experience in maternity cases, was accurate in her estimate of the ages of many Beaverton residents.

Hospital services for the local community were very limited. Not until 1897 was the Tuberculosis Sanitorium in Gravenhurst opened. The year 1919 saw the opening of the Soldiers' Memorial Hospital in Orillia. The

"*LINIMENT RECIPE* 1877

2 oz. Imonia
1 oz. oil hemlock
1 oz. Sweet oil
1 oz. terpentine
1 oz. halcihall
1 oz. camphor gum

Mich those togethor in a bottle with a good cork. Drink all the lemmon juce you can when you are aplying the linamont you must be sure and get the lemmons. Aply the linenmont where the pane is."

Clerk was instructed to try and collect from Rev. Mr. Tucker the costs of $2.40 for cremating his horse.

Beaverton Council minutes, August 7, 1897.

On Thursday afternoon of last week, Dr. Bowerman, dentist, extracted 33 teeth. One lady had 23 out at one sitting without making any noise or fuss of any kind. A good local anaesthetic was used hypodermically.

Beaverton Express Sept. 27, 1896.

Toronto hospitals were available if the seriously ill patient could survive the long train ride. In fact an older resident remarked recently, "Only the sickest patients were sent to Toronto. Then, they usually came back in a box."

However, on occasion, the resources of the city were appreciated. The Beaverton Express reported in the issue of June 23, 1893: "A special Council meeting was held to consider a petition to have Mrs. H.B., an aged woman suffering from cancer sent to the Home for Incurables in Toronto." The Council acted on the request and paid for the transportation and maintenance of Mrs. H.B. in the Toronto facility.

Without the benefit of medical insurance, the early residents of Beaverton tried out many home remedies and called the doctor only as a last resort.

The list of home remedies was long and varied. Goose oil and turpentine were considered a cure-all for colds. Coal oil was a standard treatment for head lice. Sulphur and molasses as a spring tonic was a universal favourite. Liniments of various ingredients were effective if applied vigorously to aching areas. Poultices were made from household supplies such as bread and milk, linseed and mustard. Two of the home remedies seemed to be specific to the Beaverton area: Turkish Rhubarb[2] and White's Salve.[3]

Despite the competition from local remedies, Beaverton supported two drug stores as early as 1894. The June 1 issue of the *Beaverton Express* reported: "Mr. Elliott bought drug business of Mr. Smith Thompson" and also "Mr. W. Williamson opens out next week in drug business in A.D. Morrison's old stand."

Apparently a side line of the druggist was the operation of the telephone exchange in his drug store. For the period 1894 to 1898, Mr. A.T. Elliott was the manager of the telephone exchange. He was succeeded by Mr. W. Williamson who operated the exchange from his drug store on Simcoe Street until 1916.

As well as the doctor and the druggist, the dentist played an important professional role in the village.

One of the prominent Beaverton dentists was Dr. C.J. Devine who was in practice here from 1913 until his death in 1950. Not only did he have the reputation as an excellent dentist but he also had a deep concern for the village. In his municipal positions he acted as a councillor, a member of the School Board and as Reeve of the Village. Finally in 1944 he was elected Warden of Ontario County, a unique position for a member of the dental profession.

Beaverton has been well served with conscientious doctors, dentists and druggists. In addition, the municipal representatives have shown a persistent concern for a healthy community, as recorded in the minutes of the Board of Health.

As early as 1850 a relationship between cholera epidemics, polluted water and poor sanitation had been recognized in Ontario. Although Thorah Council introduced, in 1854, a by-law to appoint health officers,[4] there is no record of any appointment at that time.

No doubt it was the Public Health Act of 1884 that provided the impetus for the formation of a Board of Health in Beaverton. This legislation compelled local governments to set up health boards and to enforce health and sanitary regulations. Beaverton responded, and in 1889 Mr. D. McNabb was appointed Chairman of the Board of Health with Messrs. Bruce, Murray and G. Smith Jr. as the other members.

[2] Recipe for Turkish Rhubarb:
diced rhubarb root
pinch of baking soda
and a drop of peppermint
used as a spring tonic

[3] White's Salve — a secret mixture developed by John Edward White.

[4] Thorah Council Minutes. Sept. 30, 1854.

These Premises are

QUARANTINED

on account of

WHOOPING COUGH

All persons except the Attending Physician, Health Officer, Clergyman, Nurse, Sanitary Inspector, or, in case of death, the Undertaker, are forbidden from going to or leaving these premises without the permission of the Medical Officer of Health, and no person shall carry off, or cause to be carried off, any material or article whereby such disease may be conveyed, until after the disease has abated or quarantine has been lifted and the premises, dwelling, clothing and other contents have been rendered free from danger by means of such disinfection and cleansing as the Department of Health may direct, and the Medical Officer of Health shall prescribe the precautions to be taken.

Any person or persons removing this notice without the permission of the Medical Officer of Health shall be liable to a penalty of not less than $5.00 nor more than $50.00, in the discretion of the convicting Magistrate besides costs, which may also be inflicted, pursuant to the provision of the Public Health Act.

BY ORDER OF ______________________ **M.O.H.**

Everyone knew when you had it.

One of the first activities of the Board was to tackle the problem of sanitation. With the appointment of Mr. William Brain in 1890 as Sanitary Inspector, regular reports on the sanitary conditions of the river and the water closets in the village, were received.

By 1893 Mr. Brain in his report to the Board struck an optimistic note: "I think it (i.e. the village) is in a very good sanitary condition. About all the old privy pits are done away with and earth closets is substituted in their place."

He continued with enthusiasm: "I think Beaverton got the best cleaning up this summer that it ever got. There has been only one house where there was any infectious disease — that was Mrs. Birchard's with typhoid fever and that was imported from Toronto."[5]

Pollution of the Beaver River was another of the early concerns of the Board of Health. This was clearly stated in a motion:[6] "that the Inspector was to notify all parties emptying soap suds or other filthy waste into

[5] Annual Report, Beaverton Board of Health 1893.
[6] Beaverton Board of Health Minutes. Sept. 9, 1892.

PAID WITH INTEREST!

Tradition reported that a local doctor on checking over his accounts, discovered an old maternity bill. When he realized the infant had now become a successful business man he presented him with the unpaid bill. Cheerfully the account was settled and the business man reported "I would have paid it at the time but I didn't have the money on me."

"SEND THEM BACK"

The Medical Health Officer reported an outbreak of Scarlet Fever in the Cook family in Orillia and that some of the children had been sent here. The M.H.O. recommended that the Board take prompt steps to have the said children sent back as there would be great danger of the disease breaking out here.

Beaverton Board of Health Minutes Dec. 20, 1900

drains having their outlet in the river or mill dam to cease the same in ten days." Apparently the practice of polluting continued, as in the following years circulars were distributed to householders repeating the warning regarding pollution of drains.

Occasionally the Beaverton Council was reminded about the link between poor drainage and infectious disease. In the Council meeting of March 25, 1889 "a certificate was read from the Medical Health officer showing that the diphtheria in Roger Thompson's family was caused by lack of drainage."[7] Three years later the Board of Health made a strong request to the Council "to complete the drain on John St. immediately, as this Board has reason to believe for want of such drains, the recent outbreak of typhoid fever was caused."[8]

Within a year Mr. Brain, the Sanitary Inspector, observed in his 1893 report:

"The Corporation is doing a great deal of improvements in the way of draining. It will be a great benefit to the village as there was a great many cellars flooded in the spring with surface water." He was concerned about drainage from the hotel yards as both the Ontario Hotel and Hamilton House yards needed attention. "The Board of Health must see that something is done at the back of the Hamilton House stables to prevent the manure and all the soakage from going into the river."[9]

[7] Beaverton Council Minutes. Mar. 25, 1889.
[8] Beaverton Board of Health Minutes. Sept. 9, 1892.
[9] Annual Report Beaverton Board of Health 1893.

As well as checking the drainage of surface water, the Board of Health kept watch over the quality of the drinking water in the Village. Water samples were sent by express to Toronto for analysis as early as 1890. Householders were urged to clean out their wells routinely. Even the hotels were not exempt from inspection. In fact, in 1895, because of poor water tests, the proprietors of both hotels were advised to boil all their drinking water. Regular testing of water from all public wells was continued until 1949. Then, with the installation of the municipal water supply, safe drinking water was available in Beaverton. But as late as 1955, the Home and School Association in correspondence[10] with the Board of Health urged that the use of the common pail and dipper at the Arena be discontinued.

With the growth of the Village, garbage disposal became a problem. In 1893, when the population of Beaverton was about 850, land was leased "for the purpose of depositing the garbage, dead animals and other matter of the village."[11] Mr. Brain, the Sanitary Inspector, mentioned in his report for that year that "there were about 200 loads of rubbish drawn away."[12] Perhaps the citizens were over zealous in their use of the dump. Early in 1894 the Council received a notice from the owner forbidding the Corporation to use his property as a dumping ground. The search for a suitable area ended in 1897 when the Council accepted Mr. Veale's offer of free land for a dumping ground.

But not all garbage reached the municipal dump. In 1926 the Board of Health registered a strong protest over making the Park a dumping ground for garbage. This protest was turned into a by-law in 1928 whereby any dumping on the Park was prohibited.[13]

With the issue of new government regulations, the role of the Sanitary Inspector was gradually enlarged. By 1913 the Inspector was requested to check bake shops, slaughter houses and pig pens "and to notify all parties having manure on their premises to remove the same forthwith."[14] In the following year he was instructed to visit all premises twice a year and report to the Medical Health Officer. Regular inspection became a ritual by 1933. Residents were reminded by a newspaper notice to clean up their premises and to pump out their wells before May 24.

Although the Sanitary Inspector was the visible employee of the Board of Health, it was the Medical Officer of Health who interpreted the many provincial regulations and directed the activities of the local

[10] Beaverton Board of Health Correspondence. Jan. 1955.
[11] Beaverton Municipal Records. May 6, 1893.
[12] Annual Report Beaverton Board of Health. 1893.
[13] Beaverton Board of Health Minutes. July 25, 1928.
[14] Ibid. May 26, 1913.

DR. ANDREW GRANT in reflection.

Board of Health. It was significant that the Board of Health minutes of January 28, 1913, reported "that the chair was taken by the Medical Health Officer (Dr. A. Grant) as provided by the new public health act." His leadership role had been reinforced by provincial legislation.

Two men who acted as secretaries for the Board of Health provided long service records: Major C.A. Paterson for the period 1890-1922 and George R. Yule for the years 1923-1941. They left behind for their successors precise and legible records.

These records show the concern of the Board of Health for the control of communicable disease. At the first recorded meeting of February 19, 1889, printed placards for diphtheria and typhoid were requested. At that time, quarantine of cases and placarding of the houses were the only control measures. On occasion, the meaning of quarantine and isolation had to be underlined. A special meeting of the Board of Health was called August 9, 1897 to discuss a complaint regarding a family quarantined in Thorah for diphtheria. The family members were visiting Beaverton regularly, despite the quarantine. As a result of the meeting, the family promised to stay at home and the nurse on the case was notified to remain with the family. As well, the Township Board was to be notified "to stop anyone where diphtheria is from coming into the village."[15]

When diphtheria occurred in a family in 1900, the directives for quarantine were explicit. Not only was the family to be isolated, but the Sanitary Inspector was to arrange for supplies to be taken to the family. Terminal disinfection of the premises was also discussed and arrangements were made for the family to receive diphtheria antitoxin.

Positive protection against diphtheria came only with the use of diphtheria toxoid. After an intensive publicity campaign, diphtheria immunization was introduced to Beaverton in 1934. In his annual report of that year, Dr. J. Masson Smith stated "approximately 80% of the public school children have been toxoided."[16] No longer was diphtheria a threat to the community.

Another dreaded disease in the early years was smallpox. Vaccination for smallpox had been available generally since 1885. At that time, children had to show proof of a successful vaccination before they entered school.

However, 1901 was a year of concern regarding smallpox. Both the Municipal Council and the Board of Health called special meetings to discuss the smallpox threat. The Reeve issued a proclamation regarding the Vaccination Act and the Council agreed to share costs with the Township of Thorah for a pest house. The Sanitary Inspector was instructed "to place all persons in quarantine who came from any infected district where smallpox is reported to be."[17] Certainly, all possible measures were being taken to prevent an outbreak of smallpox in the Village. Individual protection could be obtained for the fee of twenty-five cents, the charge for vaccination.

Although only occasional cases of smallpox were reported in the records of Beaverton, some concern was expressed in 1927 over the prevalence of smallpox in the Peterborough district.[18] The Board of Health in Beaverton did not respond to Dr. Grant's suggestion for a general vaccination of the community. Apparently, none of the Peterborough contacts travelled to Beaverton, as there was no further mention of the outbreak.

A more recent threat was the poliomyelitis epidemic in 1936. Although Beaverton reported only six cases, the mortality rate was very high, as three of the polio victims died. In order to alleviate the high level of panic

[15] Ibid. Aug. 9, 1897.
[16] Ibid. Dec. 18, 1834.
[17] Ibid. Mar. 10, 1901.
[18] Ibid. June 24, 1927.

DR. J. MASSON SMITH, with the Snowmobile of the 1920's.

in the community, Dr. Smith ordered the schools closed for a two week period. Children were advised to avoid public meetings and the Joint Field Day for Thorah and Beaverton Schools was postponed. A special meeting was called on October, 6, 1936, by the Medical Health Officers of Beaverton and Thorah Township to discuss the outbreak. Dr. Hartman from the Provincial Board of Health advised the meeting "that everything was being done that could possibly be done to prevent the disease from spreading."[19] With the widespread use of the Salk vaccine in 1955, fear of repetition of such an epidemic had been wiped out.

For many years the Board of Health was involved with the quality of milk sold in Beaverton. The results of the milk tests varied, and by 1927 the Sanitary Inspector made regular visits to inspect the premises of the milk vendors. Improvement in test results came slowly. In 1930 the Board threatened to publish all results in the *Beaverton Express.* This threat was never carried out, but inspection was tightened with the licensing of all milk distributors and vendors in 1934. This was followed by a Beaverton by-law which permitted the sale of milk only from tuberculin-tested cows.

All this preoccupation with a safe milk supply ended in 1939 when Beaverton became one of the first communities in Ontario to put into

[19] Ibid. Oct, 6, 1936.

effect the legislation for compulsory pasteurization of milk. Undulant fever and typhoid fever from an infected supply of milk would no longer be a threat.

Throughout all the changes in the history of Beaverton the local Board of Health was supported by a central organization. This Provincial Board of Health provided the legislation, the regulations and the expertise for the enforcement of the legislation. The local group did not operate in isolation but had the support and the consultative services of the central group. In turn the Beaverton Board of Health fed back to Toronto the required information and statistics on the local community. From the reporting of Beaverton and countless other communities in Ontario, the total state of the health of the province was assessed. And so, in viewing the changes in the past hundred years in Beaverton, we were also viewing the changes which took place in philosophy, knowledge and techniques of developing healthy communities throughout the province.

BARTER

A busy housewife on her weekly visit to the village, might trade a basket of eggs for a pound of sugar or a plug of tobacco for her husband's pleasure.

In the "recession" of the early 1890's, people were really not as "hard up" as the meagre church collections at the time would seem to indicate.

The scarcity of dollars was made up by the wholly natural process of barter.

A farmer from the fourth concession might barter a set of winter shoes for his horse at McMillan's Blacksmith Shop. In return, he would leave a sack of wheat at Calder's Mill to be ground into flour. Mrs. Glassford might exchange a winter of piano lessons for a new dress for her spring recital, made at Miss Ellen McInnes' dressmaking shop.

True, Dr. Watson did not receive a large stipend in 45 years ministry at St. Andrew's, but throughout the week, church members were leaving plump chickens, eggs by the dozen, sacks of potatoes, and corn, squash and beans at the back door of the manse.

The barter reached such a point that Dr. Andrew Grant had to reserve a corner in the ice box at Fred King's butcher shop to keep all his chickens, roasts and fish that patients offered in lieu of money for his services.

Reference: Conversation with Miss Mary Fowler.

WHICH ALEX DO YOU MEAN?

In bygone years to speak of Alex McRae in Thorah was to anticipate the question: "Which Alex do you mean?" There were many McRae families and such names as Alexander, Christopher, Duncan, Farquhar, and Donald were common among them. It must be remembered that the traditional system of naming the eldest son after the paternal grandfather, the second after the maternal grandfather, the third after the father, and others after uncles resulted in the predominance of certain given names in families.

In Eden School Section living where his grandson, Paul, resides today was E-e-e-asy Alex, so named because of his manner of speaking. Reeve Alex, who lived farther east of the second line was Thorah's reeve for many years as well as a farmer and auctioneer. Long Alex, tall and slim, was a carpenter, responsible for the building of many Beaverton and Thorah houses, barns, and other structures. Big Alex, sometimes called Red Alex, Proctor Alex, or even Alex By Golly, managed the John Proctor farm for many years. Having lived in London, Ontario, before coming to Thorah, London Alex McRae retired to Beaverton, to reside on Simcoe Street East.

One-fingered Christopher McRae, although a barn framer by trade, was well remembered as a violinist and violin-maker in Beaverton. When Christopher was a small boy, his brother was demonstrating how to chop the head off a turkey. Christopher's right hand was on the chopping block and when his fingers were severed, his little voice was heard to exclaim, "Good God, Farquhar! Look what you've done!"

Christopher-in-the-Swamp lived with his sister, Flora, on a farm just east of the present Beaver Downs Golf Course. Duncan-on-the-Hill lived at lot 10 concession 3 which more recently was the Brailey farm.

The Buidhe (Gaelic meaning yellow or golden to refer to this family's hair colour and pronounced boo'ey) McRaes lived in the first concession at lot 9. John Buidhe McRae settled there about 1848. His son, Phil Buidhe (Finley Joseph) and grandson, Charles, farmed the property in more recent times.

Beavertonians may now send parcels to their friends in China direct at the rate of sixteen cents per pound, cash strictly in advance. The goods will be carried by way of Vancouver.

Beaverton Express Nov. 8, 1896.

Chapter 18

THORAH ISLAND

Thorah Island lies two and a half miles from Beaverton harbour and adds much to the beauty of Lake Simcoe. The Island, which is irregular in shape, is two miles long with an area of eleven hundred and forty acres. Excavations done by Paul Sweetman on the Bristow site at the north end of the Island prove that it was once all Indian fishing camp ground.

Before settlers came to cultivate the land, timber was cut, and cattle from the mainland were pastured. George Proctor, C.H. Davidson and Henry Furniss owned land but didn't reside there. Two salt water sailors, Captain McCulloch and John McLean found their way to the Island, but were not land owners. The latter with his two-masted sailboat hauled limestone to Beaverton.

One of the first families to settle on the island was that of James White. James was the son of the first white male child born in Thorah Township. Today his great-grandsons, James and Sydney White, own valuable lake front property and a handsome brick residence.

John Furniss purchased the adjoining land in 1878 from Mr. Lee who had acquired it from George Proctor, the original owner. Six years later a barn was built, then followed by a brick house. Both were constructed by John McInnis of Beaverton. This land has also remained in the family. Kenneth Davidson, a grandson, is the present owner.

Another pioneering family was that of Thos. Warren Sr. whose property was deeded from the Crown. On a choice site overlooking the Lake, he built a spacious home known as "Thorah House". Cottages have sprung up along the shore, but Ted Warren, a grandson, owns the farm.

The Wm. Warren farm lot is owned and prized by grand-daughters, Isobel Mitchell and Lorraine Westlake. Fogals, Jewels and Emes settled the north shore. A portion of the Emes property is still owned by June Emes. Frank Furniss Jr. owned and farmed the Jewel land for many years. It is now owned by Wm. Smith and J. McFeeters.

Mr. Wm. Woodman was an Englishman who had travelled all over the world in search of a suitable climate for his respiratory ailment. His quest ended on the Island where he spent the rest of his life. He built a fine brick home which is now owned by the Jim Warren family. Woodman's shoal is well known to bass and trout fishermen.

The "Wawanessa" with Captain Tom Warren on deck is seen leaving Thorah Island Harbour.

Courtesy Edward Warren

Thorah House which was built by Thomas Warren Sr. on Thorah Island overlooks Lake Simcoe. It is now owned by Robert Curl of Toronto.

Painted by Mary Hodgson and loaned by Edward Warren.

A beautiful spot such as Thorah Island was not destined to remain a farming community. A group of Toronto men established a campsite there, and in 1892 began what became an annual holiday. Four of the men: Nick Sweetman, Tom Crashley, Jim Corin and Archie Wardell who were married to sisters, soon built cottages on the site. Today their descendants are enjoying this area which is still called "the Camp Ground".

A seven acre Indian Reserve at South Point was sold and subdivided. Mrs. T. McLennan and Duncan Macpherson have lots there. The fourteen acre marine allowance at Middle Point cannot be sold as it is reserved for emergency landings.

Prior to 1903 when the "Belle of Thorah" was built by Thos. Warren Sr., transportation to the mainland in summer was by sailboat. Until recently the Warren family continued to own and operate the ferry service. Captain Tom Jr. safely carried passengers, cargo, and mail for which he was given a contract in 1915. When the "Thorah Belle" became no longer seaworthy, the stern was removed, stood on end, and served as a post office. The "Wawanessa" was his last boat.

Education in the early days presented a problem. Miss Harriet Furniss gave lessons and conducted a Sunday School in her home. In 1921, By-law 296 formed Thorah Island into S.S. No. 7, and allowed Island children to attend Beaverton school.

When an underwater cable brought hydro to the Island in 1952, it became possible to enjoy all modern conveniences.

Snowmobiles and ice fishing have made the Island even more popular in winter than in summer.

One of the newer cottages on the Island is owned by John Furniss' great-grandson, Donald Nicholls and his wife Gwen.

When John Furniss Sr. bought land on Thorah Island, this shanty and corn-crib were the only buildings on a spot of cleared land. Bill (St. Thomas) Smith painted the scene in water colour.

Courtesy Kenneth Davidson

This is one reason why the Beaverton area is even more popular in Winter than in Summer. This trout which is 36 inches long and weighs 20 pounds was caught off Thorah Island in Lake Simcoe.

Chapter 19

FROM FARMS TO RECREATION

The Beaches of the Beaverton area have been used as summer holiday centres and picnic areas as far back as 1884. However, most of the cottage areas evolved after the coming of the Canadian Northern Railway in 1907. The railway was completed in 1909. The water front of the farm properties became useless for agriculture because of the tracks but this land made excellent cottage sites. Many of the farms were land grants made by the Crown, after the Napoleonic Wars.

The Beaches referred to in this article extend from Thorah Beach in the South to the Talbot River in the North. They are Thorah, Maple, Cedarhurst, McLennan, Cedar, Ethel Park, Alsop and lastly Riverside Beach.

William Turner of Cork, Ireland had been Ensign in the Sicilian Regiment of Wellington's army. After arriving in Canada about 1820, he and his wife started out in York (Toronto), went up the Humber River and portaged to Lake Simcoe. It is recorded that they landed at what is now Thorah Beach and built a log cabin.[1] The only inhabitants living near them at that time were friendly Indians. The land was a Crown Patent issued by the Province of Upper Canada under the name of George IV. The Patent was authorized May 1821, recorded July 1825 and was finalized on Dec. 20th, 1827. The Patent bears the signature of John Beverly Robinson, Attorney-General.

The Turner property passed to two daughters, Sophia a spinster, and Elizabeth. Elizabeth later married Robert McTaggart. The property passed on to their son, Robert William McTaggart. In the early 1900's Robert William created Thorah Beach with a plan prepared by Morton M. Gibson, Ontario Land Surveyor. The plan was dated and certified on Nov. 14th, 1921.

Mr. Robert W. McTaggart assumed responsibility for the roads as the Municipality would build only the necessary culverts.

The original log cabin was restored to a summer cottage and was known as "The 1822 Cottage." The logs have now been covered with clapboard. The structure is standing on the same site and is still in use as a dwelling.

[1] Information supplied by Mr. Donald McTaggart.

MISS SOPHIA TURNER was the daughter of Ensign Wm. Turner and one of the first children born in the Township.

The 1822 Cottage-Thorah Beach
WILLIAM TURNER Log Homestead

Mrs. Robt. William McTaggart, the grandmother of Mr. Donald McTaggart laid the cornerstone for the Beaverton-Thorah Town Hall on July 22nd, 1910. The silver trowel used for the ceremony, bears this inscription "Elizabeth Turner McTaggart was born on May 31st, 1827, the first female white child born in Thorah Township". The silver trowel is still a treasured possession of the McTaggart family.

The first house at Maple Beach[2] on this section of the lakeshore was a farm house owned by Mr. Irwin Hamilton. The story is told that in the spring when the Indians were on their way north to fish, Mrs. Hamilton would feed them breakfast and in return they would leave her some fish. The farmhouse burned down and Mr. Hamilton then purchased the red brick farmhouse and property which was later occupied by Mr. Stanley Tindale. Mr. A.L. Sanagan and his partner, a Mr. Richardson, purchased the property along the lake from Mr. Hamilton about 1914 and the cottage colony came into being. Sometime before 1921, Mr. Sanagan bought out Mr. Richardson. By 1921, there were about 25 cottages built almost entirely by Mr. Sanagan. They were selling for about $2000.00 for the lot and cottage. He operated a water system from a spring across the tracks. It was operating until 1981.

In 1921 there was no road connecting Maple Beach with Thorah or Cedarhurst Beaches. These connecting roads were not built until the early 1930's. There was a trail to Thorah Beach with a foot bridge over the creek at the Second Line.

In the late 1920's a complex was built by Mr. Sanagan on the railway side of the road. It consisted of an Inn with 3 cottages on either side of the main building. These cottages were rented on a weekly basis. "Maple Beach Inn" as it was called, lasted only about ten years, as the neighbours objected to the Saturday night dances. The buildings were then moved to vacant lots, added to, and improved. Some are still in use.

Bill Parker, an Indian of pottery fame, built a house on the corner of the 3rd Line and old Highway 48. The house burned down in the late 1950's and he moved to Woodville. There is still an area, on that property, of Indian sweet grass which he planted. It is the grass used in Indian basketry.

The area now known as Cedarhurst Beach[3] was originally a land grant to a Colonel Jones after the Napoleonic Wars. He never saw his approximately 250 acres, as he sold it in Scotland to the three Grant brothers of Bonar Bridge Scotland. The three brothers George, John, and Angus came to Canada in 1846, to their property on the shores of Lake Simcoe.

[2]Ibid., Miss Mary McGill.
[3]Ibid., The Grant family.

Some time after 1877, John entered the coal business in Toronto and George went to Sault Ste. Marie. Angus bought their shares of the property and it was his grandson Angus who named the beach and farm "Cedarhurst".

The property along the shore line was sold in lots for cottages and summer homes. Mr. Grant built and owned a number of these cottages. There is a water system still operating from an artesian well, similar to the one at Maple Beach.

The first cottage on the beach was the small Quigley cottage on the Quigley-Baker property. This cottage is now owned by the Jennings family. The Rev. McKee McLennan had purchased property from Angus Grant north of the 4th Line (Cedarhurst Road) and he in turn sold it off to a group of businessmen connected with the railway. After the railway went through in 1907 the lake shore lots were sold to members of the above group, and others. The new owners included A.J. Mitchell, Gerald Ruell, Messrs. Gibson, Waugh, Waddington, and Senator Nichols. The A.J. Mitchell cottage was built in 1908 and is now owned by Dr. Arthur Squires. Mr. Ruell's home is now occupied by Mrs. James Sissons.

In the early days of the railway, there were flag stations at the various beaches. The cottagers commuted between Toronto and the lake in this manner. The flag stations were no longer used after the 1940's.

An unusual situation occurs at Cedarhurst Beach, in that a few cottages south of the 4th Line (Cedarhurst Road) own the water rights.

In 1911 there were 5 cottages that were served by a private telephone system. This system was purchased by the Bell Telephone in 1916.

The first rural mail delivery in this part of Ontario was established in 1913 through the efforts of Mr. Angus Grant.

In one of the editions of the 1920 *Beaverton Express* it was suggested that the townfolk make a trip out to view the beautiful gardens at Cedarhurst Beach.

Originally the McLennan Beach[4] property extended from the 4th Concession (Cedarhurst Road) to the 5th Concession north of the ravine and east to the old 48 highway (Durham Rd. 23). To the south it bordered the Grant property and to the north it extended to the Ross property (now Lightfoot). The original owner was Mr. Wm. MacRae. The farm was later purchased by Mr. Herbert Furniss in 1899. In 1907 the Rev. J. McKee McLennan bought the farm from Mrs. Herbert Furniss and called it "Lakecroft". Mrs. McLennan was one of the founders of the W.I. in 1913. Part of the farm was given to the Anglican Church and

[4] Ibid., Mrs. Wilda McLennan and Mr. Harry Furniss.

MAPLE BEACH INN — Maple Beach. This complex was also known as THE COURT.

Courtesy Calvin Calder

DR. ANDREW GRANT, family and friends in front of his cottage at ETHEL PARK.

Courtesy Margaret E. Baillie

Moorelands Camp was opened on June 20th 1918 by Bishop Sweeney.[5] The Camp is no longer in operation here.

After the First World War, a son of Rev. McLennan, Dr. Trevor McLennan, convinced his father to subdivide the lake property into 100 foot lots. Dr. Trevor McLennan was in practice in Sunderland, in partnership with Dr. Arthur Berry. Thus most of the lots were sold to people from the Sunderland-Uxbridge areas. There was just a verbal agreement to keep the lots at 100 feet; consequently many have since been divided into 50 foot lots.

Dr. Arthur Berry still has his cottage on McLennan Beach and "Lakecroft" is now owned by Mrs. R.L. Brown.

According to the *Ontario Atlas 1877*, the original land owners in the Cedar Beach area were Wm. McCrae, A. Murray, Joseph Furniss, and H. Hodgson. The McCraes or McRaes were the holders of the greatest acreage on this part of the lake shore. The house now owned by Mr. C.K. Bastien, the oldest on the Beach, was once the home of Mr. and Mrs. Gordon McRae. The Gordon McRaes were great grandparents of Mr. Lorne McRae who at present resides on Cedar Beach. Mr. McRae's great-great-grandmother died without a will and so the land was split between her nine children. When Mr. McRae's great-grandmother died with no will the land was again split amongst the children and so the later generations received only very small plots.[6]

Main Street ran west out of the village to the lake. When the road turned south along the water, it became known as Cedar Beach Road. Due to the erosion caused by the water and ice, the township needed a new road allowance. The McRae family gave permission to go through their property but no permission was granted by the Hall-Batt families; hence the jogs in the road around what was the Hall Estate. With the new road completed, the land between the road and the lake made ideal cottage lots.

The Halls lived in the log and brick house set back off the present Parklawn Boulevard. Mrs. Batt, their daughter, lived in the brick house by the lake, which became part of the Music Camp. There were cottages to rent on the Hall Estate.

The log house, now owned by Bishop Parke-Taylor, was originally the farm home of Mr. Walter Mitchell and his family. It was situated at the end of the Nine Mile Road and was built well before 1890. It was moved intact over the fields, during the winter to its present location on Cedar Beach. It is unusual to move a log house by that method rather

[5] *Beaverton Express* June 20, 1918.
[6] Information supplied by Mr. Lorne McRae.

BARBER'S GROVE

Just to the south of Ethel Park, between Victoria Avenue and the harbour, was a picnic area known as Barber's Grove. Before 1888 Mr. and Mrs. Leonard Barber and their seven sons lived in a house in the midst of this park-like setting. In July 1884, about 1000 people used the picnic facilities in one week. Mr. Barber had a boat rental service. He later sold the property to Mr. Alex Hamilton and in April 1897 this site was purchased by Messrs. Veale and Way. A summer hotel "Victoria Park" was built adjacent to the harbour and facing the lake. The hotel was operated by Mr. and Mrs. George Veale. They also had a boat rental service and also built bathing houses. This activity started the trend towards summer cottages being built along Ethel Park.

than dismantling it log by log.

In 1884, the *Woodville Advocate* advertised for people to build summer cottages on the lots for sale at Cedar Beach. In the early 1900's it was reported that summer residents had arrived. Mr. James Ritchie built one of the first cottages, soon followed by Messrs. Walter Beauchamp, Wm. Williamson and J.R. Robinson.

Ethel Park was originally part of the farm of Mr. C.H. Davidson and was purchased by Mr. Alex Hamilton and called Ethel Park after one of his daughters. This community extends from Victoria Ave. to White's Creek and is one of the oldest summer settlements in the Beaverton area. The north end of Ethel Park, next to White's Creek was owned by the Misses Davidson. They sold it in 1945 to Mr. Andrew Dobson. Cabins were built and they were known as the "Beaver Bungalows."

In 1887 Mr. A.D. Morrison built a cottage and called it "Jubilee". Dr. Andrew Grant also had a cottage on the east side of Morrison Ave. and it was named "Sunlight Cottage". Two other early cottages in this area were the How and Edwards summer homes.

On June 3rd, 1915, a petition was signed by 26 residents asking that electric power be supplied for 263 lights for the summer months. Thorah Council turned this matter over to the Beaverton Council and the installation was completed for the sum of $518.43. This Community now has Town facilities and the main street is called Morrison Avenue.

Alsop Beach[7] begins at White's Creek at the north end of Ethel Park and extends across 100 acres. It was settled in 1822 by John Edward White. John's son James was the first male white child born in the township. The White family owned the property until 1870 when it was pur-

[7] Ibid., Misses Margaret and Barbara Alsop.

VICTORIA PARK HOTEL, a summer tourist hotel, built by George Veale in 1898 where Victoria Ave. meets Lake Simcoe. This hotel catered mostly to vacationers from Toronto. In conjunction with the hotel was a baseball diamond, a picnic grove and a dance pavilion. It was destroyed by fire in 1928.

chased by Mr. John Proctor.[8] He farmed it until it was bought by John and Catharine Alsop in 1904.

In 1948, the Alsop family sold a portion of the farm, between the railway tracks and the lake to Messrs. Bratty and Sartori. They had it surveyed and developed into lots. Soon after this, 21 cottages were built and at the present time there are several families that have permanent homes on Alsop Beach.

In years past, it was thought that the Riverside Beach area,[9] formed by the wash of gravel and shells from the Talbot River, was of no value. Originally traffic across the Talbot River was by a floating bridge, which was held to the shore by chains. It often came adrift and after a storm might be found out in the lake. The second bridge, built on piles, was of a more permanent nature. The third bridge was called the Champlain Bridge, as the river was part of Champlain's route in 1615 from Georgian Bay to Lake Ontario.

In 1907, Mr. A.R. Warren purchased three acres, more or less, from A. and D. Holmes, as a fishing spot. With the help of a firm of Orillia engineers — Cavana and Watson — and with a great deal of fill, he was able to gain more than 3 acres of property. This low-lying, swampy area

[8] Beers, J.H. & Co. *Historical Atlas of the County of Ontario, 1877.*

[9] Information from Gamebridge Tweedsmuir History — article written by Mr. J.B. Warren and from Mr. Harry Furniss.

was noted for its many huge bull frogs and tree stumps. In 1909, the first cottage was built and many more sprang up in the ensuing years. In 1910, Mr. and Mrs. Warren moved from Toronto to a permanent home on Riverside Beach. He had a small store which he called the "Royal York". The Warrens also built a dance pavilion and it was operated until Mrs. Warren's health failed. Mr. Warren then established a boat service which he ran for many years. The remains of his first dock can still be seen upstream from the bridge.

Mr. Alex Cameron operated a saw mill in this area around 1890.

With the coming of the railway, a swing bridge was built over the Trent Canal. In the summer time, when the train had to stop for the swing bridge, the Riverside Beach cottagers used this as a jumping-off spot to get to their cottages. The train was the major means of transportation to this area until the introduction of the automobile.

Thorah Centennial Park is situated at the west end of Concession 9, just west of the railway. This was formerly known as "Farm Forum" Park. The Farm Forum group rented it from the railway for $5.00 per year. The purpose was to have a good public beach for the residents of Thorah. Ratepayers were given stickers for their cars. The Council installed a culvert for access to the beach. In 1951, there was a covered building or shed, a picnic area, a camping site and a location for the launching of boats. In 1965, Council bought the land from the railway. In 1967, it was renamed "Thorah Centennial Park." There is no longer a camping area or boat launching facilities, but a caretaker looks after the grounds.

There is a cairn in the park with the following inscriptions; — West Face — "This Park founded by the Gamebridge Farm Forum in 1951." North Face; —

"1867-1967

Centennial of Confederation
Township of Thorah
Centennial Park
Developed by the Township of Thorah
In permanent Commemoration of the Centennial of the Confederation of Canada in 1967.
Developed and made possible through the co-operation of The Province of Ontario and the Government of Canada."

These beaches have added greatly to the prosperity and life of the community.

THE GAMEBRIDGE INN in 1926. Built in 1863, it was formerly known as the Golden Oak Hotel. Today, Gamebridge is a pleasant community with an inn, store, Women's Institute hall, Presbyterian Church, Kenco Manufacturing Ltd. and a number of homes. In the past a creamery, blacksmith shop, two railway stations, as many as three stores operating at one time, and a garage were found in this small hamlet on the Talbot River.*

* Information from the *Tweedsmuir History*, Gamebridge Women's Institute.

A game of Quoits will be played here on Friday next, the 13 inst. at 3 p.m. between Mr. A. Muir of this place, Champion Quoit player of the Dominion, and Mr. G. Sheppard of Scarborough, another Champion.

Beaverton Express, September 12, 1878.

Chapter 20

THE CHAMPION CHECKERS

The game of Lacrosse originated with the North American Indians, and became so popular throughout the country that a Canadian Lacrosse Association was formed in 1887. It was a kind of field hockey played with a hard rubber ball and a long handled racket called a crosse. On one end was a taut raw-hide mesh bag which made real skill necessary in order to trap a ball.

Although the game had been played in Beaverton for a few years, the Club was reorganized on March 26, 1883, with: President, Duncan McKenzie; Captain, John McLean; Secretary, Ken Davidson; Treasurer, Peter McMillan.

Many a hard fought game was played in Barber's Grove near where the marina is now located, and in the old Osborne Street Fair Grounds. Many there were who bore the scars to prove it. On one occasion when the players and spectators differed with Referee Waghorn's decision, he made the wise choice and made a hasty exit from town.

Members of the championship team of the Checker Lacrosse Club,
Back row left to right: W.M. Cameron, H. McKinnon, K. Davidson, W. Cameron, D. Calder, P. McMillan, W.J. Dunn
Centre: A.M. Cameron, Manager, T.J. Overend, President
From row left to right: H. Cameron, A. West, D. McNabb, O.E. Rainey, C.B. McKinnon, B. Coombe

In spite of the game being very rough, the Checkers whose colours were red and white, survived to bring much honour to Beaverton when they became Intermediate Champions of Ontario in 1899. Year after year they fielded teams that were more than a match for much larger towns. Some of the trophies they won can be seen in the Beaverton Public Library today.

In the days before automobiles, the team travelled by train and steamboat. A treasured collection of badges remains to tell against whom some of the games were played such as: Independent Club Woodville 1883, Young Club Richmond Hill and St. Thomas 1884, Tolocoo Club Newmarket and Albion Toronto 1885, London East 1885, Seaforth Beavers 1886, Kincardine and Norwood 1888.

Members of the championship team were: Billie Cameron, Hector McKinnon, Ken Davidson, Harry Cameron, Ab West, Billie Dunn, Bennie Combe, Peter McMillan, Dan Calder, Bailey McKinnon, D. McNabb, William Cameron, Ernie Rainey, Angus Cameron, Manager, and T.J. Overend, President.

It is quite possible the Checkers' yell inspired them to many of their victories:

"Red and white, red and white,
Red and white is our delight.
Hobble, gobble, razzle, dazzle,
Sis cum bah!
The Checkers, the Checkers,
Rah! Rah! Rah!

"According to the gazetteer of the world at the public school, there are seven places by the name of Beaverton on this continent," stated the Beaverton Express of July 22, 1887.

In 1876, Donald G. Ross and his wife, Rebecca Fraser, moved to Michigan taking the name Beaverton to that state. Ross, along with his parents, George Ross and Margaret Gunn, as well as his brothers and sisters had arrived in Thorah in 1837. He planned and built the drill shed which was originally situated on the old fair grounds but was later removed to the present grounds. In Michigan, he set up a lumbering business.

CURLING

Curling is not a recent sport. Beaverton has had its devotees for many years. The Orillia Times of November 3, 1898 reported:

> *"Work has commenced on the curling rink and the building when completed will be one of the most modern and best equipped in the province. The 'roarin game' has caught on here and the club will start with a membership of between thirty and forty players."*

View shows back of the TOWN HALL and LIBRARY taken from the corner of Osborne and John Streets. This was the location of the IRON BLOCK, bounded by Osborne, John and Simcoe Streets.

The Iron Block

John St.

Simcoe St.

The Hamilton Iron Block, so called because of the shape of the lot, was located where present Town Hall & Library now stand. It was made up of many businesses and shops, with some living quarters above.

Osborne St.

The following are some of the establishments that were situated in the Iron Block over the years.

1887 - Photographic Studio - owned by Mr. W.A. Madill - opened Jan. 17th 1887
1887 - Harness - Making - G.H. Williamson
1887 - Hairdressing & Barber Shop - C.A. Cole
1887 - Wagon Shop - Farm Implements - John Cameron
1888 - G.T. Chapman's Business
1888 - Shoemaker - Lachlan McDonald
1888 - Bootery - Frank Lapp - Sam Weeks
1891 - Beaverton Enterprise - J. McCartney
1895 - Blacksmith Shop - James Birchard
1895 - Livery Stable
Tin Shop - Andrew Murray
Shoe Shop - Gilbert McEwen
Tailoring Establishment - Hector Logan
Tailoring Establishment - Williamson

On March 22, 1895 a defective chimney in Mrs. Macdonald's part of the block caught fire. The large building owned by John Cameron and Duncan McRae's rough cast one succumbed to the flames. Only the blacksmith shop and the livery stable were saved.

Chapter 21

OUT OF THE NINETEENTH INTO THE TWENTIETH CENTURY

The two decades from 1890 to 1910 characterized for Beaverton and Thorah a period of transition. Not only was this era a time of saying "good-bye" to the Nineteenth Century and a hearty "hello" to the Twentieth, and, of course, seeing the Victorian age end and a new monarch ascend the British throne, it was a period when the old ways were giving way to the new advances made in communication, transportation, and many other areas of life. Of course, many of the changes experienced in those twenty or so years were being felt in communities throughout this province and beyond.

Surely no earlier age had seen such rapid developments in science and communications. In 1890 one could place a long-distance telephone call from Beaverton; however, he could make no local calls for it would be three more years before local service was put into operation.[1] Before that time, of course, Beavertonians had the benefit of telegraph service, the Dominion Telegraph Company setting up that system as early as 1872.[2] The marvels of electricity would be demonstrated during the next few years and the age of the automobile would begin.

After 1884, the year of Beaverton's incorporation, this village's population continued to increase, yet Thorah's numbers declined for the next fifty years. Mechanization on the farm cut down the number of hands required. The Canadian West was opening up and many young men, farm boys and town boys alike, hopped onto the train to seek their fortunes in Assiniboia and farther west.

Taking Thorah names to Manitoba were: William Turner Jr. and his family and William McRae to Griswold; James Galloway, William Suter and his family, James, John, and William McHattie to Napinka; James Ritchie and his son Norman as well as the Dougal Gillespie family to the Swan River district; John McRae to Roland; and John Adamson to Michie. Robert Donnell died in 1902 at Moose Jaw. His brother

[1] *Beaverton Express*, May 21, 1969.
[2] Mary H. Ritchie, *A Township on the Lake*, Beaverton, 1952, p. 50.

The north side of Simcoe Street taken from near the MILL 1908 (c.). At the left edge stands the "NEW PROCTOR BLOCK." Next right is Percy Byrne's Jewellery store which had previously housed Harry Waller's shoe shop and Henry Westcott's Hardware (1895c.-1900c.) Next is the store purchased by W.D. Rodman in 1902.

Referred to as the "NEW DAVIDSON BLOCK" the red brick building later housed Dobson & Carey's enterprise. Next is the Cameron & Cameron Hardware. This firm, founded in 1895, succeeded James Cameron's Hardware business. Next east is the F.S. King butcher shop.

James was on the mission field in Alberta. Charles Lawrence, Rod Logan, Charles Young, and Bob Abbie made their way to British Columbia while Henry Jude took up residence in Seattle.[3] These are but a few of the many Thorah citizens who settled in the western regions of Canada and the United States.

In Thorah the farm economy was gradually changing from grain to livestock. One result of this change was increased production of wool. The Ellis woollen mill had been in operation for many years but Charles T. Young had seen that there was business for another woollen establishment. His building, formerly a shoe shop which was moved across the river in December of 1881,[4] stood by the north side of the bridge on Mara Street. For a short time James Ritchie operated this mill,[5] but Young

[3] *Beaverton Express*, various issues.
[4] *Beaverton Express*, December 29, 1881.
[5] Assessment Roll, Beaverton, 1891; *Beaverton Express*, May 25, 1894.

OSBORNE STREET, circa 1910. On the extreme left is Wm. McHattie's former blacksmith shop with his house, the "split-the-wind" adjacent. On the extreme right is Snelgrove's Planing Mill with the steeple of the Knox Church showing behind.

repurchased it in 1896 and returned to Beaverton to carry on for several more years.

The year 1882 brought to Beaverton a man who leased the old Ellis mill[6] and provided some strong competition for Young. Alexander Dobson would play a very active part in the business of the community for the next thirty years or so. Born in Innerleithen, Scotland, Dobson came to Canada with his parents in 1873, settling a little later at Cannington where his family operated a woollen mill.[7] With new machinery the North Ontario Woollen Mill was operated by Dobson until 1885.

In that year Alexander Dobson and Archibald Campbell leased the flour and grist mill which John Proctor had built of brick in 1873.[8] The following year they purchased the mill, refitting it in 1887 with new machinery and the flour dressing system which Dobson had patented.[9] The partnership dissolved in 1893 with Campbell purchasing the mill at Woodville and Dobson retaining the Beaverton operation.[10]

In 1889 the Beaverton Council passed a motion that two lamps be placed on each end of the bridge. Someone would be hired to light and attend them. Alex Dobson appeared before Council in 1894 with the idea of lighting the streets by the incandescent system. Soon poles and lamps were being put up on the main streets. During the next few years different groups of citizens petitioned Council for the placement of lamps on their

[6] *Beaverton Express*, Christmas issue, 1882.
[7] *Cannington Gleaner*, October 11, 1978, story of Dobson family.
[8] *Beaverton Express*, August 26, 1887.
[9] Loc. cit.
[10] Ibid. June 9, 1893.

SIMCOE STREET, BEAVERTON, looking east, about 1908.

At the left foreground is William Williamson's Drug Store. This is now Millar's Mens Wear and Shoe Store. Note the telephone wires crossing the street and entering the drug store. The switch board was at the rear of the store. Next, in what is now the Stedman's Store, is seen Dugald A. Campbell's Furniture Store. Some examples of his stock can be seen in front of the store. Where the drug store now stands, was L.J. Cameron's Store, which at the time of this picture was about 15 years old. It was later destroyed by fire.

Alexandria Hall and the Hamilton Hotel stood then much as they do now. Note the change in the balcony. Behind the balcony stands a small building possibly constructed by D.A. Cole as a barber shop in 1887. He built on the townhall lot in return for ringing the town bell for seven years. Above the small building, the large chimneys of the old Proctor Block can be seen. On the south side of the street is Williamson's brick harness shop which was built about 1904. At the corner of Simcoe and Osborne is the Ontario House Hotel. East across Osborne is a livery stable. St. Andrew's Church stands in the background.

Photo courtesy of Bill & Win Stabback

respective streets as well as asking for longer hours of illumination.[11]

F.S. King had a two-horse-power motor installed to drive a large sausage machine in his butcher shop in 1895. The current was supplied by electric light dynamos; Alex Dobson did the wiring.[12]

In 1896 Dobson placed in his grist mill an engine and boiler to develop power not only to drive the mill but also to supply electricity to spare.[13]

The Misses Jardine, two sisters who for many years were a familiar sight delivering milk in the Village, were driving along the street when their horse caught sight of this strange-looking apparatus lying by the mill ready for installation. Frightened, the creature took off, turned into the lane beside the Hamilton House and headed straightaway to a shed which backed the river. Crashing right through this building, the badly-wounded animal drowned in the Beaver River.

Another of Dobson's proposals was to be of great benefit to the downtown section. He offered to allow the businessmen to attach 250 feet of hose to his large mill pumps to be used in case of fire.[14]

Just in time for Christmas of 1902 L.J. Cameron, a merchant selling boots and shoes where the present drug store is found, had an acetylene gas plant installed "with the result that his store is most brilliantly

[11] Beaverton Council Minutes.
[12] *Beaverton Express*, October 4, 1895.
[13] *Cannington Echo*, May 8, 1896.
[14] *Beaverton Express*, March 13, 1896.

ANNIE JARDINE and the milk delivery wagon, a familiar sight on Beaverton streets for many years.

lighted."[15] Knox Church was also fitted with an acetylene generator. However, electricity would be the illuminant of the future.

In fact, in 1901 the Beaverton Council and Dobson entered into an agreement for the construction of an electric street railway in the Village.[16] However, this project did not materialize. Nevertheless, at that time, Dobson was given the contract to light the streets for three years and his name continued to be almost synonymous with electricity in Beaverton for the next decade.

Sir Adam Beck was on hand at the Beaverton Fair in September of 1914. He was to push the button which would turn on the electricity. However, when the moment came, the esteemed gentleman decided that the honour should be given to the Reeve, Mr. Harry S. Cameron, who had played such an important role in bringing electricity generated at Wasdell's Falls to Beaverton.[17]

The Fair of that year featured an exhibition of mechanical utilities available to users of electricity. Electric meters were being installed throughout the village during the fall season and the hydro was actually turned on November 1 of 1914.[18] The tragic death of a young lineman, Clarence McKenzie, killed when he came in contact with a high tension live wire on a pole at the corner of Mara and Victoria streets,[19] surely dampened the spirits for a time of those looking forward to hydro-electric power.

In those early years the electricity was turned off at a certain hour

[15] Ibid. December 25, 1902.
[16] Ibid. April 11, 1901.
[17] Recollections of Mr. Harry Furniss.
[18] *Beaverton Express*, November 5, 1914.
[19] Ibid. September 24, 1914.

THE CAMERON BLOCK, built by Alex (Stonehouse) Cameron, 1883-84. On the right, John Hodgson had his store. For a few years, W.C. Latimer, who started business in Beaverton in 1902, operated both stores. He sold the grocery business (the right store) to W.H. Parr in 1914. Note the alley in the middle through which the delivery waggons passed to load at the back door. About 1930 the alley was closed in for Smiths' Barber Shop.

in the evening and anyone having a party and requiring illumination for a longer time had to make arrangements to have the power left on later and as a consequence was charged extra. Needless to say, the other townspeople were always glad to hear about a party in town for they benefited from the longer hours of light.

A fire on Sunday evening, March 19 of 1905, destroyed the grist mill at a loss of between 35 and 40 thousand dollars.[20] Dobson rebuilt the mill using the brick walls which were still standing; he owned it until 1914[21] when it was purchased by George Veale.

Dobson had other enterprises too. His Peat Works was located south of the Village on land which was later the Township Dump but is now the site of Ferndale Kennels. A fire in August of 1900 meant that new buildings had to be erected the following spring.[22] A dryer, just one of the machines patented by Mr. Dobson himself, was put into operation at that time and proved to be a success.[23] By November of 1901, thirty tons of peat were being produced each day.[24] This fuel was advertised in July of 1902 at $3.25 per ton at the Works, or $3.50 delivered in

[20] Ibid. March 23, 1905.
[21] Index to Abstract Land Records, Village of Beaverton.
[22] *Beaverton Express*, April 4, 1901.
[23] Ibid. June 6, 1901.
[24] Ibid. November 14, 1901.

FROM AN ACCOUNT BOOK OF 1892

Feb. 9	Paid for one car of lumber	$57.64
"	Paid for freight	13.20

Beaverton.[25] Dobson's son, James, went to various places including Caledonia Springs, Fort Frances, and Paterson Falls, N.J., to set up similar peat operations.[26]

The year 1897 saw another establishment start up in the south part of the Township. The Eden Creamery, a co-operative venture and Thorah's first, started operation in June of that year at lot 13 concession 2 in a solid brick building which, at present, is the home of Mr. and Mrs. Theodore Parliament. Mr. D. Gunn of D. Gunn, Flavelle and Company, made arrangements for the Creamery's entire output, and by July the first export of butter to the amount of 5,400 pounds was shipped to Bristol, England.[27] Mr. Stonehouse, the manager, won several prizes that year at the Toronto Exhibition[28] for his exhibits of the Eden Creamery product. When this enterprise ceased operation, the equipment was brought to Beaverton to be used in the creamery on Victoria Avenue.

As already mentioned, Beaverton had telephone service for long distance calls in 1890, but is was not until 1893 that the first exchange for local service was opened. Situated in Smith Thompson's Drug Store, the exchange had six subscribers,[29] mainly business people. By 1899, it is said, the subscribers had dwindled to one.[30] However, the popularity of Bell's invention soon increased, for by April of 1902, there were twenty subscribers[31] in and about the Village. That spring a new line was put up by the Independent Telephone Company to serve the rural areas.[32] After a short period of operation this company was purchased by the Bell Telephone Company. By 1904 fifty-eight subscribers were listed in the Beaverton exchange.[33] The drug store operated by William Williamson in the building where Millar's store is now situated, housed "Central" for several years.

Before electricity was in common use, machines were being driven

[25] Ibid. July 17, 1902.
[26] Ibid. Nov. 3, 1904; July 6, 1905; March 20, 1908.
[27] Ibid. July 15, July 22, 1897.
[28] Ibid. September 23, 1897.
[29] Ibid. May 21, 1969.
[30] Loc. cit.
[31] Ibid. April 18, 1902.
[32] Ibid. May 29, 1902.
[33] Ibid. May 21, 1969.

Photo of Beaverton 1896 (c.) taken from the Mill. On the right horizon is the KNOX PRESBYTERIAN CHURCH. Next is the ANGLICAN CHURCH. In the centre horizon stands the Bay Street PUBLIC SCHOOL. At the left horizon is the ST. ANDREW'S PRESBYTERIAN CHURCH.

Along the street, partially behind trees, is the CAMERON BLOCK. Next is JOHN MCRAE's BLOCK with a small shop at its east wall. After the old SHORTISS HOTEL stands J.J. GLOVER'S HARNESS SHOP. On the corner of Simcoe and Osborne is the ONTARIO HOUSE. Across Osborne is the LIVERY STABLE and the JIM BIRCHARD'S BLACKSMITH SHOP at the corner of Simcoe and John Streets.

by other forms of power. The one-horse tread mill sold by Wm. Smith at the Phoenix Foundry dispensed with the service of one man and one horse in its operation. To harness wind, many farmers erected windmills. While many of these devices were erected on towers to be used to pump water, others were put on barns and the power they produced was used for grinding grain, pulping turnips and performing other tasks. In fact, George Veale had a windmill installed to supply water for his hotel.[34]

In 1902 James Birchard paraded a shipment of machinery from Frost and Wood of Smith's Falls through the streets of Beaverton with a band in the lead and 31 teams following with over $1700 worth of machinery. After photos were taken, adjournment was made to the hotels for dinner.[35]

The Beaverton Pump Factory operated by Thomas Hodgson sup-

[34] Ibid. June 2, 1904.
[35] Ibid. June 20, 1902.

plied pumps for the wells of many of the citizens of Beaverton and Thorah. In 1903 Hodgson was awarded the Diploma and Gold Medal of the French Academy of Inventors for his force pump.[36] Hodgson's house was situated where the Prophet home now stands and in a building to the west he displayed his products.[37] In a newspaper advertisement of 1904 Hodgson declared: "The age of wooden pumps is now passing away and is just being replaced by the more durable article IRON."[38]

When new fences had to be put up many farmers and villagers alike were looking to the new wire types sold by W.A. Barrett. Wooden bridges, too, were giving way to metal ones. In 1902 a new iron bridge on Mara Street, 112 feet in length between the cement abutments, was completed at a cost of $4800.[39]

THE FIRST IRON BRIDGE on Mara Road, built in 1902.

In the same year a new bank building was erected between the post office and J.M. Gordon's store. Today it houses the Farmer's Kitchen. Reputed to be the second in Canada to be constructed of cement blocks,[40] it provided quarters for the Standard Bank, of which Benjamin Madill was the manager.

By 1897, and perhaps at an earlier date, concrete walks were making their appearance in Beaverton,[41] yet wooden walks were put down on Mara and Main Streets as late as 1900.[42] In 1908 a 400-dollar suit was brought against the Village by a resident of the Nine Mile Road who declared that his broken leg was caused by a loose plank in the sidewalk on Bay Street.[43]

[36] Ibid. may 22, 1903.
[37] Recollections of Mrs. Gilbert McMillan, 1979.
[38] *Beaverton Express*, October 24, 1904.
[39] Ibid. November 13, 1902.
[40] Ibid. August 14, 1902.
[41] Ibid. March 26, 1897.
[42] Ibid. June 21, 1900.
[43] Ibid. January 17, 1908.

SIMCOE STREET, BEAVERTON 1911 (c.)
On the left margin is the ONTARIO HOUSE HOTEL. At the end of the street is the old TANNERY and the MILL. The trees to the right centre mark the location of the OLD TOWN HALL lot. To the right is the "OLD PROCTOR BLOCK" which housed the POST OFFICE. Next right is the cement block building erected in 1902 by Ben Madill to house the STANDARD BANK of which he was manager. At the right margin lies a store owned by James Morrison.

C.T. Young had a shop built beside his woollen mill in 1905 using a novel type of siding at that time, a veneer of cement which was said to closely resemble stone. The work was done by George Drake[44] whose skills at bricklaying and masonry were practised for years in the Beaverton area; yet Drake's name was more often associated with the making of bricks and pottery at his brickyard at lot 10 concession 5.

Undoubtedly, the new buildings were more fire-resistant than earlier ones but the fear of their property going up in flames was a constant threat to the townspeople. Improved fire-fighting measures were needed. We are told that in 1892 the fire-fighting equipment consisted of five buckets and a ladder. About that time mischievous boys found it great sport to shoot holes in the buckets so that they had to be replaced at fairly frequent intervals. By 1896 a ladder truck had been added.[45] In September of 1905 a fire brigade was reorganized with J.F. Givens as chief.[46] About the same time, a new gasoline fire engine was purchased. A month or so later, fire broke out in Neil Black's furniture store in

[44] Ibid. September 7, 1905.
[45] *Tweedsmuir History*, Beaverton Women's Institute.
[46] *Beaverton Express*, September 28, 1905.

Chinese Starch
CHOCOLATE

The interior of the McRAE Store sometime shortly after 1902. During this period John McRae was renting his large brick store to McCRORIE & McINTYRE and continued his operation in a small store adjacent to the east wall of the large store.

Later the McRaes returned to the original store. Seated is John McRae. Farquhar McRae is standing behind the counter.

Courtesy of Donald & Ina McRae.

"There is at the present time a swindler operating the country who is making money in a new way. It is said he goes and extracts teeth without cost providing a new set is ordered. He calls again in a short time and gets half the price of the plate and disappears leaving the victim minus cash and teeth. There is wailing and weeping, but owing to the circumstance, no gnashing of teeth."

Beaverton Express, December 5, 1901.

Looking west along Simcoe Street from John Street, 1911. The then new TOWN HALL is to the left. At the centre stands the ONTARIO HOUSE. It was built in 1869 and operated by David Glover, Angus McKinnon, John Kennedy, Thomas Overend, Ed Hepburn and Fred Sutor to name a few.

This building was demolished about 1935 to make room for a service station. This is now the site of the new I.G.A.

Photo courtesy of Bill & Win Stabback

FROM AN ACCOUNT BOOK OF 1904

Oct.	5	Paid to Mr. A. Glassford for 1½ Bl cement	$3.38
″	5	Paid to Cameron & Cameron for glass	.95
″	6	Paid to A. Murray for cistern pipe	.35
″	6	Paid to Harold Martin for work	.25
″	6	Paid to Joseph Gobiel for digging cistern	1.10
″	8	Paid to Ted Leigh for cartage	.10
″	8	Paid Cameron & Cameron for wire screen for cistern	.15

FROM AN ACCOUNT BOOK OF 1897

3000	shingles at $1.25 (per m)	$ 3.75
32	lb. shingle nails	.96
500	feet lumber at $8.50 per m	4.25
6	windows at $1.25 per window	10.50

the Hamilton Block. This was a grand opportunity to demonstrate the usefulness of the new engine, but alas, before the firemen got the engine out and ready for use, the efficient bucket brigade had the fire extinguished.[47]

It is quite likely that Beaverton people made special visits to John French's store in October of 1905 just to see his new cash register in operation. It was the very latest model, "a marvel of mechanism, rendering mistakes of any kind absolutely impossible."[48]

French operated a general store but also carried a line of violins, advertised in 1906 "from the cheapest at $1.25 up to the high-class Academy Leipzig models at $25.00."[49] French, a blind man, played the violin well himself. In 1904 he was selling graphophones for $12.50, $17.50, and $25.00. In fact, if one wished to use one of these newfangled contraptions for party entertainment, French rented them at 50 cents per evening.[50] The latest sheet music was also available at French's Osborne Street store.

In 1895 A.M. Pentland was advertising new pianos for $200 and organs for $75 and up. Second hand organs and wood were accepted as part payment.[51] Mrs. Pentland gave music lessons as did several others, including Miss Jessie Drake, Miss Jean Ritchie, Mrs. Willard Glassford

[47] Ibid. November 2, 1905.
[48] Ibid. September 28, 1905.
[49] Ibid. December 13, 1906.
[50] Ibid. November 17, 1904.
[51] Ibid. January 24, 1895.

MAJ. C.A. PATERSON, Clerk of Beaverton for many years, and connected with the 34th Battalion

whose husband operated the hardware store where Wright's store is presently located, Mrs. D.M. Smith, wife of the auctioneer and baker, and Miss Allie Watson who later married Rev. David Best.[52]

One Beaverton boy, Leslie J. Hodgson, son of John Hodgson, a local merchant, became quite an accomplished pianist. After graduating from the Toronto Conservatory of Music in 1901, he left for Germany to study under the famous masters.[53]

Many young people were receiving training in vocal and instrumental music yet, strangely enough, high school education was out of their reach unless they were prepared to board in Uxbridge, Port Perry or some other larger centre. Certainly there had been talk of a possible high school in Beaverton, but it was only talk until 1906. In February of that year, Mr. J.J. Cave presented to Beaverton Council the petition of 124 ratepayers requesting that a high school be established jointly with the

[52] Ibid. various issues.
[53] Ibid. June 20, 1901.

Fancy Pin Cushion	50	25
Tea Cosey	50	25
Fancy Tidey	50	25
Sofa Pillow	50	25
Toilet Set	50	25
Embroidery on silk and satin	50	25
" on Linen	50	25
Sideboard Scarf	50	25
Berlin wool work, Flat	50	25
" " " Raised	50	25
Best made apron	50	25
Braiding on silk	50	25
Braiding on Cotton	50	25
Painting—In Oil	50	25
" In Water Colors	50	25
Fancy Knitting	50	25
Crazy Work	50	25
Button holes—on any material	50	25
Panel—painted	50	25
" Worked	50	25

CLASS 13.

Best collection of House Plants	1 00	50
" " of Cut Flowers	50	25

SPECIAL PRIZES.

Best single Driver under 15½ hands high Pickle Dish value $2.00 by Cameron & Cameron.

Best two year old Draught, goods value $1.50 by John McRae & Co.

Best Draught Team,—Scuffler value $7.00 by Wm. Smith.

Best Roadster Sucking colt—Whip value $1.50 by J. J Glover.

Best Herd of Cattle (Durham)—Lamp value $2.00 by A. W. Kelly.

Best bag of Fall Wheat—50 lbs Flour by A Dobson.
Best 12 lbs Dairy Butter in 1 lb rolls—Hat or Bonnet value $3,00 and best 50 lbs Tub Dairy butter—Hat or Bonnet $3,00—both exhibits to be owned in Township of Thorah prizes by John Hodgson,

SWEEPSTAKES PRIZES.

Best Draught Mare or gelding any age—Neck Yoke by P. McMillan & Sons.

Best General Purpose Mare or Gelding any age—Neck Yoke by Jas. Birchard.

Best Road or Carriage Mare or gelding, any age—Bridle and Martingale value $3,00 by Geo. H Williamson.

PRIZE LIST of the Annual Fall Exhibition of Thorah Agricultural Society, 1897.

> "A very fast and exciting game of hockey was played on the rink last Saturday between the Union Jacks of English Town and the Cracker Jacks of Victoria Avenue resulting in a victory for the Unions by a score of 7 to 3."
>
> *Beaverton Express*, February 23, 1899.

Township.[54]

In 1909 Mr. A.C. McKenzie donated $300[55] toward the purchase of land on King Street directly across from the present Beaverton Public School. Mr. Thomas Doherty was given the contract for building the two-storey brick structure. The new continuation school was opened in February of 1910.[56]

Many new developments were taking place in Beaverton and Thorah during these two decades yet, with few exceptions, the buildings in the downtown area remained unchanged. Of course, businesses were changing hands in this era as in every other period. Ritchie Dunsheath had taken over James Gordon's store on Mara Street in 1887.[57] In 1901 Donald McNabb of Mount Forest, who had formerly done business in Beaverton, returned, setting up shop in the Dunsheath stand.[58] J.J. Holmes, general merchant, sold out to J. Stroud in 1897.[59] W.D. Rodman and E. Edwards set up tailoring shops in opposition to Hector Logan. Coming to Beaverton in 1899, Percy Byrne carried on his jewellery and watchmaking business for many years. George Veale sold his livery business to James Lytle in 1897.[60] W.C. Latimer and John McRae & Co., general merchants, Henry Westcott and Cameron & Cameron selling hardware, W. Williamson, J.W. Mitchell and A.C. Kay, druggists, and George Williamson, harness-maker, were well-known businessmen during this time. Martin Roach and T. Ernest Godson set up law practices. In 1906 F.M. McRae opened up a store for "gents' furnishings."[61] a business he carried on for more than fifty years.

Before the first decade of the Twentieth Century closed, automobiles made their appearance on Beaverton streets from time to time. One day in June of 1905 Mr. Wm. McKenzie's auto brought a group to the Village. The newspaper of the day commented: "The machine seemed to be in

[54] Beaverton Council Minutes, Feb. 6, 1906.
[55] *Beaverton Express*, July 16, 1909.
[56] Ibid. February 25, 1910.
[57] Ibid. February 4, 1887.
[58] Ibid. June 20, 1901.
[59] Ibid. May 7, 1897.
[60] Ibid. October 28, 1897.
[61] Ibid. April 26, 1906.

perfect control but not sufficiently so to prevent running into a rig on Simcoe Street."[62] Certainly the next few years would see many confrontations, some tragic, others simply amusing, between automobiles and the horses they would eventually replace.

Anyone living at the time might have doubted that the importance of the horse would decline, for Thorah residents took pride in their horsemanship and the breeding of fine-quality animals as they never had before. Hodgkinson and Tisdale of Simcoe Lodge were showing their prize-winning Clydesdales at shows not only in this province but in Chicago and other centres. Donald Gunn of Dunrobin owned fine Clydesdales and Hackneys as did others in the Township. Men matched their horses' speeds against others on the road, and bragged in their conversations. They probably would never have believed that some day the automobile would surpass the horse in speed and endurance and the tractor would eventually take over almost all of the field work in the Township.

As people looked back over the last decade of the Nineteenth Century and the first few years of the Twentieth, many must have marvelled at the developments they had seen. In the 1880's who would have believed that within a score of years Beaverton residents would be riding in buggies without horses, talking across great distances over wires strung between poles, and simply pushing a button to illuminate a room more brilliantly than a lamp had ever shed light? Truly amazing!

THE BEAVERTON CONTINUATION SCHOOL, opened in 1910, was used until 1952. The four classrooms were finished throughout in Georgia pine with metallic ceilings. Mr. J. Osborne was the first principal.

[62] Ibid. June 29, 1905.

TOM LONGBOAT winning the Beaverton Marathon 1909.

THE BEAVERTON MARATHON

Boston may have a famous marathon race, but did you know that Beaverton used to have one which drew runners from far afield? Tom Longboat, a famous Indian runner from early in the century, ran in the Beaverton Marathon, and left his closest competitor far behind.

In the *Orillia Times* we read "Beaverton, Sept. 8, 1908. The third annual ten mile road race was run here yesterday, and proved to be by far the best yet held — The telephones were kept hot as the crowds awaiting the finish were accurately informed on the progress of the race — The first man to cross the tape was another Indian, James George, from Georgina Island, his time being 61 minutes — he finished fresh and strong — The record made this year is over five minutes better than last year and thirteen minutes better than 1906."

Mr. Cephas Doherty recalls that the marathon started at the corner of Simcoe and Mara streets, in front of the mill, went east on Simcoe to Osborne Street, south on Osborne (Regional Road 17) to the Eden School on the corner of Second Line, Thorah where it went east two miles to Centre Road (Highway 12 and 48) where it turned north. Upon reaching the Fifth line (traffic lights) the runners came west along Simcoe Street, south to old Osborne Street Fair Grounds.

One runner earned the nickname "Short Cut" by taking the Third Line, rather than the Second Line, to get to the Centre Road.

THE FRATERNAL SOCIETIES

The January 24, 1895 issue of the Beaverton Express listed five fraternal societies, the Masons, the Orange Lodge, Independent Order of Oddfellows, Independent Order of Foresters, and Ancient Order of United Workmen.

The Order of United Workmen no longer exists, and the Independent Order of Foresters no longer has a local lodge. The other three are still active in the life of the village.

Separate, but affiliated, are three women's lodges. The Order of the Eastern Star is related to Murray Lodge, AF & AM, The Rebekahs are connected with the I.O.O.F. There is a women's branch of the Orange Lodge.

SONS OF SCOTLAND

Another fraternal society that flourished locally in the late 19th and early 20th centuries was the Sons of Scotland.

In the *Beaverton Express* of January 24, 1895, we read "Douglas Camp, #27, meets in the Sons of Scotland Hall, Beaverton, on the first Wednesday after full moon, each month at 8 o'clock."

The Beaverton S.O.S. hall has disappeared, but the Gamebridge building of the Sweet Afton Camp, S.O.S., is still in use today by the Gamebridge Womens' Institute.

The Sons of Scotland were organizers of many excursions:

June 30, 1893, the S.O.S. held an excursion of 500 people to Strawberry Island.

Douglas Camp, S.O.S. held an excursion to Niagara Falls, May 14, 1903.

"Sweet Afton Camp", S.O.S., Gamebridge, will run an excursion from Lock 5 of the Trent Valley Canal to Balsam Lake on Tuesday, June 2, 1908. A Highland Band will be in attendance.

Before the days of automobile travel, Beaverton people managed to see much of our province on boat and train excursions, organized by local societies.

Chapter 22

THE CHURCHES: THE 1900's

By the early 1900's after the end of the primitive settlers' days, communities across Canada had had many years of working together in early cooperative ventures, and playing together in community team sports. It was no small wonder that the possibility of church union was discussed.[1]

In 1902, at a meeting of the General Conference of the Methodist Church in Winnipeg, a visit was paid by a deputation from the General Assembly of the Presbyterian Church in Canada. The Congregationalists, too, were interested in union.[2]

By 1911 a proposal to communicants of the Presbyterian Church to unite with Congregationalists and Methodists was accepted by a vote of 2 to 1.[3] So church union was in the air!

Patronage and state support, which had led to the separation of the Free Church from the Church of Scotland, were practically non-issues in Canada. After much discussion, the Presbyterian congregations of St. Andrew's (Church of Scotland) and Knox Church (Free Church) resolved on March 12, 1914, that: "The best interests of the Work of Christ and Presbyterianism in Beaverton be served by union of the two churches."

It was agreed that services be held in each church for two months at a time.[4] In a few years it became more expedient to use the Simcoe St. church for Sunday services and the Osborne St. church for Sunday School and midweek activities.

In a community so strongly Presbyterian the Methodist church of Beaverton was never very strong. Realizing that the national church bodies were discussing union, the Beaverton Methodists approached the Presbyterians with an idea of uniting. The Presbyterian congregation was unanimous in its assurance of a cordial welcome.[5]

On July 1, 1918 the local Methodists and Presbyterians united under the name of "Presbyterian-Methodist Cooperative Church."[6] Within a

[1] Chown, Rev. S.D., *The Story of Church Union in Canada*, Toronto, 1930.

[2] Loc. cit.

[3] Loc. cit.

[4] Pamphlet "Prepared Basis of Union between the Presbyterian Congregations of St. Andrews and Knox Church, Beaverton."

[5] *St. Andrew's United Church, Beaverton, 1879-1979.*

[6] Loc. cit.

KNOX PRESBYTERIAN Church
demolished 1927.
Courtesy of Mrs. Grace McElroy

few years the much simpler name "Beaverton United Church" was adopted.

For several more years, the national churches carried on discussion of organic union, culminating in the passage of the United Church of Canada Act of the Federal Parliament on June 6, 1925.[7]

This Act required that all congregations of participating churches hold a vote on whether they should or should not go into Union. The Beaverton vote in February 1926 was 286 for Union, 137 against Union.[8] The 137 who did not want union wanted to remain Presbyterians, so they, as the Continuing Presbyterians, held services in the Town Hall, called a minister to serve them, and in 1927 opened the present Presbyterian church.[9]

Dissension between the United Church and the Presbyterian Church of Beaverton was very strong for several years, resulting in unchristian acts on both sides.[10] However, time is the healer, and we now see cooperation between the two churches. Summertime sees joint services that allow holidays for the respective clergy.

Church cooperation functions in a wider way now. World Day of Prayer, started in 1937 as a primarily women's movement, sees people of four faiths, United, Presbyterian, Roman Catholic and Anglican, worshipping together.

Members of all the churches take part in the mission outreach programs of their national church bodies. However, many participate in individual world-wide efforts. In 1919 the Presbyterian-Methodist Cooperative Church donated $466.50 to Belgian Relief.[11] In 1981 the Anglicans donated funds to build a church in the mountains of Taiwan.[12] A group at the United Church sends parcels to Zaire, including such things as vegetable seeds.[13] The Roman Catholics list among their outreach, the support of the work of the Christian Island mission in Georgian Bay.[14] Members of all the local churches support individuals, mainly children, not only with their prayers, but financially.

Our churches have sent men and women into the wider service of the Church. Father John Walsh, first Roman Catholic priest at Vroomanton, became second Archbishop of Toronto.[15] Former rectors of the Anglican

[7] Chown, op. cit.
[8] *Toronto Evening Telegram* Excerpts copied from issues in 1926, 1927.
[9] *Beaverton Express*, February 26, 1926 to July 29, 1926.
[10] Loc. cit.
[11] Annual Report 1918 Presbyterian-Methodist Cooperative Church, Beaverton.
[12] 1981 Minutes, Annual Vestry Meeting, St. Paul's Anglican Church.
[13] Private Communication.
[14] Loc. cit.
[15] *History of Roman Catholicism in Georgina Township* 1963.

ST. JOSEPH'S CHURCH — Concession 4
demolished 1909.
Courtesy of Mrs. Grace McElroy

Choir of ST. ANDREW'S Church
Beaverton about 1910.

church, Rev. George Rix, and Rev. W.G. Hallam, became bishops of the Anglican Church.[16] Dr. Alex Calder of Peterborough is a local boy who has distinguished himself in the Presbyterian Church.[17]

Jack Scott, a boy from St. Andrew's church went west early in the century directly after leaving elementary school. A chance encounter got him interested in the ministry. From local ministers he learned Latin and Greek. Finally, after earning title to his homestead, he came back east to enrol at Queen's University. After graduating in Arts, he enlisted in the Medical Corps in World War I, where he saw service in England and Egypt. Invalided back to England, he served as a chaplain. Upon his return to Canada he completed his theology courses, was ordained, and gave many years of devoted service in Ontario centres.[18] Father Matthew Nealon from a local Roman Catholic family, served in nearby parishes. Watson Westcott, Malcolm Profitt and Robert McLellan, sons of other local families have pursued careers in the ministry. Lillian Roberts, wife of Rev. Gordon Roberts, present United Church minister of Beaverton, is engaged in studies for the ministry.

[16]The First Hundred Years St. Paul's Anglican Church 1872-1972.
[17]Conversation with Miss Mary Fowler, great grand-daughter of Rev. David Watson.
[18]*Sketch of Church Life in Beaverton 1929.*

Two Beaverton sisters, Winnifred and Marion Lytle, distinguished themselves as Sister Winnifred and Sister Mary André of the American order of Sisters of Mercy.[19] Miss Isabel Ross, daughter of John and Mary Ross, was sent by the Presbyterian Church to Indore, Central India, in 1882. After eleven years' work, she resigned, and married Mr. H. Broad. They returned to Canada and Mr. Broad studied for the ministry at Knox College. On his graduation, the Broads went to Vancouver, where Mrs. Broad worked among the Hindus.[20] Another Beaverton girl, Miss Kate Calder, went to India in 1892 as a missionary.[21]

A desire for the word of God on the part of the early residents built our churches. Their presence has been a continuing influence for good among the people of the community.

THE BEAVERTON WOMEN'S INSTITUTE

A prominent and active part in the life of Beaverton is the Women's Institute.

It was organized on January 15, 1913, with Mrs. J. McKee McLennan as its first president. She was succeeded by many able women whose services to the Institute have been noted by presentation of life membership pins and citations for many years of active membership.

The Women's Institute over the years has been noted for good works, such as providing help for needy mothers and children in Toronto, knitting socks in two world wars, and giving prizes for beautification of school grounds.

Among the valuable contributions that the Institute has made to the community are the Tweedsmuir Histories. These scrapbooks, made on the suggestion of Lady Tweedsmuir, wife of a former governor-general, are a constant source of information for people researching local history.

Quite a record of achievement for a 71 year old lady, the Beaverton Women's Institute!

[19] Private Communication.
[20] *Sketch of Church Life in Beaverton 1929.*
[21] Loc. cit.

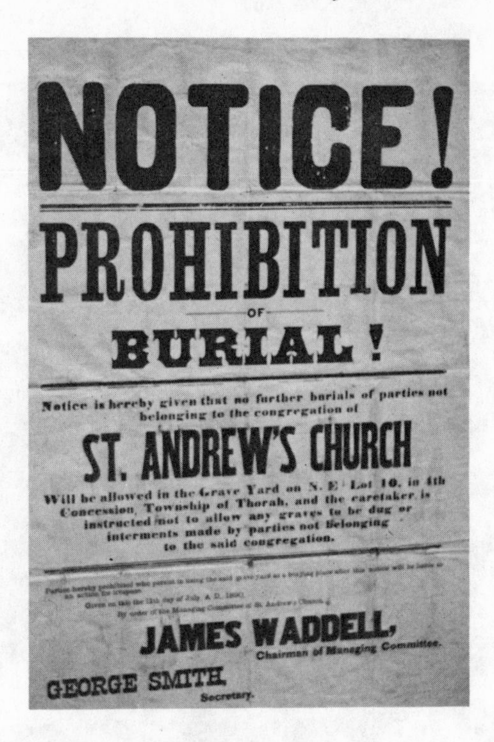

UNWELCOME GUESTS

The Council of the Village of Beaverton passed this by-law #7 1889: "To prohibit the internment of deceased persons within the limits of this Corporation."

This meant there could be no more burials in the cemeteries of the Methodist Church or the original Knox Church, both on Main Street.

As a result, burials were made in St. Andrew's Church Cemetery, on the NE section of lot 10 in Fourth Concession of Thorah.

This was a private cemetery, supported by the people of St. Andrew's Church. Hence this notice.

It was not until 1907, that Dr. Best, minister of St. Andrew's, and Angus Watson, his brother-in-law, established the Old Stone Church Cemetery as a municipal cemetery.

They borrowed from the expertise and experience of Mt. Pleasant Cemetery in Toronto. They set up a plan for burials and record keeping. As well, they initiated a program for perpetual care.

An Aerial View of Beaverton's Business Section 1920

Photo courtesy of Marion Speedie

Chapter 23

THE HARVEST OF THEIR DREAMS

And so Beaverton has lived and grown throughout the years. Now in the last part of the twentieth century it remains a pleasant, prosperous village on the shore of a lovely lake. The later years have brought many changes. Wars and rumours of wars have been a disturbing element in village life. Technological evolution has had a powerful influence. Life style has changed here as it has elsewhere. Education has developed and has become truly universal. Even the status of Beaverton as an incorporated village is gone. The social conscience of the town has developed until poverty, illiteracy and illness are no longer ignored, but have become the responsibility of the community as a whole. The village scene has changed and the small settlement of early days is, in 1984, a much larger, modern town.

Two world wars affected the lives of Beavertonians as they did those of countless other villages. Beaverton lost precious young lives and saw many of the youth of the community leave "to fight for freedom" on foreign soil. During the first "Great War" life at home was changed, business was disrupted and the local society was geared to wartime needs. The women of Beaverton formed "The Patriotic Society"[1] and met to sew and knit for the Canadian soldiers, especially for those of their own community. They also raised money to supply soldiers' needs. The council notes of 1914 tell us of a tea held in the market hall by the Patriotic Society for this purpose.

On October 21, 1915, "Trafalgar Day", a tag day was held in the village to raise money for the British Red Cross. A letter from Lord Lansdown had been sent to all Canadian municipalities asking for money for the "care of soldiers in England". The tag day was Beaverton's way of responding.

In 1919 a framed certificate and a $5.00 gold piece were presented to each "returned" soldier and to the family of those who never came home.[2]

At the time of the second "World War" the Beaverton chapter of the

[1] Beaverton Council Notes.
[2] Ibid.

The JOHN PROCTOR House. Present site of the Canadian Imperial Bank of Commerce.

Thanksgiving Day — 1978. The old mill burned.

Red Cross Society took on the work for the soldiers.[3] The auditorium of the town hall was turned into a work room. There local women produced many hundreds of shirts for the army. Wool was given out and socks, balaclavas and scarves were knitted and sent off to the local boys in the various branches of the service. Once more, life in the village was disrupted and once more young lives were lost.

The Korean war, the Vietnam War and the occupational forces also took Beaverton men many miles from their native village. Today, boys from the local community are in Europe and the near East in N.A.T.O. and U.N. forces.

The Beaverton Mill had, for some years supplied power for the electricity used in the village. When this came to an end, the coming of Hydro played a large part in bringing Beaverton into the twentieth century.

The Beaver River still meanders its way to the lake and the Beaverton dam still holds back its waters. But no longer does the old mill stand at the side of the dam; a fire destroyed the old building on Thanksgiving Day, 1979, and forever changed the town's street scene.

The amazing advances in technology of all kinds have affected the life of Beaverton in many ways. School children here, as elsewhere, are learning the wonders of computers. Through the magic of television they have watched man walk on the moon, and have taken part in the ongoing conquest of space.

Teams of horses hauling their loads over unpaved roads in summer, and through snowdrifts in winter are part of the past life of the community. Now paved highways cross the country and great snow plows keep the roads clear in the winter. All year long villagers are able to drive their cars where they will.

The changes which have taken place in Beaverton since the early days of the century were well illustrated in an article by A.E. Brodie in the *Beaverton Express* of April 18, 1962. Quoting the words of Dr. Devine, the local dentist, who, in describing the Beaverton he had moved to in 1913 said, "In many ways Beaverton had been lagging behind the times. The old McMillan skating rink was about done for. There were few modern sidewalks, no pavements, no parks, and a bleak, obsolete old school, a few cottages, an old iron bridge and an ancient post office."[4]

This dreary description could in no way describe the Beaverton of today. Soon sidewalks were constructed, a new bridge spanned the river, property was designated for parks, a new school, many fine cottages and

[3] Minutes Beaverton Red Cross Society.
[4] *Beaverton Express.*

BEAVERTON-THORAH COMMUNITY CENTRE

a modern post office all came into being during the next three decades. The village has continued to progress throughout the years.

In 1967 a new bridge was completed.[5] It takes the place of the cement arched bridge in use from 1922 to 1966, and it in turn, replaced the old iron bridge. The new bridge is the third to have been built within living memory, and probably the fourth or fifth to have spanned the river since the early settlement of the town.

Simcoe Street remains much as it was some years ago. The "Hamilton House", now called the "Beaverton Hotel", is still a dominating feature. A new supermarket stands where the "Ontario House" once was, and another recently enlarged one is in the "Cameron Block" which once held a village general store, and later, Brunning's Groceries, and Latimer's Dry Goods. A modern bank has been erected where the John Proctor house stood for many years. There is a hardware store on the site of the "old" Town Hall, and the present town hall occupies the area of the "Iron Block" of earlier days.

Instead of carriage makers, potteries and harness shops, the town now has one factory manufacturing car parts, another producing articles made of welded wire, a large lumber yard, car washes, laundromats, and

[5] Information from clerks office-Beaverton.

many varied shops.

Many of the present village houses were built over one hundred years ago, some of them of bricks produced in the local brick yards. New houses on new streets have enlarged the village and have brought many young families as well as older retired people to enrich the life of the community.

The five churches of the town and the old stone church in the nearby country are very active and play a large part in the religious and social life of the people.

The Beaverton library, since 1974 part of the Brock library system, and one of the last Carnegie libraries[6] to be built in Ontario, continues to serve the village residents as it has since the first library was established over one hundred years ago. The recently opened David Annesley gallery in the library basement has made it possible for local artists to display their work. It also serves as a fine children's library. This gallery was established as a memorial to David Annesley, a well known artist and cartoonist who lived in Beaverton and was a much loved figure in the community.

An important step to guard the health of the village was taken in 1948.[7] Under the leadership of Mr. J.A. Hawtin, then reeve of Beaverton, a by-law was passed authorizing a vote to be taken on September 4, 1948 to enable the council to borrow $150,000.00 for the purpose of constructing a water system for the village, "the said system to include intake pipe into Lake Simcoe, standpipe on high ground in the municipality and a water works distributing system including gate valves and hydrants on various streets." The electors voted in favour of the by-law and construction took place in the following years. This system is being constantly enlarged and improved as the needs of the village grow. In 1979[8] the Region of Durham started construction of a new Water Treatment Plant. The building, located in the park by the Beaverton Harbour was completed in 1980 and the official opening took place in September of that year. The contamination of local wells had been a much feared health hazard. This danger has now been eliminated.

Another important health measure was taken in 1968 when construction of sewers was started. This was done under the council of which Mr. W. Gillespie was reeve. The work was done in two phases, the last of which was completed in 1981. The days of the septic tank were over.

Some years ago concern was felt about the great load that was being carried by Dr. Harold Ames, who was, at that time, the only doctor in

[6] Minutes Brock Township Library Board — January 1974.
[7] Information Municipal clerks office — Beaverton By-laws 7 and 8 of 1948.
[8] Building permit issued March 23, 1979.

LAKEVIEW MANOR — Beaverton.

SENIOR CITIZENS APARTMENTS — On site of Way Side Inn Main Street and Mara Road, Beaverton.

Beaverton. Working from an inadequate office on Simcoe Street he had tried, for some time, to find a doctor to work with him. Some came, stayed for a short time, and went on to other things. In 1972 a committee was formed under the co-chairmanship of Mr. Earl Windatt and Mrs. Margaret McGibney. Money was raised through various community efforts such as annual "Pioneer Days" and through donations from interested members of the public. In 1974 the Medical Centre on Main Street was opened. There, three doctors, a dentist, a denturist and a physio-therapist have their offices.

The senior citizens of the area have not been forgotten. Lakeview Manor, a project of the County of Ontario, and later of the Region of Durham was opened in September of 1966 by the Hon. John P. Robarts. Present on this occasion were the Hon. M.D. Dymond M.D., who was the local provincial member of parliament, Mr. Charles Healy, warden of the County of Ontario, and Mr. William Gillespie, Reeve of Beaverton.[9] Many hundreds of concerned and interested people made this a gala affair. The beautiful Home is situated in view of Lake Simcoe, across the road from the Fair Grounds. It has the facilities to care for up to 150 residents and employs a staff of 100 of whom 50 are full time workers.[10] In June of 1978 a large, fully equipped "activities room" was opened. Here many entertainments for the enjoyment of the residents are held, including monthly birthday parties which are produced by various organizations of the community. Under Mr. Everit Quantrill and his staff, Lakeview Manor is one of the finest homes in the province.

In 1978 an Auxiliary to Lakeview Manor was formed with Mrs. Isobel Gillespie as its founding president. Through the years this group of volunteers has done much to make the life of the residents more comfortable and more enjoyable. Money is raised to buy needed extras, to pay for many bus trips, run a tuck shop and to serve the residents of the Manor in many ways. This organization has become a very important part of the residential care.

Another important aid to seniors, invalids and convalescents is the "Meals on Wheels" programme.[11] These meals delivered by different groups on a monthly basis, ease and simplify the housekeeping chores of those who need such assistance. The meals are prepared in the kitchens of Lakeview Manor under the direction of the manor dietitian, Mrs. Harold Ames, and are picked up there by the volunteer drivers. During 1983 twenty-two meals were delivered twice weekly. Such extra touches

[9] Program — official opening of Lakeview Manor September, 1967.
[10] Information from office of Lakeview Manor "Mirror on the Manor."
[11] Minutes — Meals on Wheels Programme.

as special Thanksgiving, Christmas and Easter meals are very much appreciated.

On the site of the former "Wayside Inn" on the corner of Mara Road and Main Street, senior citizen's apartments have been built by the Province of Ontario. These enable many older people to continue to live an independent life.

In the fall of 1972, under the chairmanship of the Rev. David Williams a meeting was called "to set up an educational programme, family counselling, councillor training and community and family life education."[12] From this beginning grew three social service programmes of great value to the residents of Beaverton, and of all of Brock township. These have become very important to the senior citizens of the community.

"Information Simcoe", "Brock Good Neighbours" and "Brock Counselling Service", all came into being as a result of this first meeting. These three fill an ever growing need for the local citizens — Beaverton, Cannington and Sunderland and the surrounding country all benefit from these "Community Care" programmes, and all provide volunteers under the "Community Involvement and Volunteer Programme" (C.I.V.P.) which is a unique feature of Durham Regional Community Care. With all these services Beaverton Seniors are really cared for with efficiency and with love. As proof of this, one senior citizen said "I wouldn't ever leave Beaverton. It is a wonderful place to live. We are not only cared for, but the people who give us that care become our true friends."

Another proof of care beyond the strict boundaries of duty is given in an article in the "History and Development of Community care in the Region of Durham." It tells of a maiden lady who requested in her will that only lady pallbearers serve at her funeral, explaining that "men have not driven me during my life" and she was "darned" if they were going to after her death. "Brock Good Neighbours" did supply the pallbearers at her funeral! It is evident that they look after their people during their lives, and beyond!

Add to these services such groups as the various church organizations, the Women's Institute, the Service Clubs, the Cancer Society and Beaverton can be seen to be a truly caring community.

The lake and the beaches remain a most important part of local life. Many of the cottages have been winterized and are being used as permanent homes. The harbour is a busy spot, winter and summer. The

[12] History and Development of Community care — Region of Durham.

MEDICAL CENTRE - Main Street, Beaverton

WATER SUPPLY PLANT — Beaverton.

Brock Township FIRE DEPARTMENT — Osborne Street, Beaverton.

large, modern marina offers safe anchorage for hundreds of boats, which, during the summer months ply the waters of the lake. The proximity of the Trent canal, finally completed in 1913, makes possible long scenic trips to other lakes and other rivers. In winter the gaily painted fish-houses dot the lake. Fishermen come from "near and far" in search of the lake trout, white fish and herring.

Summer is a busy time. Cottagers make the beaches gay and active spots. They are a very important part of village life. Their active support of community projects is much appreciated.

Many sporting activities take place during the year. The Red Cross Swimming lessons at the pier, financed by the local Lions Club, teach children water safety and give excellent swimming instruction. Two golf clubs are near by, with others a short distance away. Tennis courts are situated on the Beaverton school grounds where the "Continuation" School once stood. Baseball diamonds, also on the school grounds are well used by young residents of the area. Baseball is nearly as popular in Beaverton as lacrosse once was and many organized leagues play their games on the diamond in the fairgrounds, the girls and women being just as active in this sport as are the boys and men. Soccer, basketball and football are all played in the local schools.

Winter games are as popular as summer ones. Hockey and figure skating in the fine community centre, opened in 1972, and curling in the new curling club which had its official opening in March of 1977, make the winter very busy. Skiing on hills within easy driving distance, is popular with many of the young and not so young people as is cross country skiing.

Every year a Winter Carnival is held. This includes figure skating,

MR. and MRS. BRAIN — former owners of "Heritage House". Now part of Beaver River Museum.

hockey, curling and snowmobiling as well as a well attended dinner and dance. This raises money for various town organizations and provides a pleasant break in the long winter.

Outside the village the many fine farms produce goods for the market as they have since early days. Now the Belgians, Percherons and Clydesdales have given way to modern farm machinery and horses are kept rather as a hobby than to labour in the fields. Many of the local farmers are grandsons and great-grandsons of original settlers. Others have come from other parts of Canada and from Europe, bringing their special agricultural expertise with them.

The Beaverton Fair, 100 years old in 1953 and still held annually, offers an opportunity for friendly competition and a place to display examples of the years' work. The new community centre and the curling club, both situated in the fair grounds, serve as excellent display and show buildings. They add greatly to the success of the fair.

In recent years a Historical Society has been formed in Beaverton. In November of 1976 a group of interested people met to discuss the possibility of establishing such a society. On a motion by Tom Harrison it was decided to go ahead. Great enthusiasm was shown and in January of 1977 the first meeting of The Beaverton, Thorah, Eldon Historical

Old Pine Cupboard — BEAVER RIVER MUSEUM

Fire Place — Log Cabin — BEAVER RIVER MUSEUM

THE SERVICE CLUBS

Beaverton is well represented by three service clubs, the modern day outgrowth of the fraternal societies. All have begun since the Second World War — The Lions Club, the Kinsmen, and the Junior Farmers.

They meet once or twice a month, generally at dinner meetings, where good fellowship is the keynote. Their very name, "service club" indicates their purpose, service to the community. All have most impressive records of good works.

The Royal Canadian Legion was started to serve the veterans in their readjustment to civilian life. The "Legion", in both men's and women's branches now does many good works, similar to the other service clubs.

Society was held. Since that time it has flourished. In June of 1981 the first stage of the museum, a project of the Society was opened by His Honour, Alan McPhail, mayor of Brock Township. In June of 1982 the Lieutenant Governor of Ontario, the Hon. John Aird officially opened the log cabin. These two buildings along with the driving shed erected by the Kinsmen of Beaverton make up the three buildings of the Beaver River Museum.

Beaverton has many groups which are important to the social life of its citizens. The Beaverton Lions Club is a very active service group. They give much financial support to various village activities as does the Kinsmen club.

Such groups as the Junior Farmers, the Business Men's Association, the Horticultural Society, the Women's Institute, the Local Legion, the Senior Citizens club and the Beaverton Firemen make Beaverton a very vibrant village and add to the quality of life of its residents.

Though no longer an incorporated village Beaverton continues to grow and to prosper. It remains a very strong reality in the lives and hearts of its people. The hopes and dreams of its pioneer settlers are being realized in the Beaverton of today. This is the true harvest of their dreams.

Index